IRVIN MILLMAN GROSSACK, Professor of
Business Economics and Public Policy,
Graduate School of Business, Indiana University, is co-author of *Managerial Economics* and
co-editor of *Regional Perspectives on Development.*

The International Economy
and the National Interest

The International Economy and the National Interest

Irvin Millman Grossack

Bloomington

INDIANA UNIVERSITY PRESS

London

Library of Congress Cataloging in Publication Data
Grossack, Irvin Millman, 1927–
   The international economy and national interest.
   Includes bibliographical references and index.
   1. International economic relations.   2. Invest-
ments, Foreign.   I. Title.
HF1007.G722   382.1   78-13817
ISBN 0-253-36775-1   1 2 3 4 5 83 82 81 80

This book is dedicated to my parents,
Murray and Nettie Grossack,
who always did their best for me.

CONTENTS

ILLUSTRATIONS

TABLES

Preface

The growth of the multinational corporation and the increase in international trade and money flows have unquestionably been among the most important economic phenomena of the post–World War II era. These developments have spurred new interest in international economic matters among economists and others who monitor the economic scene, and have even led to interest in this subject among the general population, as perhaps best evidenced by the way figures on trade balances and currency values are often accorded headlines by even the popular press. Although interest appears to have grown in all aspects of international economics, the growth of the multinational corporation has attracted more attention in the professional literature than has the growth of international trade. There are good reasons for these differences in the engagement of professional attention. International trade is a subject that has been debated and discussed for centuries, and elegant theories explaining trade patterns and assessing their consequences have been developed that are so widely accepted that they border on being conventional wisdom. The multinational corporation, on the other hand, is a more recent phenomenon and has only lately received great attention. Although economists have not been amiss in proposing theories to explain the emergence of the multinational corporation and to assess its consequences, it can be asserted that the state of theory on this subject is still in flux and that no one proposed theory has come close to attaining the status of, say, the law of comparative advantage in the theory of international trade.

When it was suggested to me that I consider writing a book on the multinational corporation—similar suggestions apparently must have been made to many other economists—it was clear to me that the subject was sufficiently important and complicated to warrant my interest. There was initially some hesitation on my part, particularly as to whether I had anything fresh and of value to add to what had become a burgeoning literature. I also had not done much writing in the area of international economics; most of my work has been in microeconomic theory and industrial organization. But I proceeded on the grounds that the multinational corporation was also of interest to the field of industrial organization, and that my graduate work under Professor Nurkse and a stint as a foreign service officer would provide for me sufficient background to deal with the recent literature. I was also able to convince myself that my unfamiliarity with the recent literature might in some ways be an advantage, enabling me to take a fresh look at the field of international economics.

My first plan was to do an empirical study of the multinational corporation: this was the method in widest use, and the data being made available by governmental agencies and the work at Harvard under Professor Vernon virtually cried out for statistical analysis. But I shortly became convinced that what was more needed, and what I could do best, was a thorough reexamination and reformulation of *trade* theory, and then to build upon this reformulated trade theory a theory of international investment. There were several reasons for choosing this path. First, colleagues in the applied area that has become known as "international business" assured me that nobody with a practical bent was taking trade theory as it is recently evolving very seriously. Second, my review of recent developments in trade theory led me to believe that this branch of economics was becoming somewhat "precious." Third, it seemed to me that the conventional trade theory had no basis for explaining the multinational corporation, and that those trying to explain the multinational corporation by beginning with the current trade theory were engaged in an exercise in futility. Fourth, I became convinced that much of the empirical work on the multinational corporation was leading to contradictory and disappointing results because the lack of a theoretical framework made it difficult to ask the right questions and to assess properly the available data.

The book that emerged is therefore primarily one on theory. But, I like to think, the theory presented in it is not so abstract as to be inapplicable to an understanding of the real world. There will be a number of new ideas, most conspicuously a redefinition of the term "international trade." The theory will not always be elegant, in the sense that it takes the form of making deductions from a set of assumptions. Rather, it tries to point up the types of information required to assess international trade and investment. And the theory will contain no predilections that free trade and free foreign investment always lead to desirable results.

A number of acknowledgments of help I received are in order. Richard Robinson, of MIT, who reviewed an earlier manuscript, made many important suggestions and challenged me to explore more fully a number of difficult areas. Another reviewer, not known to me, and apparently somewhat taken aback by my attacks on conventional trade theory, contributed to the book by forcing me to reassess what I had written and by making me present my arguments with a bit more circumspection. Conversations with a number of my colleagues, Richard Farmer, Paul Marer, and William Travis in particular, encouraged me to believe that many of my new views were on the right track. The International Business Research Institute, funded by the Ford Foundation, and chaired at Indiana University by Harvey Bunke, sprung me free for a whole summer from other duties. Our departmental secretaries, Beverly Ball and Ruth Shannon, uncomplainingly (at least to me) provided me with fast and accurate manuscript typing. Various students helped, through their questions, by inducing me to clarify my exposition. Although it is customary to thank one's family for the sacrifices in not seeing too much of its author/father/husband, my family demonstrated no great suffering, except perhaps for my wife, who possibly had to feign interest while listening to me talk about my work.

The International Economy
and the National Interest

CHAPTER ONE

An Introduction

This book takes on two interrelated tasks. One is a critical assessment of what may be termed the "established" theory of international trade and investment, with regard to both its positive and its normative aspects. The second is to propose alternative models when the established theory is found unsatisfactory. This introductory chapter sketches the growth of international trade and investment following World War II, some of the problems and controversies to which this growth has led, and some reasons why the established theory requires this critical assessment.

The postwar growth of international trade in goods has been well documented, with exports and imports for the industrial nations in particular rising faster than their gross national products. Largely because of the growth of international banking and multinational firms, huge sums of financial capital flow with increased freedom among nations. But the most spectacular growth of the international economy has been in direct foreign investment, in which firms owned and controlled by members of one nation locate and operate in other countries. For example, the recent value of American-owned firms located abroad is on the order of $150 billion.[1] Another indication of this growth in direct foreign investment is that the value of the output of foreign-located American firms engaged in manufacturing has been recently estimated at some two to three times that of manufactured exports from the United States.[2] Although direct foreign

1

investment is not a new phenomenon, its current scope and importance have no antecedent in economic history.

Although some more or less natural economic forces have contributed to this growth, the major impetus has come from conscious decisions of national governments to reduce trade and investment barriers. In these endeavors, the United States has played the leading role. With the Reciprocal Trade Agreement Act of 1934 the underlying legislation, the United States has sponsored a number of tariff-cutting conferences. The success of these negotiations is reflected in the estimate that the average ad valorem tariff on imports into the United States has been reduced from 50 percent in 1945 to about 8 percent in 1967, when the "Kennedy Round" was completed.[3] The United States has been a leading member of the International Monetary Fund and a semiofficial member of the General Agreement on Trade and Tariffs (GATT), organizations designed to promote international trade. The United States has even promoted freer trade among other nations: the important European Community was organized with the encouragement of the United States.[4] In international investment, particularly direct foreign investment, American foreign investment has been encouraged with special tax provisions, an insurance system, bilateral "friendship, navigation, and commerce" treaties, sanctions against nations who expropriate American property (the Hickenlooper Amendment), and special low-interest loans to firms in the less-developed countries that take on American partners (the Cooley loans). Admittedly these policies have not been completely without opposition in the United States; yet they have been substantially adhered to by all postwar American administrations.

Although there are well-known and widely proclaimed arguments for free trade (the arguments for investment are more in doubt), it is surely international political considerations rather than a fresh appreciation of these arguments that has underlain American policy in this area.[5] The experience of the thirties led many to believe that trade barriers and problems impeded the coalition of Western Allies against the Axis powers, and that difficulties the latter experienced in securing sources of raw materials contributed to their aggressiveness. American postwar policy has of course been dominated by the decision to resist the spread of communism. The cohesiveness and integration to which free trade among the industrialized nations could lead were considered vital to this end—being in some ways the economic counterpart to NATO. For the developing third world countries, the response was not to be integration through free trade, but rather economic aid to develop their economies. Although this aid was at first on an official basis, American business interests were able to persuade the United States government that private investment by American firms could help these economies.[6] Accordingly, private foreign investment was encouraged even to the point of using official aid as a lever to overcome the resistance of some developing countries.

Perhaps somewhat incongruously, in recent years the United States government has encouraged some types of trade (although not yet investment to any great extent) with the Soviet satellites and even with the Soviet Union and China themselves. This has undoubtedly come about as the result of a new tack in policy toward the communist countries: to reduce Soviet hostility to the United States through increased contacts, and to reduce the economic dependence of the satellites on the Soviet Union.

American encouragement of foreign investment had another political basis. The aid commitments, the military bases throughout the world, the expanded size of official American representation, all require a great deal of foreign exchange. It was hoped that the earnings of American foreign ventures would be of help in providing this foreign exchange.

The American-led policies toward international trade and investment could be considered a success with regard to some goals. They have certainly led to an expansion of trade and investment, which to some appears to be an end in itself. There has been increased integration of national economies and successful growth of some developing economies. These policies may even have been successful in helping to contain communism, although of course such a claim would be more difficult to document. But these policies have also created problems and controversies of their own.

Perhaps the most important problem stems from the fact that free trade and investment integrate national economies into part of a broader international system. Although this integration is viewed as highly desirable to many, it does conflict with other important postwar economic developments. The most important of these developments is the extent to which governments have become more active in managing their internal economies. This management includes not only macroeconomic stabilization policy, but also a host of policies on pollution control, energy use, labor standards, income redistribution, and so forth. There is little doubt that the economic integration brought on by freer international trade and investment has increased the difficulties and reduced the autonomy of individual nations in managing their economies, a situation that is reflected in the increasing necessity to hold high-level international conferences to coordinate economic policies that only a decade ago were viewed as purely internal affairs. Because nations face different economic problems, and because their economic interests can clash, these conferences have not met with great success and it is increasingly apparent that many nations resent the loss of this economic autonomy.

For most of the postwar period, the American free trade policies appear to have enjoyed wide support. But in the troubled seventies, these policies are clearly coming under increasing attack, largely because of the disappearance of an American trade surplus of many decades standing. The loss of this trade surplus forced the United States to devalue the dollar and renege on its promise to convert foreign-held dollars into gold, a situation which led to the destruction of the fixed exchange rate system administered by the International Monetary Fund. The OPEC cartel, the huge oil imports, and the drive of other manufacturing countries to export to the United States in order to earn dollars to pay for their oil imports, have by the late seventies led to American trade deficits of unprecedented size. The problems created by these deficits are of such magnitude that American officials appear loathe to acknowledge them, much less deal with them.

Although trade problems are now paramount, for most of the postwar period it has been direct foreign investment and the multinational corporation that have captured our attention and become centers of controversy. The multinational corporation has both ardent admirers and caustic critics.[7] The admirers see the multinational corporation as the prime agent in bringing about worldwide economic development, spreading the fruits of technology to all, earning foreign exchange and advancing the interests of the United States, allocating more efficiently the worldwide supply of capital. Some even see the multinational corporation as a highly revolutionary development leading to a global reorganization of production, a complete internationalization of national economies, and even a reduction in the power of the nation-state as we now know it. On the other hand, the critics contend that the multinational corporation has led to a loss of jobs and exports for the United States, a decline in productivity and income in the United States, a decline of social control of business, undue exploitation of foreign labor and natural resources, the support (by the United States) of unpopular and undemocratic foreign governments. These claims and counterclaims have by no means been resolved, partly because the vested and ideological interests have made dispassionate dialogue difficult, but mainly because of deficiencies in those portions of economic theory dealing with this subject.

It is my central contention that the generally accepted international economic theory is incapable of dealing with many of the problems now facing the international economy, and also domestic economies. The established trade theory is open to many criticisms. To a considerable degree, it has wandered far from the brilliant formulation by David Ricardo, and even from the writings of such important modern theorists as Eli Heckscher and Bertil Ohlin. My major complaint is that the development of trade theory in the last few decades has stressed logical rigor and intellectual consistency at the expense of relevance and common-sense insights.[8] All models have to make some sacrifices of reality if they are to be tractable, and rigor and consistency are certainly in themselves not undesirable. But it can be argued that trade theory has gone much too far in its adherence to these qualities, making extensive use of highly dubious theoretical constructs and disregarding such important problems as oligopolies, labor unions, inflation, trade imbalances. One major objective here is to reformulate trade theory, to make it more relevant, simple, and consistent with the main body of economic theory.

The state of the established trade theory is also largely responsible for the lack of any generally accepted theory of international investment—particularly direct investment—and has even impeded the search for such a theory. This is so mainly because the established trade theory leaves little room for international investment. First, this theory is based upon the assumption that all factors of production are internationally immobile. Second, an important theorem derived from this theory is that free trade will equalize the returns to the factors of production in the trading countries, so that incentives for foreign investment cannot exist under these conditions. Any attempt to build a theory of foreign investment upon a trade theory that both first assumes and then deduces that foreign investment does not and cannot come about will surely be a futile exercise. A great deal of my effort will be devoted to developing models that can both explain international investment and assess its consequences.

This assessment emphasizes the economic welfare of the individual nation. Some will surely view this welfare criterion as too narrow and would bring other matters into consideration, such as obligations to help the struggling less-developed countries, to contain communism, to promote international unity, and so on. I do not reject these other considerations out of hand, but only point out that we may have to be aware of their economic costs. Furthermore, as an economist, I feel constrained to remain in my area of competency.

The major theoretical contribution I hope to make is to integrate international trade and investment into a single model. This will be done largely by a redefinition of "exports" and "imports." The term "international trade" as now used connotes goods, services, or money being traded between residents of different territorially defined nations. In my terminology, I refer to "transnational transactions," and define international trade as occurring when citizens or organizations of different nationalities transact business, regardless of their locations. This redefinition will enable us to see that indirect foreign investment (or foreign loans) is simply another type of trade while direct foreign investment *enables* new types of trade, such as the purchase by one country of the labor or land services of another.

Modern economic analysis has become increasingly characterized in its exposition by the use of mathematics and highly technical terminology. This development presents problems to all writers in this field. What training on the part of the reader is to be assumed? How much explanation and background of various concepts is required? The approach taken here is to make my work intelligible to the general economist as well as to the specialist in international economics. It is also my hope to make the work accessible to those who do not consider themselves professional economists—but they will have to have some familiarity with the tools of economic analysis. My attempts to reach a broader audience will at some points require discussion that will appear elementary to professional economists, but I hope that my colleagues will bear with me in these instances.

CHAPTER TWO

The Closed Economy

This chapter employs well-known tools of economic analysis to provide a model of an economy prior to any international economic dealings. Such a pretrade model is required for two reasons. First, both international trade and international investment may be expected to respond to international differences in the monetary prices of goods and returns on investment prior to these transactions. Second, if we are to assess the impacts of international trade and investments on a nation's welfare, we must be able to measure this welfare prior to these international transactions. Our model assumes a capitalist free-market economy, but one that is not necessarily purely competitive: that is, such a model will be capable of accommodating various types of market imperfections and governmental controls.

The model presented here is very conventional, adhering closely to the rather prosaic "partial equilibrium analysis" associated with Alfred Marshall. However, although conventional, it differs markedly from the model currently employed by most theorists in international trade. Modern trade theory, together with a few other branches of economics, has adopted the analytical method that has become known as "general equilibrium analysis," which attempts to relate all aspects of an economic system to one another—in sharp contrast to partial equilibrium analysis, which focuses upon the behavior of individual markets. Although there is much that is intellectually satisfying about general equilibrium analysis, it is my central contention that its inherent complexities require that it be presented at such a high level of abstraction that it can shed no light on a multitude of real problems. In opting for the admittedly less intellectually satisfying partial equilibrium approach, it is my belief that the choice is for relevance and flexibility, even at the expense of rigor and elegance.

A. GENERAL AND PARTIAL EQUILIBRIUM COMPARED

Since the general equilibrium approach is so important to modern trade theory, it appears necessary to show how this approach operates and to comment on its shortcomings. The nub of general equilibrium analysis—at least as it is used in trade theory—is that there is some fixed amount of each productive factor—labor, land, capital—at least in the short run. Thus, given some general state of technology, there must be some upper limit to the combinations of quantities of different goods that can be produced. These limitations are summed up in the "production possibility frontier" (PPF), shown for a two-product economy as figure 2.1.

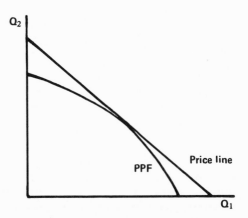

Figure 2.1 Production Possibility Frontier

Given the notion of a production possibility frontier, the supply curves of the two products must be consistent in the sense that more of one product supplied must result in less of the other product supplied. To obtain one point on the supply curve for each product, a price line is chosen, as shown in figure 2.1, whose slope reflects the relative prices of the two goods. The tangency of this price line to the production possibility frontier then provides the points—based on the argument that these output levels should come about in a purely competitive market economy. By varying the price line, the supply curves of both products could be generated, as shown in figure 2.2. It will be noted that the "prices" are not in the usual monetary terms, but are rather price ratios, which are useful if these supply curves are to be consistent with the production possibility frontier.

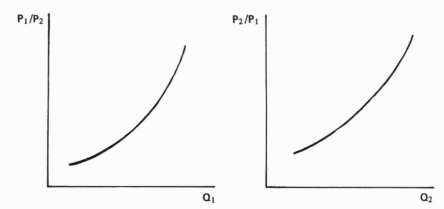

Figure 2.2 Supply Curves: General Equilibrium
Analysis

Let us discuss some of the shortcomings of this model. The first is the very notion of a production possibility frontier, which depends upon a fixed quantity of each productive factor. Perhaps the greatest problem is with labor, which this model takes to be absolutely fixed in size. This assumption is in contradiction to most other branches of economics, which generally view the labor force as variable in size, responding to the wage rate. It is also at odds with the admittedly long-run labor supply curves of Adam Smith and David Ricardo—two economists to whom trade theory owes immense debts—who saw the supply of labor as greatly expandable at the subsistence level wage rate or above. Even land, or at least the land put into productive use, can be expanded. It is a widely accepted proposition, originally advanced by Ricardo, that the amount of land put into production is not constant, but will vary with the prices of food and other raw materials. Of course, once it is admitted that these factors of production can be increased, the production possibility frontier itself is virtually indeterminate.

A second shortcoming of the general equilibrium model is its dependence on the assumption that all markets are purely competitive. Once we introduce labor unions, oligopolies, governmental policies —all surely important in the modern world—there can be unemployment, and there is thus no reason the output mix must lie on the production possibility frontier. With unemployment or a variable sized labor force, the supply curves need therefore not be constrained as in figure 2.2. Of course we should be very dubious about the value of a model that disregards the problems of noncompetitive markets that have been such major concerns of economic theory for the last five decades.

A third shortcoming of the general equilibrium approach is its reliance upon price ratios rather than monetary prices. Price ratios are useful not only for obtaining consistency between product supply curves and the production possibility frontier, but their use more importantly reflects a nineteenth-century view that only relative prices, rather than absolute monetary prices, are important. It is true that general equilibrium analysis permits the expression of prices in terms of money, but the internal logic of this approach is greatest only if the money supply is constant. This use of price ratios has made modern trade theory quite different from the Ricardian formulation, and has hampered modern trade theory from considering many problems revolving about exchange rates and price inflation.

The distinguishing feature of partial equilibrium analysis is its focus upon the behavior of individual markets. The rationale for such a narrow focus is that there are large numbers of markets in an economy, so that the operation of one market will not have *significant* impacts on *all* other markets, but rather only on those that are somehow closely related. One must concede that, in ignoring some of the interdependencies among markets, partial equilibrium analysis does not give as complete a picture of the whole economy as does general equilibrium analysis. But because partial equilibrium analysis is less ambitious in its scope, it does not have to make the same sacrifices in reality and relevance as does general equilibrium analysis in order to remain tractable.

B. OUTPUT MARKETS

Although partial equilibrium analysis assumes a large number of products in an economy, we here assume a small number for the sole purpose of keeping our models reasonably manageable. Though we often assume for simplicity that the economy consists of only two productive sectors, we work with a larger number in our broader framework. There will be two sectors producing manufactured consumer goods (C_1 and C_2), a sector producing raw material (R), a capital goods sector (K), and a "services" sector (S). The nature of the markets for these different sectors have distinguishing features, to which we now turn.

The manufactured goods are assumed to require three inputs: labor, capital, and raw materials. For C_1, for example, the production function is taken as follows:

$$C_1 = a\, L^\alpha K^\beta \qquad (2.1)$$
$$R = k\, C_1 \qquad (2.2)$$

In the use of these two equations we take capital (K) and labor (L) to be partially substitutable for each other—using the Cobb-Douglas form—while the raw material is in fixed proportion to the output level. Parameters α and β can be interpreted to reflect the extent to which production techniques are labor- or capital-intensive. The higher the value of α, the more labor-intensive the technology. The short-run supply curve will depend on the production function, the amount of fixed assets, and the prices of the variable inputs. The more labor-intensive the technology for a given product, the more price-elastic will be its short-run supply curve.

An important characteristic of most manufactured goods is that their quality can be changed through time. As a general rule, product improvements take place by applying increasing amounts of labor and capital to the raw materials, thus "working up" the latter into more highly fabricated finished goods. As a result, through time, raw material costs tend to become a smaller proportion of total production costs. An important exception to this general rule is fuels, which tend to be linked to the use of machinery rather than to output.

The demand for a particular consumer good depends on a number of variables, the most important of which are its price; the income of consumers; the portion of income saved; the "closeness" of substitutes; the prices of substitutes and complements; tastes. Given the demand and supply curves, the market-clearing price and the output level could be determined with the familiar supply/demand analysis.

The most important characteristic of the supply of raw materials is that they require an input of "nature" (land, climate, etc.) in addition to man-supplied inputs. Since the quality of nature with respect to any particular raw material can vary so greatly, this implies production costs for a raw material can vary dramatically among nations. With limitations on land, there is also a strong tendency for production costs to rise greatly through time for a growing nation as it has to put more of its marginal lands into production—which can also lead to large differences in production costs among nations. Other important considerations about raw materials are that minerals are depletable and that the production of agricultural goods can, because of weather, be unreliable.

The tendency for manufactured goods to use smaller proportions of raw materials has important implications for the demand for raw materials. In general, we should expect the demand for a broadly defined raw material to be highly price-inelastic; this is almost always true for any input that is both necessary and used in quantities that are small compared to other inputs. One result of a highly price-inelastic demand is that the market price depends heavily upon conditions of supply. The tendency for manufactured goods to use a smaller ratio of raw materials to other inputs also implies that in a growing economy demand for raw materials grows more slowly than that for other goods. Fuels, again, are an important exception to this general rule.

The capital goods sector can be broadly defined to include not only the production of these goods, but also engineering, product design, financing, research, and education. This sector can be characterized as producing individualized products, and also uses a high proportion of skilled labor. This is the sector most responsible for the development of new technology, capital formation, and the growth of the economy. It can be considered somewhat more complex in organization than the others, and an advanced capital goods sector is perhaps the most important feature that distinguishes the highly developed economy from others. The growth of this sector depends heavily upon the educational/training system.

The demand for capital goods depends upon a number of well-known variables: profit prospects; the rate of interest; the development of new technologies. The position of the demand curve, so heavily dependent upon long-run forecasts, tends to be more volatile than those of the other sectors. Since buyers of capital goods are generally more concerned with quality, service, dependability, and financing than with price, the demand for capital goods probably tends to be rather price-inelastic.

The services sector can include both personal and business services. Its most important characteristic is that there must usually be physical proximity of the provider and buyer of a service. As a result, services are usually not transportable and tradeable over international boundaries. It is largely because of this sector that international trade cannot completely integrate national economies.

C. LABOR MARKETS AND
INCOME DISTRIBUTION

The analysis of labor markets enables the determination not only of wage rates and employment but also of returns to capital. Trade can be expected to affect wage rates and sectoral profits, and thereby provides the incentives that underlie the intersectoral movement of productive resources and the transformation of an economy. Differences in wage rates and returns to capital among nations are also important to international investment.

1. The Supply of Labor

The nature of the labor supply curve—that is, the relation between the wage rate and labor offered—depends upon a number of conditions. One is the nature of the purchaser(s) of labor services: a firm, a sector, a group of sectors, the whole economy. A second is the nature of the labor, whether homogeneous or varying by skills. If we disregard skill differences and take labor to be homogeneous, there is only one labor market in a country. But if we consider skills, there would be a separate labor market for each category of labor skills. There is also no reason why a skill category must be specific to just one producing sector; thus more than one sector may be in the same labor market.

According to variations in these conditions, the labor supply curve could take one of the three "basic" shapes shown in figure 2.3. Shape (a) implies a fixed supply of labor willing to work at any wage rate. Shape (b) implies an expandable supply of labor willing (or able) to work only at some minimum wage rate or above. Shape (c) implies a labor supply that will expand only with higher wage rates. (Shape (c) need not always be linear.)

Let us assume there is only one labor market in the economy. There have been a number of views on which of the three types of supply curve best describes reality—and these views have had important effects on the conclusions drawn from economic analysis. Modern trade theory, so dependent upon the production possibility

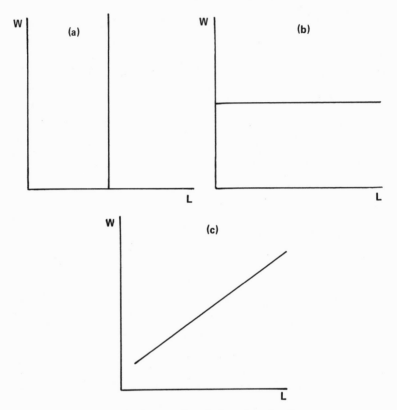

Figure 2.3 Alternative Labor Supply Curves

frontier, takes the labor supply curve as in (a). Ricardo, however, who did much of the pioneering work in trade theory, takes the long-run labor supply curve to be as in (b). He assumed a virtually infinite supply of labor at the subsistence level of real wages. John Maynard Keynes also took the labor supply curve as in (b), but for a different reason, namely that labor unions will not permit the monetary wage rate to fall. Neoclassical economists, making use of utility analysis (which includes the disutility of work), take the labor supply curve as in (c). One can appreciate how markedly modern trade theory in this important area differs from classical, neoclassical, and Keynesian economics.

To a firm, the labor supply curve would be as in (b) (assuming the firm is not a monopsonist), with the wage rate determined either in a free labor market or by negotiations with a labor union. If a producing sector is only one of a number of sectors using a certain type of labor, it too would face a labor supply curve as in (b). If, however, that sector is the only employer of a certain skill category of worker, the labor supply curve could be any one of the three types shown in figure 2.3. Which one would occur would depend upon whether or not labor could transfer from one labor market to another, and whether the wage rate is determined by free markets or is negotiated with a labor union.

2. The Demand for Labor

The study of the demand for labor begins with the "representative" firm. If this firm sells in purely competitive markets, its demand for labor is determined by the value of the marginal product of each incremental worker—a procedure well explained in all microeconomics textbooks. However, since we have chosen to include raw materials in the production function, this procedure has to be expanded. If raw materials are ignored, the profit-maximizing firm hires labor up to the point where the value of the marginal product equals the wage rate. But with raw materials, the firm would have to subtract the value of the raw materials used by a worker from the value of his marginal product to determine whether it is worth hiring him. The difference between the value of the marginal product and the value of the raw materials—or more broadly any variable input complementary to labor—can be called the *net* value of the marginal product (NVMP). We take the curve for the net value of the marginal product as the demand curve for labor.

The market demand curve for labor is of course the summation of the net value of the marginal product curves of all the firms in a labor market. The wage elasticity of this demand curve for labor will depend mainly on how labor-intensive the technologies are. (A high value of α relative to β in equation 2.1 reflects a labor-intensive technology.) The more labor-intensive the technology, the more wage-elastic will be the demand curve for labor. It is well known that the labor demand curve will shift either to the left or to the right with: a decrease or increase in the prices of outputs; disinvestment or investment in capital assets by existing firms in that labor market; exits or entries of firms. Our consideration of raw materials gives one more reason why this demand curve could shift its position. A decrease in prices of raw materials will increase the net value of the marginal product of each worker, and thereby shift the demand for labor to the right. An increase in these prices will of course have the opposite effect.

3. The Factoral Distribution of Income

Using the conventional supply/demand analysis, we can readily determine the wage rate and the distribution of income between labor and capital—either for a firm, a sector, a group of sectors, or the whole economy. This is shown in figure 2.4 for a sector. Al-

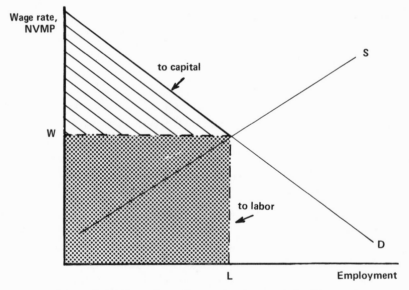

Figure 2.4 Wage Rate Determination and the Factoral Distribution of Income

though we use a supply curve as in (c) of figure 2.3, the curve could also take on other shapes. The returns to capital would of course have to be divided by the investment level to determine the rate of return on investment in that sector.

D. REAL NATIONAL INCOME AND WELFARE

For reasons to be discussed later, we take real national income (RNI) as a measure of a nation's welfare—as opposed to the alternative of maximizing some "social welfare" function. In national income accounting, the national income for a closed economy must equal the monetary value of all final goods produced during some accounting period. When this value is divided by a price index (we use consumer prices), the real national income is obtained. Assuming the final goods of the economy consist of two consumer manufactured goods (C_1 and C_2), capital goods (K), and personal services (S), then real national income would be as follows:

$$RNI = (P_1C_1 + P_2C_2 + P_kK + P_sS) / (w_1P_1 + w_2P_2 + w_3P_s) \qquad (2.3)$$

In this formula, C_1, C_2, K, and S represent the quantities *produced* by each sector, while the P's represent unit prices. The w's represent the weights in the price index—with the weight for a particular consumer good determined by the proportion of all consumer expenditures devoted to that good in some base period.

Of course real national income can only grow with increases in output levels. For a closed economy, this would normally take place with increases in capital formation, new technologies, or perhaps a larger labor force. When we turn to trade, we will also find that real national income can grow—and sometimes decrease—as a result of trade by itself. It should be noted that, in an open economy, intermediate goods that are exported become part of a nation's real national income, while imported intermediate goods must be subtracted in its calculation.

CHAPTER THREE

The Explanation of Trade

The introduction of international trade will have a number of consequences which we should want to measure and explain. First, there is the trade pattern itself: types, quantities, and prices of exports and imports for the trading partners; terms of trade; adjustment to trade imbalances. Second, trade will affect the internal economies of the trading partners: prices, output patterns, consumption patterns, the distribution of income. Trade will also affect the levels of real national income, but these "welfare" implications of trade are deferred until the next chapter. We would also wish to explain what it is that underlies trade. These tasks, except for the welfare implications of trade, are undertaken in this chapter.

There is a widely used model that purports to demonstrate how, given certain production possibilities and consumption preferences, trade will take place. This is based on so-called "offer curves." We consider this offer-curve approach to be inadequate. The main portion of this chapter is devoted to constructing an alternative model which is simpler, more realistic, and more capable of investigating a wider range of trade problems.

A number of assumptions are maintained throughout this chapter. First, it is assumed that all trade is carried on by private profit- and utility-maximizing firms and consumers. Second, we restrict ourselves to two trading nations, A and B, to keep the model simple. Third, we adopt that most important assumption in the development of trade theory, namely that the factors of production are internationally immobile. Except for movements of money, this assumption is maintained until we turn to the chapters on international investment.

A. THE OFFER-CURVE
APPROACH: A CRITIQUE

The offer-curve technique is so widely explained in textbooks that we need do no more than sketch its main characteristics.[1] The derivation of a country's offer curve begins with its production possibility frontier and "social indifference curve map," and for simplicity only two products are assumed. Then some price ratio between the two goods is selected—this being a potential posttrade price ratio—and the optimal consumption and production pattern is determined for this price ratio. This is shown in figure 3.1 for products C_1 and C_2.

According to this diagram, at the price ratio shown, the incentives are such that this country would produce the product combination denoted by point $a,$ but consume the product combination denoted by point b. This country would then offer to export ad units of C_1 to its trading partner in exchange for db units of C_2. There is then a unique quantity of each product "offered" (both to buy and to sell) associated with this particular price ratio. This procedure can be repeated for each possible price ratio; and, by so doing, a whole schedule of buying and selling offers associated with all alternative price ratios can be established. When this procedure is repeated for the trading partner, a similar "offer curve" can be drawn. When the two offer curves are drawn on the same diagram, a market-clearing trading price ratio can be found such that the reciprocal offers to buy and sell the two products will be equalized— that is, trade is in balance. Export and import levels for the trading partners in both goods are also determined.

Let us turn to criticisms of the offer-curve approach. The first is its manifest dependence on the notion of a social indifference curve map. There are many who doubt even the theoretical existence and meaning of such a map. Note the guarded language and reservations

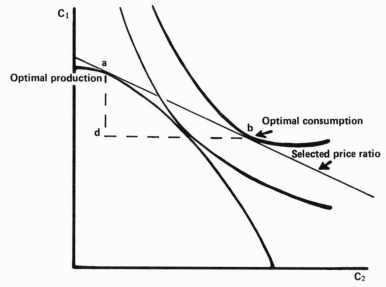

Figure 3.1 Optimal Production and Consumption
Pattern

in the following passage in which Caves and Jones decide to use
such maps.

> Using indifference curves for a community of individuals (say a
> country) as well as for any single individual would be extremely
> *convenient.* Under *strict assumptions* this can be done—e.g., if all
> individuals have identical tastes and initial endowments of food and
> clothing. We have *decided to assume* in this book that community
> preferences may be represented by a set of non-intersecting indiffer-
> ence curves. Later we shall point out some of the implications of
> this assumption. Here we state explicitly that such an assumption is
> made in full awareness of its *abstraction from reality* and is *justified
> by its facilitation* of *all* our subsequent discussions of the welfare ef-
> fects of trade, commercial policy, and growth.[2] [emphasis added]

Perhaps even more questionable is the relation of a social indifference curve map to laissez-faire economics. An important proposition underlying the advocacy of a free market system is that only

the individual can judge his utility in consumption, a proposition tenaciously adhered to by generations of libertarians. If this proposition is accepted, then even the notion of a social indifference curve map is downright seditious in its implications for individualism. Such a map implies that a governmental authority can always know the optimal pattern of consumption (and thus production) for a community, and therefore provides a strong philosophical basis for state planning. Because of this implication, most libertarians would reject the concept of a social indifference curve map. Yet, such a map quite inconsistently (on philosophical grounds) is used to advocate free trade policies.

A second problem with offer curves is also based on the social indifference curve map. These maps have meaning only for consumption goods. Thus, even if these maps could be defended, they are not readily useful in explaining trade in nonconsumer goods— raw materials, capital goods, intermediate components.

A third criticism of offer curves, as they are generally used, is the assumption that trade is in balance. (The offer-curve approach, however, allows, for a *predetermined* imbalance in trade.)[3] Of course trade imbalances are very real problems, and there are many reasons they can occur: deficit countries may have reserves of gold and other acceptable means of payment; individuals and central banks in the surplus nation may be willing to hold the national currency of the deficit country; loans can be made; the citizens of one country may buy nontraded items such as land in the other country. The important point for our purposes here is that, without an assumption of a balance in trade or a predetermined trade imbalance, the offer curves cannot determine unique price ratios and hence any unique pattern of trade.

A fourth problem with the offer-curve approach is that all prices are expressed as ratios of exchange between goods rather than in monetary terms. This was done, one may suppose, in order to get around the fact that countries have different currencies and also to reflect the view of some that relative rather than absolute prices are all that really matter. (It also reflects the general equilibrium approach.) Of course, this treatment of prices means that the offer-curve approach cannot say anything about the effects of domestic and international monetary policies upon trade. The failure of the offer-curve approach to use the usual monetary denominations of prices has led to a type of "pure" trade theory that has created a most unnatural divorce between trade theory and international monetary policy.

Fifth, the offer curves imply a "solidarity" of each of the two national groups engaging in trade. "All" As are taken to trade with "all" Bs. Of course, in reality "some" As buy or sell particular products from or to "some" Bs, and a group exporting one product need not be the same group that imports another product. This solidarity assumption also implies a complete harmonization of the economic interests of each national group in trade, which is, of course, completely at variance with the great clashes that have taken place within nations over trade policy.

Despite our malignment of the offer-curve approach, a few words can be said on its behalf. Most importantly, it has taken on an ambitious task, namely the development of a consistent general equilibrium model of a whole economy in trade with another economy. The goal is commendable. But, although the offer-curve model has had some success in terms of presenting everything in a single (though not uncomplicated) diagram, its accomplishments have been obtained only at the cost of an exceedingly high level of abstraction.

We instead turn to the more prosaic partial equilibrium tools, in which attention is focused upon the behavior of individual markets under trade. Rather than viewing a group of As bartering with a group of Bs, our model emphasizes the integration of individual markets that trade brings about.

B. THE TRADE MODEL: SHORT-RUN ASPECTS

The model developed here centers upon an individual product. Before trade, there is a separate market for any given product in each country. These markets are portrayed with the traditional supply/demand curves, with prices expressed in terms of the currency of each country. When trade is introduced, individual buyers and sellers in both countries compare *monetary* prices for that product in both countries, and make offers to buy from or sell to the trading partner country based on any price differentials. Even if some individual producers and consumers do not make these comparisons, it can be safely assumed that a class of professional traders exists which buys in the country with the lower price and resells in the country with the higher price.

It is important to emphasize that the market for an individual product is our basic unit of analysis. This view is taken because citizens of country A and country B, in dealing with each other, are generally concerned only with a single product and have no concern with whether other products are being traded or whether trade is in balance. Of course, imports of one product, if not matched by exports of another, can lead to trade imbalances that set in motion adjustment mechanisms affecting trade in all products. But in the partial equilibrium analysis we are using, trade in other goods and any adjustment mechanism are considered exogenous to the market for any particular product.

The model has both short-run and long-run aspects. In the short run, fixed productive assets are assumed to be intersectorally immobile. Hence, in this period, the supply curves in both countries for any product are fixed in their positions: output can only be increased or decreased through the use of more (or less) variable inputs, mainly labor. Short-run trade, however, will normally affect returns on capital on traded products in both countries, thereby providing incentives for capital to move from one product sector to another. These intersectoral movements of capital will be reflected in shifts in the positions of the supply curves. These shifts will then have an additional impact on trade patterns and the internal economies of both countries, and are the long-run aspects of the trade model.

1. Price Equivalents

A buyer or seller in one country, in deciding whether to deal with a foreign rather than a domestic buyer or seller, must be able to compare the prices in the two countries for any given product. Such a comparison must take into account exchange rates, transport costs, and any taxes or subsidies on imported or exported products. An A trader, for example, will have to "translate" a price in B in terms of B currency to its "price equivalent" (PE) to him in terms of A currency.

Let us define e, the exchange rate, as follows:

$$e = M^b/M^a \qquad (3.1)$$

which is the number of units of B currency that exchanges for one unit of A currency. Ignoring transport costs and taxes and subsidies, the price equivalent to an A of a price in B—P^b—is

$$(PE)_a^b = (1/e)P^b \qquad (3.2)$$

To a B, the price equivalent of a price in A becomes

$$(PE)_b^a = eP^a \qquad (3.3)$$

The subscript of the price equivalent designates the nationality of the individual making the translation—the superscript designates the other country.

If T is the unit transport cost, assumed to be paid in A currency, the price equivalent to an A buyer of the price in B becomes

$$(PE)_a^b = (1/e)P^b + T \qquad (3.4)$$

An A seller, however, subtracts the transport cost, so that to him the price equivalent becomes

$$(PE)_a^b = (1/e)P^b - T \qquad (3.5)$$

All types of taxes and subsidies need to be considered in this translation process. Thus, if an A importer has to pay an ad valorem tax of t percent on the value in B of a product (expressed in A currency), the price equivalent to him of that product's price in B will be as follows:

$$(PE)_a^b = (1/e)P^b + t(1/e)P^b + T = [(1+t)/e]P^b + T \qquad (3.6)$$

If, as another example, a B exporter has to pay this ad valorem tax on the price in A, to him the price equivalent will be:

$$(PE)_b^a = eP^a - teP^a - T = (1 - t) eP^a - T \qquad (3.7)$$

Equations such as 3.6 and 3.7 could be formulated for a wide variety of taxes and subsidies.

To generalize, we can write $(PE)_a^b = f(P^b)$ and $(PE)_b^a = f(P^a)$. This implies that, for a given exchange rate, unit transport cost, and tax or subsidy, there will be a unique price equivalent to an A of any price in B and vice versa.

2. The Model: The Supply Variation

The "market-integration" model works with just one product, and it can be any kind of product—consumer goods, raw materials, and so forth. It begins with the supply and demand curves for that product in both A and B. It can then operate in two ways: either by considering the quantities sellers in one country offer buyers in the other country—the supply variation—or by considering the quantities buyers in one country offer to purchase from sellers in the other country, the demand variation. Both variations always yield the same results, but we develop both because under certain circumstances one or the other could be more convenient to work with. In this section we show only the supply model. It is assumed pretrade prices are such that this product is exported from A to B. We also assume at this point that any product produced by both countries is identical, that there are no import or export quotas, and that there are no forms of cartels setting either selling or buying prices. We further assume that payment is made at the time of sale, and that expectations of exchange rate changes have negligible impact on the behavior of traders.

A synopsis of the model could be helpful. Assume a pretrade price exists in A at P^a. Assume now there is some price in B for that product, P^b, such that $(PE)_a^b$ $(=f(P^b))$ is greater than P^a. At that price in B—P^b—A sellers would sell to A buyers *only* at its price equivalent: that is, an A seller would refuse to sell at home for a price less than the equivalent of the price he can obtain in B. The price equivalent of the price in B thus sets an effective "floor" to the price in A and establishes a new supply curve to the A market. At the $(PE)_a^b$ of P^b, there may therefore be an excess of the quantity A sellers wish to sell over the quantity A buyers wish to buy. This excess would be offered for sale on the B market. At each alternative value of P^b there would be an alternative "excess" the As wish to supply to the B market, and the locus of these price/quantity points becomes the supply curve of A to B, which we call S_a^b. There will now be two supply curves to the B market, one from B sellers and one from A sellers. These could be added together to obtain an aggregate supply curve to the B market. This aggregate supply curve, together with the demand curve in B, determines the posttrade price in B. The price equivalent in A of this price in B then becomes the posttrade price in A. From the usual supply and demand graphs, one can readily determine: exports and imports, prices, quantities produced and purchased in both countries.

Figure 3.2 graphically derives the supply curve of A to B. Consider the left frame of figure 3.2. Ignoring lines EF and E'F', there is a pretrade supply and demand curve in A that establishes a pretrade price and the quantity produced and purchased, which must be equal. Now we introduce trade. Say the price of that product in B is $P^b_{(1)}$, and the value of $(PE)_a^b$ corresponding to $P^b_{(1)}$ is as shown in this frame. How would the A sellers react to this price in B? They would presumably refuse to sell in the A market for any price below the price equivalent of $P^b_{(1)}$. Thus, the price equivalent in A of $P^b_{(1)}$ sets the "floor" on the supply price at which A sellers would sell to A buyers. The effective supply curve to the A market now becomes EFG, and the price in A will be $P^a = f(P^b_{(1)})$. At this higher price, however, A buyers wish to buy only Q_d units of the product while sellers wish to sell Q_s units. The difference between the quantities supplied and the quantities demanded at this price, shown as ab, is the "excess" that would be offered on the B market.[4] If the price in B were $P^b_{(2)}$, by the same reasoning cd would be the excess supply offered by As to the B market. The relation between

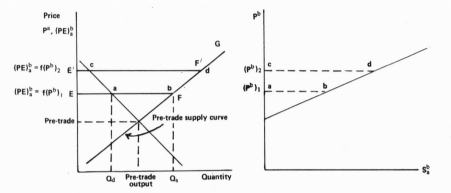

Figure 3.2 Derivation of Supply of A to B

all values of P^b and the excess supplies then becomes S_a^b, the external supply curve of A sellers to the B market, which is shown in the right-hand frame of figure 3.2.

Let us turn next to the B market, described in figure 3.3. The S_a^b curve can be horizontally added to the internal supply curve to obtain the aggregate supply curve as shown. The unprimed variables show pretrade price, output level, and purchases in B, while the primed variables show their posttrade values. Imports into B are evidently Q_d' minus Q_s'. The price equivalent to A sellers of the posttrade price in B then establishes the nature of the supply curve in the A market (in form as EFG in figure 3.2) and thereby the posttrade price, output, and purchases in A. These posttrade values of course can be usefully compared with the pretrade values.

3. The Model: The Demand Variation

Instead of working with supply, we can work with demand to obtain much the same results.

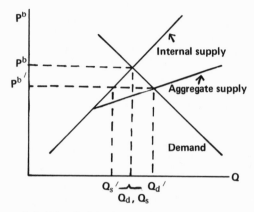

Figure 3.3 The B Market: Before and After Trade

The left frame of figure 3.4 portrays the B market, with the pre-trade supply and demand curves and the pretrade price. Let us now say some price $P^a_{(1)}$ exists in A whose price equivalent to a B buyer is below the pretrade price in B. Given the availability of goods from A at that price, B buyers would not pay above its price equivalent to B sellers. That price equivalent then sets a "ceiling" on the demand curve in the B market, which then becomes EFG. At this price, B buyers wish to buy more than B sellers wish to sell, and the segment ab measures the excess demand in the B market. The right-hand frame of figure 3.4 gives this amount of ab as the quantity Bs demand from A at $P^a_{(1)}$—and is one point on D^a_b, the B demand curve from A. By varying the value of P^a, the full demand curve D^a_b can be generated, showing how many units B would buy from A at alternative prices in A.

The D^a_b curve can now be added to the internal demand curve in A to obtain the aggregate demand curve for A's output. This aggregate demand curve, in conjunction with the supply curve in A, enables us to readily calculate all the pretrade and posttrade values for the variables. This is shown in figure 3.5, with the primed variables representing posttrade values. The price established in A then determines the exact position of a demand curve in B of the type EFG shown in the left frame of figure 3.4.

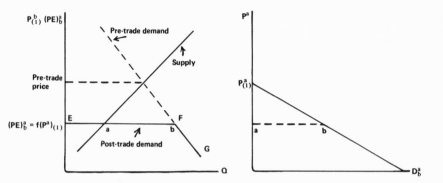

Figure 3.4 Derivation of B's Demand from A

4. A Joint Consideration of the Two Variations

Both the supply and demand variations could be shown together, as in figure 3.6. Note that in B (the importing country) the demand curve is horizontal at the price equivalent in B of the price established in A. Similarly, the supply curve in A is horizontal at the price equivalent in A of the price established in B. Allowing for price-equivalent conversions, the posttrade price becomes the same in both countries. Although either variation of the model can be used by itself to yield the results, it is well to bear in mind that adjustments to trade take place in both countries.

5. A Note on Quotas

The trade model can also take into consideration quantitative restrictions on trade. Assume B imposes an import quota on a particular product. Then the S_a^b curve in the right-hand frame of figure 3.2 becomes vertical at the quota level, the same occurring for the D_b^a curve in figure 3.4. The same methodology enables the calculation of all posttrade values within the two countries. However, the equilibrium posttrade price in one country need no longer be the price equivalent of the posttrade price in the other—the quota

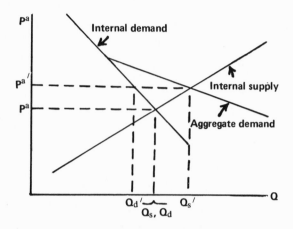

Figure 3.5 Calculation of Posttrade Price, Demand, and Production in A

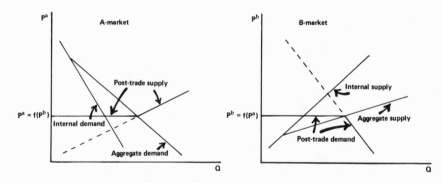

Figure 3.6 The Two Variations Shown Together

breaks the price linkage. Nor is there a readily established trading price: that price will depend upon whether there are other countries exporting or importing the quotaed product and the extent, if any, to which exporters or importers are organized in their trading with other countries.

The trade integration model can be readily adapted to account for quotas. If we assume that B enacts an import quota, then the right-hand frames of figures 3.2 and 3.4 would appear as in figure 3.7.

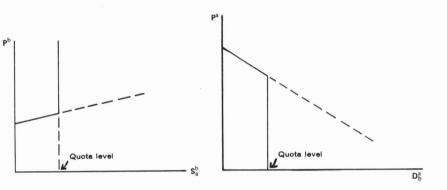

Figure 3.7 Effect of Quota on Supply of A to B and
Demand of B from A

Figure 3.8 is an adaptation of figure 3.6, which is designed to demonstrate the impact of this quota upon the internal market in each country. The unprimed variables show the posttrade values in both countries without the quota, while the primed variables display these values with a quota.

6. Product Differentiation

The trade model has assumed the traded product produced by each country is identical in all its characteristics. However, many products can be differentiated—with respect to quality, styling, reputation, tied terms such as credit or repair facilities, and the like. The trade model can readily accommodate such complexities. Although firms actually differentiate products, it is not going too far afield to think of an A version and a B version of a particular product. These

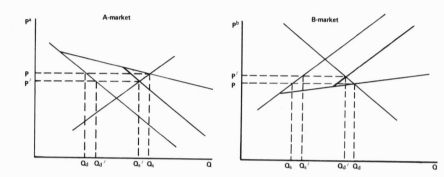

Figure 3.8 Impact of a Quota on Internal Markets

two versions could be treated as separate markets, although of course the demand curves for any version in both countries can be highly influenced by the price and product characteristics of the alternative version. If there is a demand for both versions of a product in both countries, it is quite possible that two-way trade can take place in different versions of essentially the same product.

7. A Note on Cartels

Let us assume the A sellers are organized into an export cartel. If the cartel attempts to maximize its joint profits, it would then calculate a marginal revenue curve from the Bs' demand curve from the As—the right-hand frame of figure 3.4—and then select a single offering price to the B market. The supply curve of the A cartel to the Bs will then become a horizontal line at the selected price. If the Bs were organized into a buying cartel, they would presumably assess the supply curve of A to B—the right-hand frame in figure 3.2—to select an optimal offering price at which to buy. The Bs' demand curve from the As will then become a horizontal line at this price. It is well to bear in mind that a state trading company, such as that used by centrally planned economies, combines the attributes of both a quota-setting agency and a cartel.

C. LONG-RUN TRADE PATTERNS

Since trade changes output prices, the curves for the net value of the marginal product should shift in each country (see figure 2.4) —to the right for the export sector and to the left for the import-competing sector. As a result, the rate of return on capital rises in each country in its export sector relative to that in its import-competing sector—assuming the labor supply curves are not completely vertical. Capital should then move to each country's export sector. As a result, the short-run supply curves of the export sectors also shift to the right, while those of the import-competing sectors shift to the left. Each country then further specializes in producing its exported product, and trade in both products should increase.

The long-run positions of the supply curves in both countries— assuming no restrictions on the intersectoral movement of capital— should be those at which the rate of return on capital in each sector is equalized in each country. (We assume risk is the same in both sectors.) The exact long-run positions of the supply curves are somewhat more complicated for the open than for the closed economy. In a closed economy the rates of return are equalized in the sectors by the intersectoral capital shifts affecting output prices and, often, input prices. But in an open economy, the rate of return in any sector also depends upon the intersectoral shifts of capital in the trading partner nation. Thus, the long-run positions of the supply curves in, say, A, will depend partly upon the extent of the capital shifts that take place in B.

D. TRADE AND THE FACTORAL DISTRIBUTION OF INCOME

One important result of trade-induced intersectoral shifts of capital is that the demand for labor, and possibly the wage rate, will change in each country. Such changes of course will alter the distribution of income between labor and capital. The impacts along these lines have been extensively studied in conjunction with the Heckscher-Ohlin model (to be discussed). However the Heckscher-Ohlin model assumes that production technology involves fixed proportions between capital and labor. Here I wish to offer a short informal proof that trade can alter wage rates when production technology is as represented by the Cobb-Douglas production function.

Assume: country A exports C_1 and imports C_2; both products are produced with Cobb-Douglas production functions; the technology of C_1 is capital-intensive relative to that for C_2. As a result of differences in factor intensities among the two products, the C_1 sector demand curve for labor will be steeper than that of the C_2 sector. Each unit of capital transferred from C_2 to C_1 (induced by trade) will raise the C_1 demand curve by the same amount the C_2 demand curve is lowered. But since the C_2 curve is flatter than the C_1 curve, the net result must be a reduction in the demand for labor by both sectors taken together. Of course, the opposite should occur in **B**.

If completely free labor markets exist in both countries—that is, if labor unions and governments do not affect wage rates and no intersectoral barriers exist for labor—the wage rate should fall in A and rise in B. Of course, returns on capital should rise in A and fall in B. But if the kinds of restrictions in the labor market noted above exist, the decreased demand for labor in A may result in unemployment rather than in a wage rate reduction.

E. COMMODITY TERMS OF TRADE

The measurement of commodity terms of trade has been widely discussed. In this short section a new variation in this measurement is added that could prove useful. We concentrate here on the terms of trade for country A, continuing to assume it exports C_1 and imports C_2.

One possible way to measure the terms of trade is by the number of units of C_2 imported per unit of C_1 exported. Such a formulation is, however, too restricted: it can give misleading figures when trade is not in balance and is not useful at all if a large number of products are traded. A superior measure of A's terms of trade $(T/T)^a$ is the amount of foreign exchange earned per unit of export divided by the amount of foreign exchange paid per unit of import. Expressed this way, with both the export and import price measured in terms of B currency, the terms of trade for A are as follows:

$$(T/T)^a = P_1^b / P_2^b \tag{3.8}$$

If more than two products are traded, the prices in this equation must be weighted to obtain an index.

A reformulation of this equation can provide some useful insights. If we assume undifferentiated products, an absence of quotas, tariffs, and cartels, and negligible transport costs, then with trade the price of a given product, allowing for conversions into price equivalents, must be the same in both countries. Thus, in particular, $P_1^b = eP_1^a$, and substituting for P_1^b enables us to express the terms of trade as follows:

$$(T/T)^a = (eP_1^a) / P_2^b \tag{3.9}$$

This is a useful formulation. It shows that A's terms of trade can improve for three different reasons: a higher domestic price for its exported product; a lower foreign price for its import; an appreciation in the value of its currency. It is worth noting that a country's terms of trade need not *necessarily* change because of a change in the value of its currency: in particular this would be the result if the change in the exchange rate came about mainly because of different rates of inflation in the trading partner countries.

F. TRADE IMBALANCES

The trade model presented here, based upon the integration of individual product markets, provides no assurance that trade must be in balance. This must be considered a virtue, since trade imbalances are very real and have created great problems for the international economy. If we ignore the possibilities of governmental action to redress trade imbalances, as through tariffs, subsidies, and quotas, there are three more or less automatic mechanisms that can lead to the elimination of trade imbalances. At this point we merely describe how they are supposed to work; in a later chapter we discuss why they in fact may not fulfill their tasks.

One adjustment mechanism, which received the earliest attention from trade theorists, operates through international money movements and internal changes in pretrade prices. As the result of a trade imbalance, gold, or some other acceptable type of money, should flow from the trade-deficit country to the trade-surplus country—thereby altering the money supply in each country. With the assumptions of purely competitive markets and no offsetting governmental policies regarding money supplies, monetary prices should rise in the surplus country and fall in the deficit country, which should of course redress the trade imbalance.

The second mechanism, associated closely with the Keynesian apparatus, operates through changes in income—and assumes downward inflexibilities in wage rates and therefore the possibility of unemployment. The trade-surplus country should have higher income and employment—the reverse being true for the trade-deficit country. Demand curves for goods should therefore shift toward the right in the surplus country (toward the left in the deficit country), which should act to redress the trade imbalance even if internal prices do not change.

The third mechanism operates through changes in exchange rates. This mechanism presupposes that national currencies are not all irrevocably pegged to gold and that central banks and international bodies do not interfere with the operation of the foreign exchange market. Given these conditions, the demand for the deficit country's currency in this market should fall relative to the demand for the currency of the surplus country. Thus, the relative value of the deficit country's currency should decline, and a consideration of our trade model shows this should redress the trade imbalance.[5]

At this point, it should be pointed out that monetary loans from the trade-surplus to the trade-deficit country can act to frustrate these adjustment mechanisms. If the loans are equal to the size of the deficit, then there will evidently be no change in the internal money supplies in either country, and the "internal price" mechanism cannot work. The loans will also result in an increased supply of the surplus country's currency on the foreign exchange markets, so that the deficit country's currency may not depreciate in value. And if the loans alter interest rates sufficiently in both countries, this may offset the effects of trade imbalance upon employment and income levels in both countries.

G. FORCES AFFECTING CHANGES IN TRADE PATTERNS

The underlying reason for trade in our model is differences in pretrade monetary prices in the trading nations, with allowance made for the translation of a price in one country into its price equivalent in the other country. This implies that anything that affects either pretrade prices or the "translation" process can alter trade patterns, quantities traded, and posttrade prices.

The process of conversion of one country's prices into price equivalents in the other country was shown to depend upon the exchange rate, transport costs, and any taxes or subsidies on trade. A rise in the value of A currency, for example, decreases the price equivalent of a price in B to a potential exporter from A. This shifts the S_a^b supply curve (see figure 3.2) to the left, with ascertainable impacts on trade. Any other changes along these lines can be readily studied with the model.

A wide range of changes in pretrade prices in either country can also affect trade patterns. These price changes can be brought on by either shifts or changes in shapes of the supply curves; among the forces that can affect these supply curves are changes in input prices, new technologies, new investments, taxes or subsidies, pollution laws, enforcement of antitrust laws, education, patent policy. Changes in the positions or shapes of demand curves can also affect internal pretrade prices. Among the forces that can bring such changes about are changes in monetary income, changes in tastes, changes in prices of complements or substitutes. Again the model can readily be used to ascertain the impacts of such changes on trade patterns.

H. THE ESTABLISHED THEORIES OF TRADE PATTERNS

The preceding section argued there can be a large number of quite complex variables that can influence trade patterns. Yet for the last one hundred and fifty years the theory of trade patterns has been dominated by two interrelated models, both of which focus upon production costs and ignore demand. These are of course the celebrated Ricardian theory of comparative advantage and the more modern and equally celebrated Heckscher-Ohlin model, which in many ways is a refinement of Ricardo's model.

Ricardo emphasized differences in technology in the production of goods as being responsible for price differentials between countries for a given product. The technological differences were reflected in the amount of labor necessary to produce a given product in each of the trading countries. It was Ricardo's great contribution to demonstrate that, even if one country were technologically superior to the other in both (or all) products, mutually advantageous trade could take place and each country would specialize in the production of the product in which its *comparative* advantage was greatest.[6]

The possibility of a trade imbalance, and the flow of money and its effect upon internal prices, were integral parts of Ricardo's model. Using much the same approach we have taken here, to Ricardo trade takes place in response to actual monetary price differentials. Thus, if one country were technologically superior in all goods, initially there would not be two-way trade. Rather, all the goods would flow from the technologically superior country (Portugal in his famous example) to the other country (England). However, gold would flow from England to Portugal and, through its impacts on internal prices, two-way trade should come about. It should be noted that the modern "offer-curve" model diverges from Ricardo's model in two important respects. First, Ricardo allowed for the possibility of a trade imbalance. Second, trade responds to differences in monetary prices rather than to price ratios.

Another integral part of Ricardo's model concerned the mobility of productive factors. Without any great difficulty (Ricardo considered only the purely competitive market model), Ricardo assumed perfect geographical and intersectoral mobility of productive factors within a country. However, the possibility of international mobility of productive factors was more of a problem. If, after all, Portugal were technologically superior to England in the production of both wine and cloth, incomes would be higher in Portugal, and one might expect English capital and labor to migrate to Portugal as an alternative to trade. Ricardo, somewhat lamely, argues that "experience" shows these factor movements would not take place because of the insecurities of living in a strange land. Ricardo also gratuitously adds that he *hopes* men of property will be satisfied with lower returns in their own country rather than seek more advantageous employment of their wealth in foreign countries. Adam Smith, however, did not share Ricardo's sanguine hopes about the patriotism of capitalists, writing:

> A merchant, it has been said, very properly, is not necessarily the citizen of any particular country. It is, in great measure, indifferent to him from what place he carries on his trade, and a very trifling disgust will make him remove his capital, and together with it all the industry which it supports, from one country to another.[7]

Nevertheless, despite Smith's remarks, Ricardo's rather weak defense of the proposition of resource immobility between countries, and the arguments of many that the facts suggest otherwise, the assumption of the international immobility of productive factors remains a cornerstone of trade theory to this day.

The Ricardian doctrine of comparative advantage dominated both the explanation and the defense of trade for about one hundred and twenty years, and is still important today. But in the 1920s and 1930s two Swedish economists, Eli Heckscher and Bertil Ohlin, developed another theory of trade that is now dominant.[8] In most respects this model is similar to the Ricardian model, since it is also based on differences in production costs. But the Heckscher-Ohlin model differs from Ricardo's model in two important respects. First, it assumes the availability of technology to be the same in all countries; second, it makes the more realistic assumption that there are two inputs used in the production of all products—labor and capital. (The development of the model allows for any number of inputs.) The use of two inputs also enabled the investigation of the impact of trade on factoral incomes.

The Heckscher-Ohlin model is based on two propositions. The first is that products differ in terms of their input factor intensities. The second proposition is that countries differ in the relative abundance (or scarcity) of the productive factors. Since these relative abundancies will be reflected in factor prices in the two countries, the model easily shows that production costs for the labor-intensive product would be lower in the labor-abundant country, the same being true for the capital-intensive product in the capital-abundant country. These differences in production costs then determine the pattern of trade and the specialization of production. An important deduction from the Heckscher-Ohlin model that will concern us greatly can also be noted: namely, trade between these two countries will equalize wage rates and returns to capital in both countries.

Both of these models are based upon a number of assumptions, which could limit their usefulness. The most striking assumption of both is that product prices reflect only the costs of production and nowhere consider demand. (The offer-curve model was an attempt to compensate for the neglect of demand in the Ricardian model.) Yet, from Ricardo's viewpoint, there was possibly a legitimate reason for ignoring demand. Ricardo, in his value theory, was always concerned only with the "natural" price, which we would today call the long-run price. And, given certain conditions, most importantly perfectly competitive markets, the long-run price should reflect the cost of production. In essence, Ricardo assumed a horizontal supply curve for manufactured goods, so that demand could affect the quantity produced of any product, but not its price.

Nevertheless, the usefulness of these models is circumscribed by ignoring demand and concentrating only upon the long-run price. Demand is assuredly one of the determinants of short-run prices, so that these models have little to say about short-run trade patterns. A greater problem is whether the long-run natural price would always materialize. For this to occur, there must be competition in markets with intersectoral mobility of resources within a country. But modern economics is largely concerned with the problem that many markets are not competitive and that many resources are not perfectly mobile. John Williams, for one, criticized the assumption of perfectly mobile resources some forty years ago.[9] Nor has the lack of competition and resource mobility been a concern only of modern economists. Adam Smith argued quite clearly that the natural, or long-run, price need never come about for any product if there is a lack of competition and restrictions exist on factor mobility. Thus, since the Ricardian and Heckscher-Ohlin models depend on this natural long-run price, they can have little to say about trade patterns in the absence of purely competitive markets and intersectoral factor mobility.

Many other assumptions underlying the Ricardian and Heckscher-Ohlin models are open to question. All resources are assumed to be homogeneous, thereby ignoring education, training, learning, motivation, technological differences. Products are also assumed to be homogeneous, thereby disregarding possibilities of product changes, advertising, reputation, trademarks and patents, and so forth. Another assumption is constant returns to scale, which is generally taken to be reasonable. I have shown elsewhere, however, that economies of *size*—a relation between size of plant and average costs of production—are not at all inconsistent with constant returns to scale (a relation between *physical* inputs and outputs), and that economies of size are quite common.[10]

Fortunately, economists in the last few decades have been proposing alternative theories of trade. These alternatives have attracted attention partly because empirical studies have not been too kind to the Heckscher-Ohlin model.[11] As a result, Baldwin and Richardson could report that "the theory of international trade is in flux."[12] These alternative theories invariably proceed by relaxing the various assumptions noted here underlying the Ricardian and, especially, the Heckscher-Ohlin theories. Thus, Keesing relaxed the assumption on homogeneity of labor and demonstrated that differences in labor skills could explain trade patterns.[13] Gruber, Mehta, and Vernon relaxed the assumption (in the Heckscher-Ohlin model) of identical technology, and provided evidence that international differences in technology help explain trade patterns.[14] Linder put stress on product differentiation plus similarities or differences in consumer preferences —thereby incorporating demand into trade theory.[15] Many have pointed out the effects of monetary arrangements and a host of public policies.

It is clear then that there are many variables that can influence trade patterns, and we should be pleased that they are taken into account in such leading textbooks as Caves and Jones, and Ellsworth and Lieth.[16] However, it must be reported that many modern trade theorists, in their attempts to deduce "theorems," still start only with the Heckscher-Ohlin model by itself and put aside many of the "complications."

CHAPTER FOUR

Trade and Welfare

Trade theory is concerned not only with explaining trade patterns but also with assessing the gains, or increased "welfare," attributable to trade. We here concentrate completely on the welfare of nations, and use real national income as the measure of their welfare. It is shown that, under some circumstances, trade can adversely affect a nation's welfare.

A. THE WELFARE CRITERION

Modern trade theory makes extensive use of the social indifference curve map not only as a basis for the generation of the offer curve but also as a measure of the welfare gains accruing to a country engaging in trade. Thus, referring to figure 3.1, if trade leads to a set of relative prices that differs from pretrade prices, the consumption pattern with trade must always lie on a higher indifference curve than that without trade. Why must this be so? Essentially because trade expands the choices of consumption patterns. Without trade a nation's consumption pattern is limited to the concave production possibility frontier, while with trade it becomes a straight line at the trading price tangent to this frontier.

This diagram is often employed as a welfare criterion "proving" that free trade increases a nation's welfare. But we must reject it as our welfare criterion: our skepticism of the social indifference curve was made clear in the last chapter, and even if it could be defended, this model only measures "trading" gains. Instead, we take real national income as a nation's welfare criterion. This is both measurable and used in most other branches of economics. Furthermore, it is completely consistent with the criteria employed by Smith and Ricardo in their advocacy of free trade, which, they argued, would result in higher output and incomes for all nations. Of course trade, even though it may increase a nation's real national income, can still have adverse impacts upon the real income of some economic groups. But because it is always possible to redistribute income in a country, the possibility of adverse impacts on some groups need not detract from the use of real national income as a welfare criterion—in effect, the distribution of income is another problem.

B. THE CONDITIONS NECESSARY FOR WELFARE GAINS

We now investigate the prospects for an increase in real national income from trade for country A. To keep the model simple, we assume that country A produces only two final goods, C_1 and C_2. (The model could readily be expanded to include many sectors and trade in intermediate goods.) Before trade, A's real national income will be:

$$RNI = (P_1C_1 + P_2C_2)/(w_1P_1 + w_2P_2) \qquad (4.1)$$

Posttrade real national income is defined as:

$$RNI' = (P_1'C_1' + P_2'C_2')/(w_1P_1' + w_2P_2') \qquad (4.2)$$

in which posttrade prices and output levels (but not the price index weights) can differ from their pretrade values.

Assuming A imports C_2 and exports C_1, we expect $C_1' > C_1$ and $C_2' < C_2$. Defining ΔC_1 and $-\Delta C_2$ as the output changes, we therefore have: $C_1' = C_1 + \Delta C_1$, and $C_2' = C_2 - \Delta C_2$. Let the pretrade and posttrade price indexes be I and I' respectively. The change in real national income, defined as ΔRNI, will be $RNI' - RNI$. Making the substitutions and carrying out the algebraic manipulations enables us to express ΔRNI as follows:

$$\Delta RNI = [(P_1'/I') - (P_1/I)] C_1 + [(P_2'/I') - (P_2/I)] C_2$$
$$+ (P_1'/I')\Delta C_1 - (P_2'/I')\Delta C_2 \qquad (4.3)$$

This is our basic welfare equation.

The first two terms of equation 4.3 reflect the posttrade revaluation of pretrade output levels. Since the real price of C_1, the exported product, should rise, the first term should be positive: the second term, however, should be negative. These two terms should tend to offset each other, although perhaps not perfectly. This tendency is attributable to the weighting system in the price index. Thus, if $C_1 > C_2$ (and the expenditures on C_1 are greater), then for equal changes in prices the real price of C_1 should not rise as much as the real price of C_2 falls. Thus, the larger C_1 is multiplied by a smaller price increase, while the smaller C_2 is multiplied by a larger price decrease.

It is the third and fourth terms—which together represent the real posttrade values of the changes in output levels—that mainly determine whether or not ΔRNI is positive. One obvious condition for ΔRNI to be positive is that ΔC_1 be high relative to $-\Delta C_2$—that is, the increase in output in the export sector be greater than the decrease in output of the import-competing sector. Another condition is that the real price of the exported product be high relative to that of the import-competing product.

For ΔC_1 to be high, it is necessary that the supply of C_1—viewed either in terms of the short run or the long run—be price elastic, so that the trade-induced price increase for C_1 will elicit a large increase in that product's output. For ΔC_2 to be a small negative number, it is necessary that the supply curve for that product be price-inelastic: in such an event, the output of C_2 will not decline much in response to the lower price of C_2 brought on by trade. In broader terms, A benefits most from trade to the extent the supply of its exported products are price-elastic while the supply of its import-competing products are price-inelastic. Of course, if these elasticities were reversed, ΔRNI could be negative.

For the price of the exported product (C_1) to be high, and that for C_2 to be low, the conditions in country B, the trading partner, are most important. A consideration of our trade model will show that the higher the price elasticities of both supply and demand for both products in B, the more beneficial will be the prices to A. This is because the higher these elasticities for C_1 in B, the greater will be B's demand for this product from A at any price, while the supplies of C_2 from B to A would also be greater at any price.

The output changes should be more important to A's welfare than the prices. Outputs have cumulative impacts on real national income over a period of time: prices, on the other hand, are basically just once-and-for-all weighting devices to determine the relative importance of changes in output. As a result, we concentrate only upon changes in output—on the supply elasticities.

It may be objected that it is unreasonable to expect a large change in the output of one product with only a small change in the output of the other product. This objection would be valid if there were a fixed supply of productive factors, purely competitive markets, perfect resource mobility, constant returns to scale—all of which are generally assumed in the established trade model. But once we allow for resource immobilities, downward inflexible wage rates, oligopolies, diminishing returns to a sector, increasing economies of size, a variable-sized labor force, it is indeed quite possible for the supply elasticity of one product to be high with the other low. In the remainder of this chapter we investigate these supply elasticities, and the impact trade has upon real national income, for a number of types of trade and for varying conditions.

C. SOME REASONS FOR DIFFERENCES IN SUPPLY ELASTICITIES— PURE COMPETITION ASSUMED

For advanced industrialized countries with high population-to-land ratios, the import of raw materials in exchange for manufactured goods has always been a most important type of trade. This importance can be readily explained in terms of supply price elasticities.

Limitations on land resources imply that a nation's internal supply curves for raw materials tend to be highly price-inelastic with expansion in outputs—certainly much more so than for manufactured goods not as subject to the law of diminishing returns. The price decreases in raw materials and price increases in manufactured goods brought on by trade should therefore lead to large output increases in manufactures with much smaller output decreases in raw materials. Furthermore, the nonuse of marginally efficient land, even though output will not decrease substantially, will free large amounts of labor and capital to be used in manufacturing.

Another type of intersectoral trade that might be advantageous is the export of capital goods in return for mass-produced consumer goods. The argument here is that capital goods tend to be more individual in nature and require more research and engineering. Thus, a trade-induced expansion of the capital goods sector may lead to longer production runs and spread research and design costs over a larger number of units. Such economies will probably show up as long-run supply curves with greater price elasticities than those for consumer goods. But there are some drawbacks to such trade from the viewpoint of the nation exporting capital goods: the demand for capital goods is notoriously volatile; the expensive technology embedded in capital goods may be obtained without cost by other countries.

Economies of size and diminishing returns are probably the two most important reasons why the price elasticities for supply curves can vary among products. But there can be other reasons. If, for example, the labor force has skills more appropriate for use in one product than another, this would affect their relative supply price elasticities. And, as we shall show in the next two sections, imperfections in either labor markets or product markets can have important impacts on these price elasticities and on the gains from trade.

D. MALFUNCTIONING LABOR MARKETS

It is widely acknowledged that in practice many labor markets deviate significantly from the competitive model. One aspect of this "malfunctioning," an admittedly normative term, is that wage rates are "negotiated" rather than set by the supply and demand for labor. Thus, in particular, if the demand for labor declines while the wage rate is not permitted to fall, there will be unemployment. The reasons the wage rate can be kept at a level that fails to clear the labor market are well known: labor unions, minimum wage laws, unemployment insurance, and so forth. Perhaps a less important malfunction of labor markets is the immobility of labor between productive sectors. This could be attributed to: entry restrictions imposed by labor unions and professional licensing; skill and educational requirements; inability to finance relocation; pension rights; various types of discrimination. In this section, we investigate how these labor market malfunctions affect the welfare of a nation engaging in trade.

Figure 4.1 depicts three types of labor supply curves, which can be those to a productive sector. The labor supply curve in frame (a) would occur if there were a negotiated wage rate, below which nobody would (or could) work, but with unrestricted entry. That in frame (b) reflects a complete restriction on entry (or exit), but without a negotiated wage rate; thus there would be a fixed supply of labor to each sector willing to work at any wage rate. Frame (c) shows a supply curve reflecting both a minimum negotiated wage rate and a fixed supply of labor to a sector. Also shown in this diagram are a number of labor demand curves. It can be seen that a shift in a demand curve affects only employment in frame (a) and only the wage rate in frame (b). Frame (c) is more complicated. The demand curve designated as (1) is that at which there is full employment at the negotiated wage rate. A rightward shift of demand from this position increases only the wage rate, while a leftward shift has its full impact upon employment.

Assume two production sectors, C_1 and C_2. Assume also that trade raises the price of C_1 and lowers that of C_2. These price changes will of course shift the demand curve for labor for each sector, to the right for C_1 and to the left for C_2. We now investigate the impact of trade on that nation's welfare for each type of labor supply function.

Consider first the case of perfect immobility of labor into both

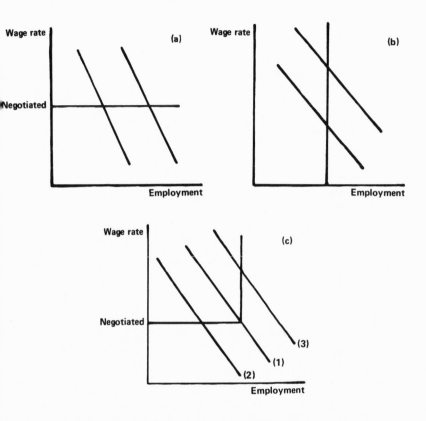

Figure 4.1 Alternative Labor Supply Curves

sectors, so that each sector faces a labor supply curve as in frame (b). Trade will then have no effect upon employment in either sector; but the wage rate will rise for C_1 labor and fall for C_2 labor. A consideration of figure 2.4 also shows that profit rates do not change, so that there should be no intersectoral movements of capital. The result is that the product supply curves are perfectly price-inelastic, so that there will be no change in the output mix and hence no significant change in real national income. Trade will, however, benefit C_1 labor at the expense of C_2 labor, and those who consume more of C_2 at the expense of those who consume more of C_1. Trade benefits the nation as a whole, then, only if these income redistributions are considered desirable.

Assume now that each sector faces a labor supply curve as in frame (a). The nonresponse of the wage rate to changes in the demand for labor by each sector, together with the intersectoral mobility of labor, implies that the output supply curves of both sectors are price-elastic. Thus, for country A to gain from trade, the price increase of C_1 should be high relative to the price decrease of C_2—a situation that would also increase employment. Trade under these conditions will raise the profit rate for the C_1 sector above that for the C_2 sector, so that there should also be an intersectoral movement of capital. If C_1 is the more capital-intensive sector, trade may bring about some unemployment as well, although it does not necessarily follow from our conditions that real national income would also fall.

Assume both sectors face a labor supply curve as in frame (c)— and that before trade the labor demand curves are as in position (1). Then the trade-induced increase in the price of C_1 leads to a higher wage rate for C_1 labor, without any increase in employment. But the decrease in the price of C_2 results in a reduction of employment by that sector, with no change in the wage rate of C_2 labor. One result of trade must therefore be some unemployment. The asymmetry of the response of wage rates to changes in the demands for labor also implies that the output supply curves for both products must be inelastic at higher prices and more elastic at lower prices.[1] Thus, a reduction in the price of C_2 leads to a large reduction in that product's output, while an increase in the price of C_1 should result in only a small (if any) increase in output of C_1. From this analysis, it is clear that, to the extent intersectoral labor immobility and downward wage inflexibility exist, trade can *reduce* a nation's real national income.[2] It should be noted, however, that this problem is not entirely connected with trade. Any changes in output demand curves, for any reason, can also reduce real national income.

E. OLIGOPOLIES

The oligopolistic market structure characterizes many industries. Although there is much that is not understood about the behavior of oligopolists, two features do stand out. One is the tendency for oligopolists to restrict entry of new firms. The second is the ability of oligopolists, generally acting in concert, to maintain an "administered" price over sizable ranges of demand for their product. If, however, demand rises high enough, the oligopolists tend to select a higher administered price. And if demand falls sufficiently, they may reduce the administered price, although such a reaction does not appear to be common.

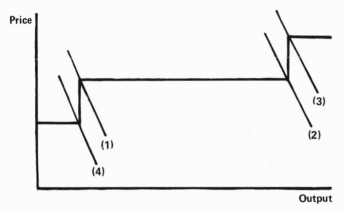

Figure 4.2 Supply Curve of Oligopolistic Sector

Based on these notions of the selection of the administered price, the supply curve of the oligopolists would take the general form shown in figure 4.2. Also shown are a number of alternative product demand curves. If demand ranges from (1) to (2), the administered price is maintained, and over this range of the supply curve it is perfectly price-elastic and any change in demand has its impact only upon output. If demand rises from position (2) toward position (3), the oligopolists may raise the administered price, so that this portion of the supply curve is completely inelastic. Whether the supply curve then becomes elastic again at the higher price will depend upon capacity and, in the long run, on new investment and new entry. We consider that range of the supply curves between those demand curves designated as (1) and (3).

A few words are necessary on the nature of the oligopolist's demand for labor. An oligopolist, like any other firm, has a curve for the net value of the marginal product. But the oligopolist does not hire labor up to the point where that net value equals the wage rate. Other firms do this because they can sell as much output as they want at the market-determined price. The oligopolist, however, in concert with other oligopolists in his sector, sets the price rather than his output. His output is thus limited to what he can sell at that determined price. Accordingly, his demand for labor depends heavily upon his expected output. Thus, assuming the output price is maintained, the aggregate demand of the oligopolists in a sector for labor is ultimately determined by the position of the product demand curve.

We turn now to trade, in which the models of chapter 3 can apply. Assume that in country A, the C_1 sector is oligopolistic while the C_2 sector is competitively organized. Assume further than C_1 is exported while C_2 is imported. Since A's output of C_2 should fall, the welfare effects of trade will depend upon whether or not the output of C_1 rises.

The demand from B for C_1 can be added to the domestic demand for that product, thus providing the aggregate demand facing the oligopolists. If the aggregate demand is anywhere between (1) and (2) in figure 4.2, then the increased demand should not change the administered price and there should be a large increase in output. With this portion of the supply curve highly elastic, A should benefit substantially from trade. But if the demand curve of the As were at position (2), then the increased demand attributable to the Bs would lead to a higher price with little or no change in output. Clearly, if the output of C_2 falls while that of C_1 does not rise, trade reduces A's real national income. Ultimately, then, whether or not A gains from trade depends upon how the oligopolists choose to respond to an increased demand for their product—by increased output, or with a higher price. Capacity utilization and entry restrictions may affect this choice, but, given the discretion of oligopolists, we cannot be certain which response will be chosen.

Assume now that country A exports C_2 and imports C_1. Under this condition, the supply curve in the import-competing sector can be much more price-elastic than that in the export sector, and it can be anticipated that A's welfare depends upon how large the reduction in the output of C_1 will be. Assume that the oligopolists maintain their administered price despite the competition from the Bs—in which event this price becomes a "price umbrella" to the Bs. Then, if the pretrade price in B is anywhere below this administered price, the Bs could have virtually the whole market for C_1 in A. The output of the oligopolists would then depend completely on how much the Bs *choose* to supply the A market. If there is any unused capacity in B's C_1 sector, or if the capacity of this sector can be easily expanded, the amount the Bs choose to supply could be large indeed—and the real national income of A could fall by a great deal. In this regard, it is well to consider the attempt of the United States to get other countries to limit their exports of items such as steel to the United States; this implies an administered unchanging price in the United States, with imports into the United States being determined completely by foreign producers.

One may object to this assessment on grounds that import competition will force the oligopolists to reduce their price. But this argument assumes that the oligopolists can produce profitably at a lower price. Oligopolists, however, because of a lack of competition, often become inefficient, and their efforts to restrict entry, such as tying up raw material sources, are often costly. In the short run, at least, whether oligopolists will reduce their prices to meet import competition is likely to depend largely on whether fixed costs are a high or low proportion of total costs.

CHAPTER FIVE

Trade, Integration, and National Autonomy

International trade, to the extent it is not controlled by quotas, sanctions, exchange restrictions, or tariffs and subsidies, must necessarily integrate the internal economies of the trading nations. One important result of this integration is that the individual nation loses some degree of autonomy in the management of its own economy. Thus, policies adopted by one nation designed only to influence its internal economy may have important consequences for other nations, may lead to trade imbalance problems, or may prove to be ineffective.

In laissez-faire economies, governmental policies are of course not important. But the postwar era has witnessed a tremendous growth in the responsibilities of governments to manage their domestic economies. Yet, somewhat anomalously, the same period has seen a reduction of trade barriers and, for most of that period, fixed exchange rates—both of which integrate national economies and reduce national autonomy. To the extent free trade and autonomy in the national economy are not compatible, the question must arise as to whether the benefits of one outweigh the benefits of the other.

By far, the greatest attention along these lines has been paid to the problems of macroeconomic stabilization policy. The problem in this area for a trading nation is the relation between its "internal balance" —that is, its attainment of full employment and stable price levels—

and its "external balance," that is, its foreign trade being in balance. But this is not the only area of concern. A whole host of internal "structural" policies—pollution control laws, labor laws, various internal taxes and subsidies—also have important international ramifications. In this chapter, we offer a brief discussion of these important problems.

A. MACROECONOMIC STABILIZATION

1. Internal Balance

Macroeconomic stabilization policy in the postwar period has been dominated by the work of John Maynard Keynes, as extended and refined by his many followers and, also, his critics. Underlying the Keynesian analysis is the view that prices in many markets are unresponsive to reductions in demand, so that such reductions have their entire impact upon output, income, and employment. Keynes himself wrote only of the downward inflexibility of the money wage rate, but today most economists agree that such downward inflexibility of prices also applies to oligopolistic commodity markets.

The Keynesian policy prescriptions are basically simple: to manage the aggregate demand for goods at a level compatible with full employment. The aggregate demand for a nation's goods has four main components: consumption, private investment, governmental, and exports. Imports play a role only insofar as a nation's expenditures on imports may reduce its expenditures on domestically produced goods. Keynes was quite aware that the aggregate demand necessary to bring about full employment could also lead to general price inflation, but he did not fully anticipate the problems this could cause and how these problems might impinge on his full employment policies.

There are various measures whereby aggregate expenditures can be stimulated. Policies can be adopted to expand exports or reduce those imports that displace domestic production. But such measures, although undoubtedly used, are not considered desirable: they imply a begger-my-neighbor philosophy that could lead to unemployment in other countries, and they can also bring about mutually disadvantageous retaliations.[1] The other measures have been widely discussed and debated: manipulation of interest rates; tax incentives to encourage investment; personal tax reductions to encourage consumption; increased government expenditures. Although there are a number of such measures, most economists probably agree with Milton Friedman that control of the money supply is the crucial policy instrument. (To see why this is so, consider a deficit in the federal budget, widely thought to be a stimulative device. This deficit would force the government to borrow, thereby raising interest rates and reducing private investment. Thus, the stimulative effects of the deficit could be offset by a reduction in private investment—unless the central bank increases the money supply sufficiently to keep interest rates from rising.)

Although the Keynesian policies to attain full employment have enjoyed much success, there is now much concern about their inflationary implications. The apparent incompatibility between full employment and stable price levels is captured in the widely discussed Phillips curve, which purports to show the trade-off between levels of unemployment and price inflation.[2] The Phillips curve now symbolizes the dilemma facing macroeconomic stabilization policy: how much inflation should be accepted in order to reduce the level of unemployment? The extent of this dilemma varies from one country to the next. It can also change within a country, and there is widespread concern that it is becoming worse; that is, the attainment of low levels of unemployment requires higher levels of inflation than before. (It must be pointed out that some economists reject the notion that inflation is needed for full employment, at least in the long run. Their argument is that inflation could so raise interest rates, and thus discourage investment, that there would be fewer jobs.)

2. External Balance: Some Consequences of Imbalance

Virtually all countries look favorably upon and desire trade surpluses. These desires have little to do with the drive for obtaining precious metals, so closely associated with the mercantilist philosophy, although even today it would be difficult to find a country that objects to an inflow of precious metals. But there are other reasons behind the desire for a trade surplus. First, a country with a trade surplus will often be the one to help finance the trade deficits of others, and this financing can be profitable and a source of foreign exchange earnings. Second, a trade surplus is a form of national saving and investment that not only can earn income but enables that country to increase imports, or decrease exports, should an emergency arise. Third, to the extent full employment policies become necessary, the negative effect of such policies on a nation's trade balance can obviously be more readily accommodated by a country already running a trade surplus; moreover, such a surplus usually means these full employment policies are less necessary. Fourth, if the deficit countries are forced to devalue their currencies, this step by itself may improve the terms of trade for those countries whose currencies appreciate, as we demonstrated in chapter 3.

For the opposite reasons, no country is happy with a trade deficit —except possibly when planned as a means to acquire goods necessary for economic development. In addition to the reasons implied in the previous paragraph, a deficit country will often have to endure lectures about "living within your means"; its international prestige, even on a political front, will suffer; and the deficit-induced possibilities of a devaluation may lead to capital outflows and difficulties in borrowing. Furthermore, since the trade surplus countries are not unhappy with their positions, all burdens of the adjustments needed to correct trade imbalances typically fall upon the deficit countries.

A persistent trade deficit can have even more dire consequences for a country. It can mean a loss of control of its productive organizations, its land, and even its political independence. A book on the history of balance-of-payments accounting makes it clear that this has been a concern of some economists for centuries.[3] This is not just theoretical speculation. A once proud and dominant England has been humbled by the necessity to sell its foreign income-earning assets to cover its trade deficits in the Second World War. Today (1979), in the United States, huge American trade deficits are leading to foreign acquisitions of American farmland, of urban properties (resulting in soaring land and housing prices), and American corporations, including banks. Even American universities and other politically sensitive institutions are increasingly dependent on dollars held by foreigners. This is now everyday news. One may even suggest that a careful study of colonialism, in which one nation came to dominate another, will show that trade imbalances played a major role.

At this point it is well to comment on the differences between trade balances and payment balances—particularly because so much more attention appears to fall on the payment balance. Payment balance, of course, is a broader concept than trade balance, encompassing international loans as well as the trade balance. Thus, it is possible for a country to have a trade deficit and a payment surplus, if its borrowings abroad exceed its trade deficit. It is unfortunate that many look only at the payment balance in assessing a nation's international economic position. Surely this approach is incorrect; it appears to suggest that there is no difference between obtaining foreign exchange by exporting goods and services, or by borrowing. An analogy would be that an individual who spends more than he earns, borrowing to make up the difference (or selling assets or drawing from savings), is no worse off than an individual able to finance his expenditures out of current earnings.

Emphasis on the payment balance, rather than the trade balance, has led to considerable confusion in assessing the consequences of the huge American trade deficit (estimated at $27 billion in 1978), largely brought on by OPEC and the failure of the American response to this challenge. Banking sources assure the American public that there is little to be concerned about, since the foreign-held dollars will be "recycled"—a euphemism for saying the OPEC countries will be willing to loan Americans the dollars (at a rate of interest, of course) obtained from their sales at cartel-determined prices. As normally sober a newspaper as *The Wall Street Journal* (9 January 1978) could seriously editorialize that the United States has found a new *export*—bonds—as if the selling of American debt securities to foreigners is no different than the sale of goods and services as a means of obtaining foreign exchange. The Citibank *Monthly News Letter* (June 1978) argued that because OPEC countries lend to the United States amounts sufficient to cover the American deficit with them—the lending euphemistically called "capital inflows"—oil imports have little to do with the decline of the value of the dollar. Fortunately, only the incredulous could fail to see that the trade deficits plus the mounting American interest payments abroad can only presage more difficulties for the dollar. *Forbes* (12 June 1978) took Citibank to task for this irrelevance, but incorrectly blamed it on "muddle-headed" economic theory rather than asking whether the interests of the large international banks might have been the inspiration for these views.

3. Shortcomings of Trade Adjustment Mechanisms

An earlier chapter discussed three automatic adjustment mechanisms for redressing trade imbalances. But, for various reasons, these may not always work. Consider first the classic "internal price" adjustment mechanism, in which the flow of gold from the deficit to the surplus country should reduce monetary prices in the former and raise them in the latter. The main reason this mechanism may not work in modern times is that countries can now better control their money supplies and have little desire to have either domestic inflation or domestic deflation. Thus, the trade surplus country will be inclined to "sterilize" any inflow of gold or foreign currencies: why, after all, should it suffer inflation, with the problems it entails, to correct a trade surplus it does not find distasteful? The deficit country, even if it chooses not to compensate for its gold outflow with an increase in the supply of its national currency, may not even have a deflation of its prices; given the downward inflexibility of wage rates and many commodity prices, the result is more likely to be unemployment. Keynes, in his *A Tract on Monetary Reform* (1923), saw quite clearly that this classic adjustment mechanism no longer functioned.[4] He charged that the United States, with a large trade surplus and gold inflow, chose to "bury the gold under Washington" rather than let it affect its money supply: the United States, Keynes pointed out, was opting for internal price stability rather than playing by the rules of the international gold standard.

Somewhat ironically, the income adjustment mechanism, so closely associated with the Keynesian tools of analysis, may no longer fulfill its task of redressing trade balances because of the full employment polices proposed by Keynes. For this mechanism to work, the deficit country must be willing to endure unemployment, perhaps over a substantial time period, even though it could use Keynesian policies to bring about full employment. This entails a sacrifice of internal stabilization goals on behalf of external balance, a sacrifice that most countries find unattractive.

Flexible exchange rates are viewed today by most, but not all, economists as the most acceptable means for redressing trade imbalances. The main point in favor of flexible exchange rates is that they can work without the internal inflation, deflation, or unemployment associated with other adjustment mechanisms. Yet flexible exchange rates are not without their problems. First, they require a severance of the linkages between national currencies and gold, which thereby removes an important constraint upon the size of a nation's money supply and hence upon inflation. Second, flexible exchange rates impart risk to all international transactions in which contracts call for a party in one country to accept or make monetary payments in terms of the currency of other nations. Third, speculative activity in foreign exchange, brought about by expectations of future changes in exchange rates, can destabilize trade and bring about larger changes in exchange rates than those necessary to correct trade imbalances. Fourth, the central banks of individual nations could interfere in the foreign exchange market in order to bring about exchange rates they deem desirable in their own interests—a problem very much a concern today of the International Monetary Fund. Fifth, flexible exchange rates may be related to the problem of oligopoly, particularly for the country whose currency depreciates. It has long been recognized that import competition is an important constraint to oligopolistic price levels; as a consequence, when the devaluation of a nation's currency raises prices of imports, that nation's oligopolists can seize this as an opportunity to raise their prices. Yet, despite these very considerable drawbacks, flexible exchange rates may still be the best of the *automatic* trade adjustment mechanisms.

The difficulties with the efficacies of these automatic trade adjustment mechanisms must of course undermine any free trade system.

The deficit country may well be forced to either restrict imports directly, by tariffs and quotas, or take some kind of action to subsidize exports.

4. Internal/External Balance Problems

Throughout his work on problems of internal stabilization, Keynes was always concerned with the impact of foreign trade and investment on the efficacy of his proposals. A catalogue of his views may be useful.

In *A Tract on Monetary Reform,* Keynes cautioned that the goal of internal price stability could be inconsistent with fixed exchange rates, because with such rates any inflation or deflation in one country would be transmitted to England. This idea was quite novel at that time, implying that national currencies must not be pegged to gold, and thus running against the free trade philosophy of the times. In *The Economic Consequences of Mr. Churchill* (1925), he argued against pegging the pound to gold, a practice which then meant an upward valuation of the pound relative to other currencies, on the grounds that this would lead to high unemployment in England. In *A Treatise on Money* (1931), a long chapter is devoted to the loss of autonomy in internal stabilization to a nation because of trade and international money movements. Keynes here was especially concerned that the internal use of monetary policy to bring about the "natural" rate of interest—that which would equate savings and investment—would be undermined by money inflows and outflows because of different interest rates in other countries. When serving on the Macmillan Commission, which was constituted to advise the British government on full employment policies in the early years of the Great Depression, Keynes advocated protective import tariffs and a tax on outflows of money. The reasons behind these proposals were that his full employment prescriptions—massive public works and low interest rates—would lead to large trade deficits and outflows of money. Roy Harrod assures us that Keynes would not have advocated the tariff if the pound were not pegged to gold; that is, if exchange rates could change.

In *The General Theory of Employment, Interest and Money*

(1936), Keynes has a chapter on mercantilism that was to become a center of controversy. He praised the mercantilists as being shrewd enough to observe the favorable effect of a trade surplus and gold inflow (which should reduce interest rates) on economic activity and the level of employment. For pointing out the relationship between a trade surplus and full employment, Keynes was criticized by free traders and called a neomercantilist, which to economists is not a term of endearment. But these criticisms were manifestly unfair. Keynes nowhere advocates trade policies designed to bring about an inflow of gold, one of the chief aims of mercantilism, but merely observes that a trade surplus could lead to higher levels of employment, which today cannot be doubted. But even more important, Keynes, by proposing alternative means of attaining full employment, really undercut mercantilism: a trade surplus was no longer necessary for attaining full employment. And he also undercut the charges of Hobson and Lenin that imperialism—and the consequent trade surpluses by the imperialist powers—was necessary to these countries to bring about full employment.

Finally, in the 1944 Bretton Woods conference leading to the International Monetary Fund and fixed exchange rates, Keynes expressed concern that these could undermine his full employment policies.[5] Harrod writes that the Bretton Woods agreement came into being only after American negotiators (before the actual conference) were willing to accept Keynes's proposal that deficit countries had the right to discriminate against imports from surplus countries, which might well be countries that did not enact full employment policies.[6]

The damper that trade can place on full employment policies is clear enough.[7] If countries A and B both have unemployment, but only A enacts full employment policies, under fixed exchange rates A will have a trade deficit—thereby also retarding the move toward full employment—while B will enjoy both a trade surplus and stimulation of its economy. Thus, a unilateral decision to attain full employment in one nation could benefit others more than itself. This problem was recognized at Bretton Woods. The American delegation proposed an international ministry to assure that all countries would enact full employment policies (which was withdrawn when it was made clear that the United States Congress would not allow any such interference with American domestic policy), and the final agreement allowed trade discrimination against countries that did not pursue full employment by means other than that of a trade surplus.

But the problem today is not so much that some countries will fail to enact full employment policies. Rather, the problem of internal/external balance revolves more about the inflation that frequently accompanies full employment. Differences in national inflation rates can have greater impacts upon trade imbalances than can changes in the levels of national income. And the nature of the Phillips curve can vary greatly among nations. Thus, if A requires a higher inflation rate than B to attain full employment, then full employment policies enacted by both countries will lead to a trade imbalance. Thus, if a trade balance is to be maintained, it is more important for both countries to align their inflation rather than their unemployment rates. But of course, the alignment of inflation rates leads to unemployment in the country with the "worse" Phillips curve. In effect, to the extent that trade deficits are of great concern, the inflation rate of the country with the "better" Phillips curve determines the unemployment rate in the other country.

A solution to this problem can be found in flexible exchange rates. Under such a regime, if both A and B pursue full employment and A has the higher inflation rate, A's currency can be expected to depreciate by about the difference in inflation rates, which should keep trade in balance. Thus, with flexible exchange rates, each country could pursue its mix of internal stabilization goals without having to be concerned about trade deficits. Flexible exchange rates thus serve the purpose of insulating national economics from one another, thereby enabling greater national autonomy.

Despite this seeming advantage of flexible exchange rates, the issue of flexible vs. fixed exchange rates is still controversial. Led by such notables as Harry Johnson and Milton Friedman, most economists now favor flexible exchange rates.[8] Johnson argues much as we have done here: only under flexible exchange rates can a nation benefit from both free trade and national autonomy in internal stabilization. Friedman argues that it is absurd to allow trade imbalances of comparatively small magnitude to dictate important internal policies and that, from the trade viewpoint, the small and continuous changes in exchange rates under a system of flexible exchange rates are much to be preferred to the large sudden changes that had become necessary even under the fixed exchange rate system.

Given these arguments, it is worthwhile asking why some economists still argue for fixed exchange rates. There are admitted drawbacks connected with flexible exchange rates, as described earlier, and the unilateral uses of devaluations in the 1930s to help employment in individual countries did lead to some bitter consequences. (The International Monetary Fund was really more concerned with unilateral devaluations than with fixed exchange rates per se.) However, the case for fixed exchange rates goes deeper than this. The essence is that there are many who fear too much autonomy for individual nations, and welcome the restraints that fixed exchange rates place upon this autonomy.[9] Thus, with flexible exchange rates a country, constrained neither by the cost of supplying money nor by the fear of a trade deficit, might find it too easy to resort to inflationary finance to solve its problems. Although there is undoubtedly much merit in this position, an important fact is that most countries, if forced to choose between free trade with fixed exchange rates and internal stabilization, would opt to restrict trade. In the long run, free trade without flexible exchange rates may be unacceptable.

5. Money Flows and Internal Balance

International flows of money may be a greater threat to internal stabilization efforts than are trade deficits. Any country using monetary policy to set an interest rate below that in others will see an outflow of money; on the other hand, there would be an inflow of money if its interest rate were set above that of others. In either case, any individual country faces difficulties in determining its internal interest rate, and such problems must emasculate the independent use of monetary policy, a point that is now being more fully appreciated.

It was noted that Keynes, in pressing for lower interest rates to stimulate both consumption and investment expenditures, was concerned this policy would lead to monetary outflows unless countermeasures were adopted. It can be argued, however, that international money inflows are more of a problem to countries trying to control inflation with high interest rates than to those trying to stimulate their economies with the use of low interest rates. Since the creation of money is now virtually costless, the country wishing the lower interest rate can respond to currency outflows simply by creating more money. Not only would such a policy meet its interest rate target: in addition, the currency outflows could stimulate its exports and earn foreign exchange in the form of interest payments. A country wishing to control inflation with high interest rates has a much greater problem. If it wishes to maintain a high interest rate, it must continuously reduce its own money supply to compensate for currency inflows— a policy to which there are distinct limits. Ironically, this country will also find itself paying interest to foreign "lenders" for the dubious benefits of having its anti-inflation policies undermined.

The unrestricted flow of money may have other unfortunate consequences. Since the country with the easy money policy has something to gain and the country with the tight money policy has something to lose, free international money movements create a bias toward the adoption of the more inflationary alternatives in stabilization policy. Moreover, while changes in exchange rates can deal effectively with trade imbalances, they may be ineffective or work perversely in their impacts upon monetary flows—a point we examine in greater detail in a later chapter.

6. Trade Policy to Enhance Internal Stabilization Policy

We have painted a rather dark picture of the difficulties in simultaneously pursuing policies of noninflationary full employment and free trade in goods and international monetary flows. But it should also be pointed out that there are conditions under which international trade may aid domestic stabilization policy (other than through a trade surplus), although this trade may have to be controlled.

First, consider the inflationary problem of oligopolies setting higher prices that are "administered" and often completely unrelated to demand and capacity utilization. This problem goes back a century to the times of the trusts in the United States, and Hans Thorelli[10] writes that the government often threatened the trusts that it would reduce tariffs on competitive imports as a way to restrain upward price movements. And, as Thorelli points out, the original "antitrust" bill proposed by Senator John Sherman (and enacted in 1890) was to institutionalize what were then informal tariff-cutting threats. This very natural response is finding an echo today. It was no coincidence that Robert Strauss, who for a time during the Carter administration took the lead in informally "jawboning" firms not to raise prices percipitously, was simultaneously the American Special Trade Negotiator responsible for the tariff reduction negotiations taking place in Tokyo and Geneva.

A variable tariff rate can also be a means for using foreign trade to stabilize the internal economy. As students of economic history know, such a device was used for some time by England, specifically in wheat. England would reduce tariffs when domestic wheat prices were rising, and raise them when these prices were falling. Such a scheme can be quite effective as an internal price-stabilization mechanism, and can readily be extended to subsidization of exports. Unfortunately such a system runs counter to the free trade philosophy now dominating trade policy—although undoubtedly it is used on an informal and ad hoc basis—and, although it may stabilize one economy, it may act to destabilize the economies of other countries. Nevertheless, the possibilities of using variable tariffs and subsidies to stabilize the internal economy should be receiving more attention than that currently devoted to them in at least the theoretical literature.

B. INTERNAL STRUCTURAL POLICIES

There are many areas of governmental policy outside macroeconomic stabilization that have important consequences for the relation between trade and national autonomy. Among these are agricultural price maintenance, labor standards and minimum wages, pollution control, subsidization or taxation of almost any type, antitrust policy. All of these policies will, directly or indirectly, purposefully or inadvertently, affect commodity prices within a nation. And since trade responds to pretrade price differentials, it follows that these policies must affect trade and provide competitive advantages or disadvantages to particular industries in the trading countries.

Much attention has been paid to how these policies affect trade, particularly the "fairness" of international competition—and this attention undoubtedly reflects the interests of writers on international trade, who have done most of the work on these problems. But it may be even more important to focus upon the problems that trade creates for the efficacy of these policies. Thus a program to compel an industry to purchase pollution control equipment, which would raise its production costs, may, because of foreign competition, lead to the economic destruction of that industry—along with reduced pollution. And a program to raise agricultural income by restricting output in order to raise prices may lead to increased imports of competing products and thus smaller income to farmers. Obviously many such examples could be offered, and it is evident that trade may reduce the autonomy of nations in dealing with what appear to be purely internal problems. The European Community has fully acknowledged these conflicts.[11] Thus, with the elimination of barriers on trade and on movements of the factors of production between its members, it was found necessary to "harmonize" internal measures affecting trade, although mainly to put international competition on an equal footing rather than to protect any nation's internal autonomy.

Harry Johnson has written on these possible conflicts between trade and internal "structural" policies, although mainly from the viewpoint of how the latter affects the former.[12] His argument is that such policies need not affect trade patterns or trade benefits if two conditions are met: if exchange rates are flexible, and if the policies are nondiscriminatory among different industries. Thus, if some internal policy were to raise the prices of all products by, say, 20 percent, trade would be completely unaffected if that country's currency were to devalue by 20 percent. And, we can argue that, with Johnson's two conditions, trade would not affect the efficacy of these policies.

Johnson's analysis provides still another argument for flexible exchange rates. But the condition that any measure have nondiscriminatory impacts on prices of all sectors would surely be only rarely fulfilled no matter what the intention. Pollution control laws, energy conservation taxes, minimum wage laws, are almost certain to affect prices more for some products than for others.

Even if the possibility is granted that internal policies could have nondiscriminatory effects, the question remains whether any nation, in order to foster fairness in international competition, should be constrained to adopt only nondiscriminatory policies. Here the dictates of fair international competition and free trade run head-on into the whole area of externalities and the attempts to align private with social costs and benefits. Dealing with externalities must, almost by definition, be discriminatory: the whole point of such exercises is to penalize or favor particular industries. James Meade, an eminent trade theorist and a follower of Anthony Pigou, took the view that trade confers social benefits only if prices properly reflect social costs.[13]

CHAPTER SIX

International Trade and Investment: New Perspectives

Trade in goods and services among different countries is only one branch of "international economics." Another major branch concerns international movements of the "factors of production"—primarily capital, labor, and technology. These two branches are by no means independent of each other: trade in goods and services should affect the movements of productive factors, and vice versa. Although they are manifestly interdependent, and both are obviously important phenomena, there is no generally accepted unified model that enables us to study the various complexities that can arise when these two branches are considered together. This lack of a unified model is largely responsible for much of the debate and confusion surrounding the multinational firm.

My objective in this chapter is to develop an accounting approach that can consider trade and factor movements together. This will be done by redefining "international transaction." As now used, this term refers to transactions between individuals or organizations located in different nations. We argue that a more relevant definition is that an international transaction is any transaction between individuals or organizations of different nationality, regardless of their location. This redefinition has greater consequences than that of just providing a different accounting of trade. It also redefines exports and imports, clarifies the international asset positions of nations, has important implications for the measurement of economic welfare, and will be of great help in uncovering the motives of firms in locating abroad. Furthermore, this redefinition allows us to see that the essence of direct foreign investment is that it enables a range of international transactions that cannot otherwise take place.

A. DEFINITIONAL CONCEPTS AND QUESTIONS

Direct foreign investment is generally defined as investment by one nationally defined group (or individual) to establish ownership and control of productive assets, generally organized as business enterprises, located in a country other than that of the owning group. We adhere to this definition. The ownership is usually evidenced by some sort of recognized title, such as common stock. By control we mean the usual commercial property rights, to buy, to sell, to produce, to pay dividends, and so forth, on behalf of an enterprise. Such control is always limited in various ways and to various degrees by policies of governments, which in this case may be the government of the country in which the assets are located and/or the government of the country of which the members of the owning group are nationals. To make use of our two-country model, there is direct foreign investment of A in B whenever A nationals own and control productive assets located in B. In this definition, it is immaterial whether the enterprise located in B is formally constituted under the laws of country A or those of country B, or whether the A nationals who control the enterprise reside in A or in B. Sometimes, especially with joint ventures involving ownership by both A and B nationals, the question of who controls an enterprise may not be readily established.

Indirect foreign investment, often called "portfolio" investment, is generally defined as the purchase of securities (bonds, stocks, promissory notes, bank passbooks) issued by members or organizations of one national group by members or organizations of another national group, but without transfer of operating control of assets or enterprises to the purchasers—a definition to which we again adhere. In our two-country model, there is indirect foreign investment whenever

A nationals or their organizations purchase securities issued by B organizations. Although these purchases are usually for cash, such these securities can also be "purchased" in exchange for anything else of value. In both cases As are making loans to Bs, either in the form of cash or in the form of credit. When the loan is in the form of cash, the money need not always be A currency: it can also be an international money such as gold, or any B currency held by A nationals (including their organizations). Any payment of interest, dividends, or repayments of principal may be denominated in any national currency or gold, according to the terms of any particular contract.

There are two important distinctions between these two types of investment. The first distinction centers about control. In the case of direct foreign investment by A in B, A nationals acquire commercial control of production facilities: but in indirect foreign investment of A to B the transfer of money or other valuable goods enables B nationals to acquire and control productive assets. The second distinction concerns obligation. In indirect foreign investment, specified B organizations have contracted to make payments to As. But in direct investment no specific Bs have taken on any such obligations. In the latter case, the B government may have taken on the obligation to convert any earnings of the foreign-owned firm into A currency for remittance to A. But the conversion of currency is not the same as making payments—and of course there may not be any earnings. These distinctions lead to a number of definitional questions.

We may first ask in what sense direct and indirect foreign investment should both be considered "foreign investment." As generally employed, this term implies that the foreign exchange position of the investing country will *eventually* improve: that is, if As invest in B the end result of a particular investment should be greater holdings by country A (or its nationals) of B currency and gold relative to the holdings of A currency and gold by country B. Barring default, this should always occur for indirect foreign investment, because Bs have taken on contractual obligations to As. Indeed, a loan of money or the granting of credit by As to Bs can be regarded as an export—A exports to B the use of its money or credit.

But there is no such assurance of foreign exchange earnings for A in the case of an A enterprise located in B. Whether this enterprise will earn foreign exchange for A depends upon its operations, specifically whether or not its sales to Bs and to other non-A nationals exceed its purchases from them. In this regard, any profit repatriation by the enterprise to A should not be viewed as analogous to interest and dividend payments to As by those Bs who issued the securities on which these payments are based. It is quite possible for the A enterprise to earn profits which are remitted to A while the net result of *its* operations leads to a loss of foreign exchange to country A. It is true that both indirect and direct foreign investment can have complicated secondary impacts upon the foreign exchange positions of both countries—a problem to which we will turn. Here, the pertinent point is that the direct results of any particular indirect or direct foreign investment is that only the former will assuredly earn foreign exchange for the investing country—again assuming no default.

Consider next the term "capital flow." As generally used, this term implies that one country either acquires control over productive assets, or its capability for acquiring such control is enhanced, the converse occurring for the other country. This definition holds true for indirect foreign investment. A transfer of funds or credit by A to B in exchange for securities enables B to construct or acquire productive assets, although the opportunity may not always be seized and may instead lead to higher consumption levels for Bs. But when nationals of A construct or acquire productive assets located in B, the Bs do not as a result of this action control any additional productive assets, as long as "control" means the usual commercial rights to operate a productive facility and not the ultimate power of a government to control anything located on its soil.

Perhaps the best definition of a capital flow is a transaction that *enables* members of one national group to acquire control of additional assets, regardless of the location of the assets. The acquisition by A nationals of existing productive facilities from B nationals is particularly instructive on this point. If As purchase, say, a plant from Bs for cash, then there is no capital flow, since nothing enhanced the ability of the As to acquire this property. Such a transaction can be termed an export from B to A, if we define an export as a transfer of national control rather than as relocation of the assets. If, however, the Bs who sold this plant obtain in return financial securities issued by the As rather than cash, we can say there has been a capital flow from B to A and indirect foreign investment of B in (or *to*) A, since the Bs have extended credit to As which enabled the latter to control more assets than might otherwise be possible. Using control rather than location as the criterion, this latter transaction is also an export from B to A, but not one in which payment is made immediately.

Consider next the term "capital formation," which connotes the construction of productive facilities, and possibly even a buildup of the capabilities of such construction. Consider the construction of a new plant located in B but owned and controlled (in the usual commercial sense) by As. There has clearly been capital formation, but it is not clear which country's stock of productive assets has increased. It would be that of B if one defines a nation's capital stock as all productive assets located on its soil, but that of A if a nation's stock is defined as assets its nationals own and control regardless of the location of the assets or of the nationals. The case can be readily made that ownership and control, rather than location, are the more relevant criteria in defining a nation's capital stock. The purpose of productive assets, at least to the individuals who own them, is to generate income, and on these grounds the A-controlled assets located in B should be considered part of the productive wealth of nation A, when this is taken to be synonymous with the wealth controlled by its citizens. We should therefore think of an A-owned plant in B, not as part of B's capital stock, but rather simply as part of A's capital stock located abroad rather than at home. This admittedly puts aside the possibility of expropriation, but we should not always assume that the risk of the loss of ownership and commercial control is necessarily greater if the enterprise is located abroad rather than at home.

The essence of direct foreign investment is that a business enterprise owned and controlled by members of one national group is located in another nation. As such, it can engage in transactions with other entities that can be characterized on the basis of both nationality and location. Thus, an A enterprise located in B may transact business with: Bs (individuals or their organizations) located in B; As located in A; As located in B; Cs located in C; and so forth. This raises the interesting question of whether an international transaction should be defined on the basis of the nationalities or locations of the transacting parties.

Virtually all the statistical data that constitute the balance of payment of individual nations are based on transactions between the *residents* of different territorially defined nations. This, of course, means that the location of the transacting parties is the basis for defining an international transaction, and that an international transaction implies that goods, services, money, or securities are relocated over international boundaries. There are some exceptions to the international movements of the goods, services, and the like, as the basis of an international transaction. Most importantly, the transactions of an individual regarded as a resident of one country, but located in another country, with residents in the country in which he is located are regarded as international transactions: clearly the *usual* location of the parties is the criterion, even though in this case goods, services, or money may not have crossed international boundaries. The most obvious type of such international transactions arises from tourism.

Although the transactions abroad of individuals who are residents of one country but who are located in another are considered international transactions, this is not true under current international accounting practices for the enterprises that these individuals may control. Thus, although an A resident, when living in B, will have *his* transactions with B residents reckoned as international transactions, the transactions carried on with B residents by a B-located *enterprise* owned by the A resident will *not* be considered international transactions. This is because the International Monetary Fund and the United States Commerce Department, among others, regard a business enterprise as a resident of the country in which it is located, regardless of the nationality or residence of those who own the enterprise. Thus, with the exception of the transactions of individual residents visiting or living in foreign countries (tourists, government officials, students), and some financial movements, all international transactions connote a relocation of goods, services, money, securities, over international boundaries.

It is my contention that a definition of an international transaction on the basis of the nationalities of the transacting parties, including the enterprises that engage in transactions on behalf of those who own them, has greater economic relevance than one based upon the location of the transacting parties. The reason for this contention is simple enough. The importance of an international transaction is not so much that something of value has been relocated. Of greater importance is that items of value have exchanged national hands, that international obligations have been incurred, that foreign exchange positions of nations have become altered, that the national incomes of countries have been affected. Furthermore, basing the definition of an international transaction solely upon the location of the transacting parties not only may fail to shed light on these important points, but may have hampered our understanding of the major significance of the multinational corporation. The following examples will help clarify these points.

Let us consider two alternative loans: in one case an A-owned bank located in B makes a loan to B nationals located in B; in the second case the transaction is the same except that the bank is located in A. In both cases B nationals obtain funds, and therefore command over goods, and incur obligations, while A nationals receive debt instruments acknowledging these obligations. Moreover, any further consequences of the loan will usually not be affected by the location of the A bank. Although such an exchange between parties of different nationalities is surely the most important feature of an international transaction, under current accounting rules it would not be considered an international transaction if the A bank were located in B rather than in A. Consideration of the location of the parties clearly introduces a spurious element into the definition of an international transaction.

Consider next a sale to Bs of the same item by an A firm located in B compared with that by an A firm located in A. With international trade defined on the basis only of a relocation of goods, only the second alternative would be considered an international transaction leading to an export from A to B. But the essential elements are the same for both cases: B nationals obtain goods and A nationals obtain some form of money or financial securities. Now the locational aspect injects a spurious element into the definition of an export: by any other criterion A has exported to B in both alternatives.

Consider next the sale of an item by an A firm located in B to an A firm located in A. If one looks only at the relocation of this item, such a sale would be considered an international transaction resulting in an export from B to A. But by any other criterion, the transaction is not international nor does it lead to an export—no Bs are involved in the transaction; As do not acquire anything from Bs that was owned by the latter; B citizens do not earn foreign exchange, and as a result their claim on A goods is not enhanced.

Clearly, once the possibility exists that business organizations owned and controlled by one national group are located in other countries, it is necessary to reexamine what we mean by exports, imports, and foreign investment. We turn now to such a reexamination, in which a distinction is made between trans*national* and trans*territorial* transactions. Although the distinctions are made in an accounting framework, their importance transcends the problem of accounting. By redefining international transactions on the basis of the nationality of the transacting parties, we will be able to obtain fresh insights into the significance of direct foreign investment and be able to unify trade and investment into a single framework.

B. THE NEED FOR ANOTHER INTERNATIONAL ACCOUNTING SYSTEM

A nation or country can be defined on two different bases. It can be defined either as a territorial unit or as a group of citizens (or nationals) who profess a national identity. A nation's property can also be defined either as assets located in its territory or as assets owned by its nationals regardless of the location of the assets or the nationals. The two definitions of a nation and its property are synonymous only when all its citizens and their property, and nobody else nor anyone else's assets, reside and are located in the nation as territorially defined.

Throughout much of recorded history, nationals of various nations have resided in or visited other territorially defined nations. This has always created problems concerning which country's laws should govern such individuals, and their property as well. It has also led to problems in defining exports, imports, payments, and a nation's foreign exchange position. Max Wasserman and Ray Ware, in their book on the history of international trade accounting, have shown that this accounting underwent changes largely in response to nationals located abroad.[1] The accounting for a balance of trade came first, in which international trade meant the physical relocation of goods across national boundaries. It was in response to the realization that a nation's gold holdings can also be affected by the transactions of its citizens located abroad, or by transactions of foreign nationals residing in its borders, that the balance of payments evolved, to also take into account transactions of a country's nationals with others in which goods and money do not cross international boundaries.

Transactions in which goods or money do not cross borders have always been difficult to account for, since they do not leave the trail of records associated with trade across boundaries. Until recently, transactions between different nationals located in the same country have not been quantitatively too important, with the possible exceptions of tourism and troops stationed abroad. But now, because of the tremendous growth of multinational corporations, these types of transactions are clearly of great importance, often greater in importance than transactions between residents located in different countries.

The important question now arises of whether the multinational corporation should be regarded as an agent of those who control it. If it should, then it does not make much sense to term transactions of, say, Americans in France (mostly with French citizens) "international," and thus reflect them in the statistics of the payments balance, while not treating transactions with French citizens by corporations owned by Americans and located in France the same way. This must bring up the definition of a multinational corporation. Although there has been debate about this definition, few would disagree with its main point, that citizens of one nation, often through control of a parent corporation, own and control business organizations located abroad. The "agency" aspect of this definition is clear. And we cannot deny that corporations have nationality designations that are those of the groups or organizations that control them. A corporation located outside the United States but controlled by American individuals or by an American corporation is universally thought of as an American firm, regardless of the laws under which that firm may have been incorporated.

That a nation's citizens and/or property they own can be located abroad also raises questions regarding the national interest and whether the primary responsibility of a government is to the welfare of its citizens or of its residents. Most political scientists, I am sure, would argue that the paramount responsibility of a government is to its citizens, and, by extention, to their property, no matter where located. That this is also the actual view taken by governments is evident in the many actions to protect their citizens and their property located in foreign countries—as by passports, consular representation, treaties, penalties, and so forth. Clearly, if governments took as their prime responsibility their residents, regardless of nationality, these kinds of actions would be unnecessary. That governments also protect their foreign residents is to some extent a mark of civilized behavior, but the underlying more basic motive for such protection is surely to secure reciprocal treatment for its citizens and property located in foreign countries.

Especially when dealing with national welfare, international trade theory has generally assumed that all residents of a country are also nationals of that country. Thus, when something is exported territorially from country A to country B, it is assumed that an A citizen sold something to a B citizen. And if country A is somehow better off as the result of this export, it is assumed that it is A citizens who are better off. Of course economists are aware that trade data are territorially defined on the basis of transactions between residents rather than between nationals. But the definition of international trade as that between residents is surely not theoretically desirable, but is rather a statistical compromise necessitated by the practical difficulty of distinguishing traders by their nationality. Even though these difficulties exist, there is nothing to prevent us from defining international transactions on the basis of nationality in theory—which will at least clarify our understanding and point to the need for better data. We already define international transactions on the basis of the nationalities rather than the location of the transacting parties when a country's nationals are abroad. (That these nationals are called "residents" is just another statistical compromise.) I will argue that a nation's enterprises located abroad should be viewed the same as its citizens located abroad with regard to the definition of an international transaction, because an enterprise is the agent of those who control it and the locations of the transacting parties are not as important as their nationalities.

To demonstrate the need for defining international transactions on the basis of the nationalities rather than the location of the transacting parties—which would lead to an accounting system based on transnational as opposed to transterritorial transactions—we can begin by examining the interpretations of trade and payment data based on a territorial definition and the uses to which such data are put. First, when an item is exported from, say, A to B, we assume the A seller and the B buyer made comparisons of this transaction with alternative transactions at home, and thus that A must have had some sort of comparative advantage in the production of the product. Second, we assume A has given up control of this product to B. Third, we assume Bs have made or will make some sort of payment to As. Fourth, we assume the product has been relocated from A to B. Fifth, we assume the export has generated income for As as the result of producing that good. Sixth, we assume that A's net foreign exchange position has or will improve. In short, we interpret such a territorially defined export as a bona fide transaction between A nationals and B nationals. It is almost needless to point out that these trade and payment data have important uses, among them the formulation of policies with regard to macroeconomic stabilization and international trade and investment.

Largely because of the multinational corporation, it is readily shown that these interpretations and uses of a territorially defined export may not be valid. To be specific, let us say a territorially defined export from A to B resulted from a transaction between an A firm located in A and an A firm located in B. In such an event, note the following: B nationals receive no goods and A nationals have not given up control of anything; no B national has taken on any obligation for payment; country A's foreign exchange holdings—if defined as foreign exchange held by its nationals or their organizations no matter where located—will not have increased. In short, such a transaction should be considered an export only in the sense that goods have been relocated.

Another drawback to defining trade only on the basis of territory is that transactions between different nationals located in the same country would not be considered international trade—yet such transactions lead to the same results we associate with territorially defined trade between different nationals. Let us say an A firm located in B purchases something from B nationals also located in B—which is not defined as international trade by territorially based accounting. But the important results of such a transaction are as follows: As acquire something from Bs; As have to make payments to Bs; country B's foreign exchange position has been enhanced. Thus, this transaction is not international trade only in the sense that goods have not been relocated from one country to another; by any other criterion it should be regarded as international trade.

Many other questions along these lines can be raised. Let us say that an A firm in B sells and ships an item to a C firm in C. This is an export from B to C on a territorial accounting basis, but should be viewed as an export from A to C if any consequence of the transaction other than the relocation of goods is considered the relevant criterion. Or say an A firm in B sells and ships an item to a B firm in A. Only on the basis of the relocation of goods would this be considered an export from B to A; by any other criterion it is A that has exported to B. Many of these same considerations hold for movements of financial capital. For example, should borrowing by an A firm in B from an A bank be considered an international capital flow only if this bank were located in A? Or should it be considered an international capital flow at all?

From these discussions, it is clear there is need for an international accounting system in which an international transaction is defined on the basis of the nationalities rather than locations of the transacting parties or enterprises. This can be called a transnational accounting system, in contrast to a transterritorial system. This proposal is really not all that novel. As pointed out, nationality is the basis for international transactions in tourism. It is also the basis for accounting in some financial transactions, transshipments of goods, free trade zones. Thus, all I am really suggesting is that the same principles of transnational transactions also be applied to business organizations controlled and owned by national groups other than those of the country in which the enterprise is located.

There are still a few questions to be considered. First, could there be some "netting out" that would obviate the need to consider transnational transactions in a nation? If, for example, an A firm in B buys from Bs located in B, would that not simply become an offset against the profits repatriated by that firm to A? I don't believe this would refute my contention of the need for transnational accounting. First, the firm may not make profits, and even if it did, there is no guarantee these will be repatriated. Second, there is the question of timing: even if such a purchase would eventually be reflected in the profit remittance, a country surely needs information on its trade and foreign exchange position in particular time periods. Third, a total reliance on net figures can be shown to be absurd. By the same logic one should conclude that only one trade or payment figure is needed— only the *net* trade or net payment figure. By this criterion all other trade figures showing magnitudes, countries, types of products, value of products, and so forth, would be deemed useless. Thus, just as we evidently really need these figures (or detail), the same should hold for nonterritorial transnational trade.

Another question to consider is whether the foreign exchange earned by a nation's firms from sales to other nationals is available to that country as a whole regardless of the location of these firms. This question of availability of foreign exchange is not new; it antedates multinational corporations. Keynes, for example, in evaluating a proposed monetary system in his *Indian Currency and Finance,* argued that one purpose of a nation's monetary system is to assure that foreign exchange is centrally available to all its importers for foreign payments. One question involved in transnational accounting, then, is whether foreign exchange earned by exporting from a home base is any more centrally available than that earned by exporting from foreign locations.

The resolution of this question depends mainly on whether there are any governmentally imposed restrictions on the movement of foreign exchange. Assume first that there are no such restrictions. The question can then be posed as follows: would the funds obtained from a sale by an American firm located in the United States be any more likely to end up with the American Federal Reserve Banks, or even in the American commercial banking system, than the funds from a similar sale carried out from a location in England? Since the American firm is free to deposit its funds wherever it wishes, there is no basis for an affirmative answer to this question. With no restrictions on the banking of foreign exchange, the problem to a nation in making its foreign exchange earnings centrally available to all its importers is independent of the location of its exporters.

If, however, there are exchange controls, then the location of the American firm is indeed crucial to the central availability of foreign exchange. If, for example, England were to allocate its foreign exchange only to its importers from abroad and not permit foreign exchange to leave England freely, then the location of the American firm would be important. Or, if the American government would permit exports only on condition that the foreign exchange earned be sold to its central bank (as is done in most centrally planned economies), the location of the American firm would again be important, because a nation can normally control its exports only from its own territory.

A consideration of such controls leads one to speculate as to why international trade was originally defined on the basis of the territorial rather than the national definition of a country. One possible answer, I believe, lies in the fact that most nations have always tried to exercise control of both its foreign trade and its foreign payments, control which could normally only be exercised on a territorial basis. These controls were especially important in the mercantilist era, when these trade concepts were developed. One can suggest that ultimately the major reason for retaining trade accounting systems based on the international relocation of goods and payments is that they provide a basis for imposing, and assessing the consequences of, controls. Thus, although it is my contention that transnational accounting yields the more complete and relevant picture, I would not suggest that transterritorial accounting be discarded.

In the next two sections I develop a system of transnational accounting, contrasting it at points with transterritorial accounting. Although the system is plausible, it is by no means meant to be definitive. Its main purpose is to show the kinds of information that can be divulged and to clarify questions as to who is selling, who is buying, and so forth. This will enable us to better understand the significance of the multinational corporation and to assess its economic consequences.

C. TRANSNATIONAL ACCOUNTING: PRINCIPLES OF CLASSIFICATION

In transnational accounting, it is necessary to define the nationality of any individual or organization, and it is assumed this can be done. In this system, the nationality of an organization is determined by the citizenship of the individuals who control it, and not by its location or the country's laws under which the organization, if a corporation, is incorporated. Control is considered to be synonymous with the ownership of assets. Sometimes the nationality of control may not be readily discerned, particularly with joint ventures involving more than one national, or even with corporations whose common stock is held by different nationals. Later, some problems of the ambiguity of nationality of control will be addressed.

We have devised a symbolic shorthand to designate the nationality and location of any individual or organization. It consists of two letters —the first designating the nationality, the second the location. Thus, an organization of nationality A, located in B, is designated an A/B organization. If this organization were located in A or C, it would be called an A/A or A/C organization.

1. Transnational Assets and Liabilities

To a nation, an important purpose of its transactions with other nations is to enable it to lay claim to goods or services, existing or newly produced, of other countries. Any instrument acknowledging such claims, whether exercisable at any time or only in the future, then becomes part of that nation's transnational assets. But such holdings by other nations lead to counterclaims on its goods and services, and are therefore that nation's transnational liabilities. In so defining a nation's transnational assets and liabilities, two points are particularly important. The first is that a productive facility owned by nationals of one country but located elsewhere is not a transnational asset of that country: it evidences no claim on foreign-owned goods. Thus, an A-owned plant located in B does not provide country A with claims on any goods owned by Bs. It is true that the operations of an A/B plant may lead to transactions that will provide A with a future claim on B goods, but this would be as true for a bushel of wheat in A that might be sold to Bs. The second point is that the physical location of instruments acknowledging claim is immaterial to whether such instruments should be regarded as a transnational asset or a transnational liability, so long as these instruments can be transferred to any party. Under these conditions, any holdings of B currency by an A/B firm are as much part of country A's transnational assets as are similar holdings by A/A firms.

Four types of transnational assets and liabilities can be usefully distinguished. These will vary according to whether the instruments evidence an immediate or a deferred claim on goods, a general claim on all goods or a specific claim only on certain goods, or whether the claim is conditional or unconditional. We concentrate on A's asset/liability position.

The first category of assets for A consists of its holdings of B currency and gold (or some other type of internationally acceptable money). Such assets are immediate in that they can be used to lay claim at any time, general in that they can be used to purchase any B goods for sale, and unconditional if Bs are required or always willing to accept them in payment. By similar reasoning, the A currency and gold held by Bs become A's transnational liabilities of the same type. For any country, the differences between its assets and its liabilities of this type is its "net immediate generalized unconditional claim" position—measuring the extent to which its claims on the goods of others are greater than or less than the counterclaims on its goods. We can take it as usually desirable for a country to have a positive net claim position.

Any transaction in which money is used as payment will change the net claim position of both countries. But the type of payment affects the nature of this change. Thus, if As sell goods or securities to Bs in exchange for B currency, then country A's net claim position improves via an increased claim on B goods: but if payment is made in A currency, A's net claim position improves via a reduction of B claims on A goods. If payment is made in gold, the impact on the net claim positions of both countries is *double* that when payment is made in a national currency. This very interesting result comes about because gold, unlike a national currency, is an unconditionally acceptable means of payment in both countries.

A second type of transnational asset consists of the holdings by one country (or its nationals) of financial securities issued by nationals of the other country and promising payment in some kind of money. Such securities differ from money in that they represent deferred rather than immediate claims. There can be a net claim position for securities as for money, but this figure may be less useful. Financial securities need not always reflect loans: they can also be created by rental agreements (as when A firms license B firms to use a patent in return for a contract specifying royalty payments), or by ordinary sales in which payment is a promissory note rather than cash.

Financial securities are often divided into short-term or long-term securities, generally on the basis of the maturity date, and this division in international transactions does not differ from that in intranational transactions. However, from the viewpoint of nations, the long-term/ short-term division may not always have much relevance. Individual borrowers and lenders often need to know the maturity date in order to plan properly: the borrower knows the period for which he has the use of the funds, and the lender knows when the principal will be returned. However, if there is a securities market on which the lender can sell his securities, the maturity date is important only to the borrower. In international lending, the borrowing *nation* cannot be assured of a continuous command of the borrowed funds, no matter what the maturity dates of the debt instruments, if an international securities market exists. Thus, even if B firms issue thirty-year bonds purchased by A buyers for A currency, country B cannot be assured it can use these funds for thirty years if Bs are able to purchase *any* securities from As for A currency.

A third type of transnational asset for a country consists of securities held by its nationals acknowledging their right to receive payment in specific goods rather than in money. An important example of a transaction in which such a security would be created is when, say, an A firm agrees to help Bs explore for and produce oil, in return for which this A firm is to receive some share of the oil. Such transactions of course become barter—though one party's payment may be deferred.

There is still one more type of transnational asset—namely, some amount of a nation's own currency. Thus, if Bs are willing to accept and hold some additional amount of A money as payment for B goods, this amount represents another claim by As on B goods. It is, however, a conditional claim, conditioned by the willingness of Bs to hold more A money. This willingness would depend upon: the amount of A money already held by Bs; whether the A money is convertible into gold; the possibilities of changes in exchange rates; and expected changes in the prices, quality, and availability of A goods relative to B goods.

2. Transnational Transactions

A transnational transaction is one in which items of economic value —goods, services, currencies, securities, rights to use property— change national hands; such a transaction is independent of the location of the transacting parties and of any physical relocation of the traded items. We discuss here a number of useful distinctions.

First, not all transnational transactions are necessarily exchanges. One country might give a gift or grant to the other, a form of unilateral transfer. Second, not all exchanges are sales. The special characteristic of a sale is that one party obtains either money in payment or a security specifying future money payment. A number of exchanges may not be considered sales in that sense: two-way exchanges of goods (barter); currency swaps. These can be considered "pure" exchanges, in which one cannot distinguish the buyer from the seller.

There are two basic types of sales: one in which, after payment, title to the sold item is transferred to the buyer; the second is one in which the buyer only rents the item. A rental of tangible goods in return for cash is an obvious type of rental sale. Somewhat less obvious, but more important, a loan of money is also a rental sale, with the interest being the payment for the use of money. Lenders, in short, are sellers, and borrowers are buyers.

A transnational export is one in which a national of one country transfers something of economic value to a national of another country, regardless of the location of the transacting parties or of the item of economic value. But not all exports favorably affect a nation's transnational assets and liabilities; a unilateral transfer is one obvious type of export in which there is no impact. And the means of payment —national currencies, gold, financial securities, goods, the right to use goods—can also have differing impacts on a nation's transnational assets and liabilities.

In the next section I provide the accounting for a large number of transnational transactions. My main purpose is to distinguish transnational from transterritorial accounting. But this is more than an exercise in accounting. It deals with other questions as well. Which country is buying and importing, and which is selling and exporting? How do these transactions affect foreign exchange positions and control of assets?

D. TRANSNATIONAL
ACCOUNTS: THEIR USE

In this section we set up a group of "transnational" accounts that can be used to record the results of all transnational transactions. The accounts we choose, of course, are by no means definitive, and it will be obvious that alternatives showing greater or lesser detail can be devised. Although the accounts chosen are both plausible and capable of recording all transactions, our main purpose is essentially illustrative. After the accounts are developed, we discuss a wide variety of transactions: how they would be recorded, problems that arise, and general comments.

i. The Accounts

The transnational accounts are drawn up for country A, defined as a national group. These accounts are divided into two major groups, one showing A's transnational assets and liabilities, the other showing A's transnational exports and imports. Any holdings of assets, or liabilities, by an A firm or a citizen of A are considered part of *country* A's assets or liabilities, regardless of the location of the firm, citizen, assets, or liabilities. Similarly, any sale or purchase by an A firm to or from Bs is considered an export or import by country A no matter where the firm or foreign parties are located. For the most part, we assume B is the other national group, but we also consider some transactions involving C, a third country. The accounts are shown in Table 6.1, and are numbered for referral.

There are three classes of measurable transnational assets and liabilities, which were discussed in the preceding section and are shown

Table 6.1 Transnational Accounts for Country A

Transnational Assets and Liabilities

Unconditional Immediate Generalized Claims

    (1) Assets: holdings of B currency and gold by As

    (2) Liabilities: holdings of A currency and gold by Bs

        Net unconditional immediate generalized claims $= (1) - (2)$

Unconditional Deferred Generalized Claims

    (3) Assets: holdings by As of securities issued by Bs and payable in money

    (4) Liabilities: holdings by Bs of securities issued by As and payable in money

Claims on Goods

    (5) Assets: holdings by As of contracts specifying payment by Bs in goods and services

    (6) Liabilities: holdings by Bs of contracts specifying payment by As in goods and services

Conditional Generalized Claims (Unmeasureable)

    (7) Assets: additional amount of A money B nationals are willing to accept and hold

    (8) Liabilities: additional amounts of B money A nationals are willing to accept and hold

Location of A Assets Abroad (Informational)

    (9) Assets controlled by A, located in B

    (10) Assets owned by A, rented to Bs

Transnational Exports

Outright Export of Goods and Services: Ownership Transferred

    (11) Payment in A money

    (12) Payment in B money

    (13) Payment in gold

    (14) Payment in financial securities

    (15) Payment in contracts evidencing claims on goods

    (16) Payment in goods (outright barter)

    (17) No payment (unilateral transfers)

Rental Exports of Goods and Services

    (18) Payment in A money

    (19) Payment in B money

    (20) Payment in gold

    (21) Payment in financial securities

    (22) Payment in contracts evidencing claims on goods

Table 6.1—*continued*

(23) Payment in goods
(24) No payment
Use of Money
    (25) Payment received for use of money

Transnational Imports

Outright Title-Transferring Imports
    (26) Payment in A money
    (27) Payment in B money
    (28) Payment in gold
    (29) Payment in financial securities
    (30) Payment in claims on goods
    (31) Payment in goods
    (32) No payment
Rental Imports of Goods and Services
    (33) Payment in A money
    (34) Payment in B money
    (35) Payment in gold
    (36) Payment in financial securities
    (37) Payment in claims on goods
    (38) Payment in goods
    (39) No payment
Use of Money
    (40) Payment by As for Use of Money

in Table 6.1 as accounts 1 through 6. The difference between accounts 1 and 2 is particularly important: it represents the net unconditional immediate generalized claims that A has on the B economy. We also show two other sets of assets/liabilities. The first, accounts 7 and 8, represent the conditional claims the two groups have on each other. These conditional claims are virtually unmeasurable, and are included mainly so that we will not lose sight of them and their importance. The last two "asset" accounts represent assets owned by A but either located abroad or rented to Bs. These are really not transnational assets, and are listed mainly for informational purposes. The first six accounts, taken together, may be thought of as A's transnational balance sheet.

The next series of accounts shows the transnational exports. There are three main groupings. In the first group are exports in which title is transferred from A to B. In the second are exports in which As rent something to Bs. The third (account 25) is payment for the use of money. This is really a rental account, and could be included in with the other rentals, but it is unique and important enough to be given its own classification. Within the first two categories, the exports are distinguished by type of payment, and the classification scheme used is self-explanatory. Transnational imports are classified by exactly the same scheme as the exports. Information on the type of payment is necessitated by our definition of the transnational balance sheet.

2. Accounting for Transactions

We now formulate a rather large number of transactions, most of them transnational. For each we show which accounts in Table 6.1 are affected. Also, most of the transactions are accompanied by comments, designed mainly to clarify concepts in transnational accounting —but also to point out issues. We use the numbering system in Table 6.1 in referring to the different accounts. We continue to identify a party to a transaction by both nationality and location, so that an A/B firm refers to a firm of A nationality located in B.

1. A/A makes an outright sale of goods to B/B, for payment in B money.
   Accounting: Raise (1) and (12) by value of sale.
   Comments: This is a straight transnational and transterritorial transaction that would also be reflected in territorial accounts.
2. A/A sells to B/B, payment in A money.
   Accounting: Reduce (2) and raise (11) by sale value.
   Comments: Same as transaction 1, except A's "net claim position" is enhanced via reduction in B claim on A economy rather than increased A claim on B economy.
3. A/A sells to A/B for B money.
   Accounting: None.
   Comments: Not a transnational transaction.
4. A/A sells to B/B and accepts interest-bearing note, payable in B money.
   Accounting: Raise (14) and (3) by face value of note.

5. After transaction 4, B/B liquidates loan, including interest payment.

   Accounting: Raise (1) by total payment; reduce (3) by face amount of note; raise (25) by interest.

   Comments: Loan payment converts A's deferred claim to immediate claim. It should be noted that A's export consisted not only of goods but also of the use of money.

6. A/B firm hires A/A or A/B workers, payable in any money.

   Accounting: None.

   Comments: Not a transnational transaction.

7. A/B firm hires B/B workers or buys any goods from B/B firm. Payment in B currency.

   Accounting: Reduce (1) and raise (27) by value of purchase.

   Comments: This is a typical transnational transaction that would not be reflected in territorial accounting. It is clear, however, that A is buying and B is selling.

8. A/B sells goods to B/B firms or consumers, for B money.

   Accounting: Raise (1) and (12) by value of sales.

   Comments: This is a common case in which a transaction considered an export by transnational standards would not be so considered by transterritorial standards.

9. A/B sells goods to A/A firms or consumers for any kind of money.

   Accounting: None.

   Comments: This is a common case in which the purchase by A/A would not be considered an import in transnational accounting, but would be so considered in transterritorial accounting.

10. A/B sells goods to C/C firms for B money.

    Accounting: Raise (1) and (12) by value of sales.

    Comments: This is a transnational export from A to C that transterritorial accounting would record as an export from B to C.

11. A/B firm sells stocks and bonds to A/A individuals.

    Accounting: None.

    Comments: This is not a transnational transaction, but transterritorial accounting would record it as a capital flow from A to B.

12. A/B firm sells stocks or bonds to B/B for B money.

    Accounting: Raise (1) and (4) by money value.

    Comments: This is a flow of capital from B to A transnationally, which would not be recorded in transterritorial accounting. Through this transaction, A is increasing its net immediate generalized claim on the B economy.

13. A/B pays interest or dividends on securities held by B/B, in B money.

    Accounting: Reduce (1) and raise (40) by value of payment.

    Comments: This makes it clear that in the purchase of A/B securities by B/B, it is the Bs who are the ultimate sellers and As are the ultimate buyers. This transaction would not be recorded in transterritorial accounting.

14. A/B buys a plant from B/B for A money.

    Accounting: Raise (2) and (26), by value of sale and record in (9).

    Comments: This is nothing more than an outright purchase by A from B. But because the plant is not physically moved, it is not recorded as an import by A in transterritorial accounting.

15. A/A firm buys plant from B/A firm for A money.

    Accounting: Raise (2) and (26) by sales value.

    Comments: This does not differ from transaction 14, except with regard to the plant's location.

16. A/B firm buys B/B firm for stock issued by A firm, dividends payable in A money.

    Accounting: Raise (4) and (26) by face value of stock.

    Comment: This is just an import by A, but for a deferred rather than immediate generalized claim on the A economy. This transaction would not be recorded in transterritorial accounting. It includes a flow of capital from *B to A*.

17. A/B firm pays dividends of A money to B/B stockholders.

    Accounting: Raise (2) and (40) by payment.

    Comment: A is paying for the use of B capital, and is thus "importing."

18. As buy stock in A/B firm from Bs for A money.

    Accounting: Raise (2) and reduce (4) by monetary value.

    Comment: Though this would be recorded transterritorially as a capital flow from A to B, it is essentially a conversion of B's deferred claims on the A economy to immediate claims.

19. A/B firm borrows B money from B/B bank.

    Accounting: Raise (1) and (4) by money borrowed.

    Comment: This is a flow of capital from B to A that would not be recorded in transterritorial accounting.

20. A/B pays interest on loan—from transaction 19.

    Accounting: Reduce (1) and raise (40) by payment.

    Comment: This verifies that it was B that was "selling" and A that was "buying."

21. A/B firm borrows any kind of money from A/A or A/B bank.
    Accounting: Neither the borrowing, the repayment, nor the interest payment is a transnational transaction, therefore no recording.
    Comment: The borrowing from A/A bank would be considered a flow of capital from A to B by transterritorial accounting.

22. A/B firm borrows money from B/A bank.
    Accounting: Raise (1) and (4) by amount of loan.
    Comment: This is transnationally no different than borrowing from a B/B bank, but it would be recorded as a flow of capital from A to B transterritorially, although transnationally it is a flow of capital from B to A.

23. A/A deposits A money in a B/B bank as a savings account.
    Accounting: Raise (2) and (3) by amount of money.
    Comment: Transnationally and transterritorially this is a flow of capital, a loan, from A to B.

24. A/A depositor paid interest in A money by B/B bank.
    Accounting: Reduce (2) and raise (25) by payment.
    Comment: This verifies that transaction 23 was a loan, and that A has exported the rental use of its money.

25. A/A deposits in savings accounts in A/B bank.
    Accounting: None; not a transnational transaction.
    Comment: In transterritorial accounting, this would be recorded as a movement of capital from A to B.

26. A/A deposits A money in a B/B bank, as a demand deposit.
    Comment: This transaction creates some subtle accounting problems. B receives A money, which can be used within limits, but A is not giving A money, since a demand deposit is also money. The checkbook is really not a financial security in the usual sense, since A and B are sharing the use of the same money—perhaps the hallmark of demand deposits. What, if anything, does A receive in return for letting B share the use of its money? The answer must be the banking services provided by the B bank. In effect, then, A is trading the rental use of money for banking services. The value of these services would have to be imputed. It would seem then that accounts (25) and (33) should be raised by the imputed value of the services. A is exporting the use of money, and importing banking services. Less clear is whether (2) should be raised by the amount of the deposit. It is true that Bs now have more A money, but their ability to use this money is restricted.

27. A/B rents a factory from B/B, pays rental in advance in B money.

Accounting: Lower (1) and raise (34) by payment.

Comments: A is importing transnationally the use of the plant.

28. A/B rents a factory from B/B, signs contract for future cash payments in B money.

Accounting: Raise (4); list in (9) for information.

Comment: This could be treated as an immediate import by A, but it is probably best to record as an import when payment is made.

29. A/B pays rent on contract of transaction 28.

Accounting: Lower (1) and raise (34) by payment.

Comment: Now record the import.

30. A/B or A/A bank exchanges A money for B money with B/B or B/A bank.

Accounting: Raise (1) and (2) by values exchanged.

Comments: This transaction is not an export or import. A and B are exchanging and enlarging claims on each other's economy.

31. A/B or A/A bank exchanges B money for A money with B/B or B/A bank.

Accounting: Reduce (1) and (2) by value of exchange.

Comment: A mutual reduction by both countries of claims on each other's economy.

32. A/B bank swaps B money for gold with B's central bank.

Accounting: (1) changes in composition; (2) is reduced.

Comments: This does not change A's unconditional claim on B economy, but it does reduce B's claim on the A economy. It is also likely that B's willingness to accept A money will rise. Thus, (7) can be thought to rise although the amount cannot be specified.

33. A/A trades goods with B/B, even-up swap.

Accounting: Raise (16) and (31).

Comments: There is a valuation problem in how much to raise these accounts. This is one trade in which neither country obtains a claim on the other.

34. A/A trades goods and A money to B/B for goods.

Accounting: Raise (2) by money payment; raise (16) by imputed value of exported goods; raise (31) by imputed value of imported goods.

35. B government contracts with A/B firm to produce something or explore for minerals. A/B firm to receive share of output.

Comment: There are alternatives here in the accounting treatment, depending on which entity is viewed as controlling the venture. If the B government is viewed as the controlling entity, then

A is exporting the rental use of property to B in return for a contract specifying claims by A on specific B goods. Thus, raise (22) by the value of A's property, and raise (5) by "expected" value of goods to be received. The second possibility views the A/B firm as controlling the venture. In this event, there is no transnational export, but B receives a contract specifying a claim on A goods. This would be recorded as a note in (6) for the expected value of these goods.

36. Goods produced as the result of transaction 35 are divided between the A/B firm and the B government.

    Comment: Accounting would follow the choice made in 35 as to the controlling entity. If it is the B government, then the share of the output to the A/B firm is A's import payment for the rental of A goods. Thus, we raise (31) by the imputed value of the goods. If the A/B firm is viewed as the controlling entity, then A is exporting the goods to B, for the use of B assets. Thus, (16) is raised.

37. A/B and B/B firms form a joint venture operating in B. Each puts in 50 percent of the cash, and the common stock is divided equally.

    Comment: The accounting again will depend on how the nationality of the enterprise is determined, and there seems to be no obvious rule to follow. If the venture is viewed as an A enterprise, then A is thought to borrow money from B in return for the stocks. Thus, raise (1), raise (4), both by the same amount. If the joint venture is viewed as a B enterprise, then A is lending money to B. Thus, (2) and (3) are both raised by the same amount.

38. The joint venture sells goods to B/B for B money.

    Comment: Accounting again depends on the designated nationality of the joint venture. If A, we raise (1) and (12) by value of sale. If B, there is no transnational transaction.

39. The joint venture sells goods to A/B or A/A for money.

    Comment: If the joint venture is viewed as an A enterprise, there is no transnational transaction. But if viewed as a B enterprise, we raise (2) and (26) by value of sale.

40. The joint venture pays dividends in B money.

    Comment: If the joint venture is viewed as an A enterprise, we lower (1) and raise (40) by payment. In effect, A is paying for the rental use of B capital. If viewed as a B enterprise, we raise (1) and (25): B is now paying A for the use of A capital.

41. A/A firm allows B/B firm to use a patent, with payment made immediately in B money.

    Comment: Raise (1) by money received. The use of the patent is an export by A, but whether it is a title-transferring or a rental sale depends on whether the patent use is revocable. If nonrevocable, raise (12) by the amount; but if revocable, raise (19).

42. A/A firm licences B/B to use patent, for given time period, with royalty payment tied to output.

    Accounting: On a cash-basis method of accounting, we simply show in (10) to note that A's property rented to B.

43. B/B pays royalty to A/A for use of patent—in B money.

    Accounting: Raise (1) and (19) by payment.

    Comment: A is exporting the rental use of its property.

44. A government makes a grant of money to B government.

    Accounting: Raise only (2) by grant value.

    Comment: This is a unilateral transfer of generalized claims on the A economy.

45. Any A makes a gift of goods to B.

    Accounting: Simply raise only (17) by imputed value of goods.

    Comment: Notice this is a type of export that does not lead to any claim by A on B.

46. A/A has shipped goods to B/B for securities, and B/B defaults.

    Accounting: Reduce (3) as worthless security. Reduce (14) and raise (17) by the value of the original export.

    Comment: The overall result of this whole transaction is a unilateral transfer, although involuntary.

47. B government expropriates an A/B facility.

    Accounting: Raise (17) by imputed value; remove from (9).

    Comment: An expropriation also becomes an involuntary unilateral transfer.

48. B government nationalizes A/B plant, and pays in B money considered less than the value of the plant.

    Accounting: Raise (1) by money payment, and divide the value of the plant among (12) and (17), with (12) equal to the money received, and (17) the difference between value and payment.

    Comment: There are obvious valuation problems. The effect of the transaction is an export from A to B, partly for money and partly as a unilateral transfer.

49. An A citizen, together with his A money, becomes a B citizen.

    Accounting: This is probably best treated as a unilateral transfer of A money, so that (2) is raised by the amount.

50. An A/B firm pays taxes, or bribes, to the B government, in B money.
    Comment: In this transaction A is buying and B is selling. What is A buying? Protection, the right to operate, and possibly some useful governmental services. Thus we reduce (1) by the payment and raise (27), the import account for purchase of services, by the same amount.

51. A/A buys bonds issued by an international organization (i.e., the World Bank) for A money.
    Accounting: Raise (2) and (3) by money payments.
    Comment: There will be an immediate claim on A goods, although who will have this claim is not known until the transfer of funds is made to a national group.

52. Interest collected by As from "World Bank."
    Accounting: Reduce (2) and raise (25) by value of receipts.
    Comment: A has rented out the use of its money, and has thus exported.

53. A citizens residing in or touring B buy personal services and other items from B, for B money.
    Accounting: Reduce (1) and raise (27) by value of purchases.
    Comment: A has imported: the treatment of tourism is one case in which transterritorial accounting correctly considers as an import the purchases by A citizens located in B.

54. A group of B workers move temporarily to A to work for A/A firm, and are paid in A money.
    Accounting: Raise (2) and (26) by payment.
    Comment: It must be clear here that A is transnationally importing the service of B workers. It will be argued that this importation of labor is the important alternative to direct foreign investment.

E. DIRECT FOREIGN INVESTMENT AS AN "OUTPOST"

The need for a system of transnational accounting arises because productive entities owned and controlled by one nation (or alternatively its nationals, which we take to be synonymous with the "nation") can be located in another country. The most important economic significance of these foreign-located entities is that, because of their location, the nationals owning them can more easily buy from, or sell to, the host-country nationals. We have defined these kinds of transactions as international trade with our transnational accounting system. Sometimes this type of trade could have been carried on from entities located at home rather than abroad. But there are other types of trade between the nationals that can be carried on *only* through the location of the entity in the foreign country. And there are types of trade that may be profitable, and therefore feasible, only from locations abroad.

It can be useful to think of a productive entity owned by one national group but located in another country as a "trading outpost" of the former country in the latter. Thus, an A/B firm can be considered a trading outpost of A in B. That such a firm can engage in a productive activity such as manufacturing should not becloud the fact that the essential *international* activity of this firm is trading with host-country nationals, although it can also trade with other As as well. Anything this A/B firm sells to Bs is a transnational export from A to B. And anything the A/B firm buys from Bs is a transnational import by A.

Some goods the A/B firm trades with B/Bs could be traded by A/A firms as well. These typically consist of items that are transportable over national boundaries. But sometimes the A/B firm, because of its location, may be able to trade with B/Bs at more advantageous net prices than can an A/A firm. This would often be the case if transport costs are high or if there are trade barriers enacted on *transterritorial* trade. Thus, in some cases A/B firms enable trade with B/B that would not be feasible for A/A firms.

Of greater significance is the fact that A/B firms can conduct transactions with B/Bs for items that cannot be obtained at all by A/A firms. These are items, generally services, that cannot usually be transported over national boundaries. The most important items of this nature that an A/B firm can buy are: B labor; the use of B land; electricity, transport, and other items provided by B's infrastructure. There are also certain items As can sell to Bs only if the productive organizations are located in B: public utility services, construction activity, retailing services. It is clear, then, that direct foreign investment makes possible some types of transnational trade that might not otherwise be possible.

In manufacturing operations, the most important type of transnational transaction made possible or feasible by a foreign location almost always is the purchase of host-country labor services. Thus, an A/B firm, by its location in B, is able to hire B labor, which is a transnational import to A. However, a location in B may not be the only means whereby an A firm can hire B labor. An alternative might be B labor moving to A to work in A/A plants. Such alternatives bear some consideration.

Let us assume the existence of two identical plants owned by American firms, one located in the United States, the other in England. Let us say both hire only British labor—with English workers coming to man the plant located in the United States. Let us further assume that both plants produce the same item in the same quantities, that the outputs of both plants are sold to Germany at identical prices, and that the wage rate paid to the British workers is the same regardless of the plant's location.

If we ignore such secondary questions as taxes, the expenditures of the workers, and so on, it is easy to show that the economic consequences of these plants are identical. Both earn the same foreign exchange from Germany for the United States—assuming the United States as a whole has identical access to the foreign exchange regardless of the plant's location. In both instances, British nationals (or Britain in general) earn the same amount of foreign exchange. The income generated by the output of each plant is divided in the same proportions between Englishmen and Americans. To the extent an American firm located in England purchases only English labor, an American firm located in England is clearly an alternative to an American firm in the United States importing British workers to man its plant. In a very broad sense, then, some types of direct foreign investment are alternatives, not to trade as is so widely thought, but to the international migration of labor.

A careful consideration of transnational accounting raises the question of whether international trade by itself can describe all transnational transactions. What we call "indirect foreign investment" is nothing more than an international loan. The lending country is simply renting out the use of money in much the same way that it might rent out the use of a plant, and this loan is therefore an export. In direct foreign investment, the setting up of the plant itself involves trade: the investing country will almost always import transnationally items from the host country—construction labor, other services and items, even possibly the whole plant (as in an acquisition). The productive activities of the plant will nearly always also involve transnational trade in which the investing country hires host-country nationals. The really distinctive feature of the foreign location is that it enables a type of trade—most importantly the purchase by one country of another country's labor and land—which would not otherwise be feasible, except for importation of workers. The foreign location also enables sales by the investing country to the host country of services for which physical proximity of buyer and seller is required. Thus direct foreign investment enables trade in essentially territorially nontransferable inputs and outputs. It is clear then that indirect foreign investment is just another form of international trade while direct foreign investment *enables* certain types of international trade to take place.

Although it is true that all international investment can be reduced to some form of international trade, one important reason remains for distinguishing investment from trade: international investment leads to a *continuing* trading relation between two nations. An outright sale or exchange of goods is a one-shot affair in which the transaction is completed once the items of economic value have exchanged national hands; but foreign investment involves a kind of continuing commitment between two nations, with its attendant risks, that is not present in simple outright sales.

F. TRANSNATIONAL TRANSACTION MATRIX AND THE INTERNATIONAL DISTRIBUTION OF INCOME

The production of goods and services, when sold, generates income for the various productive factors used in the act of production. The productive factors are people, or are owned by people, and as such have nationality designations not as easily ascribed to goods. Thus, a Volkswagen is a German car, not because of its characteristics but because it is produced in German-owned plants. But any product can consist of elements produced by different national groups, and as such can generate income for a number of national groups. Thus, a Volkswagen may also generate income for Belgian glassmakers, Malaysian rubber producers, Turkish workers located in Germany, and so forth.

In a completely closed economy, its output generates income only for the national group defining that economy. As international trade and investment become possible—that is, as that economy "opens"— various combinations of national productive factors also became possible, and as a result production may generate income for different national groups. To analyze the possibilities, we turn to the construction of a Leontief-type transaction matrix that reflects the transactions between firms organized into sectors, productive factors organized by types of productive services, and final buyers.[2] The firms constituting the sectors, the productive factors, and those who purchase the final goods, are designated by nationality—and we assume only two nationalities, As and Bs. The nationality designation is independent of location. Transactions can take place between citizens of the same nationality and between citizens of different nationalities.

This transaction matrix serves a number of purposes. First, it further clarifies the significance of international trade and investment. Second, it shows how international trade and investment can alter the international distribution of income. Third, it enables us to see more clearly a variety of relationships. Fourth, it helps us to raise questions concerning the welfare effects of international trade and investment.

A more ambitious consideration of these welfare effects, however, awaits later chapters.

The transaction matrix presented as Table 6.2 has sellers along the rows and buyers along the columns. There are four classes of sellers: the A-nationality producing sectors; the B-nationality producing sectors; the A-nationality productive factors; and the B-nationality productive factors. There are also four groups of buyers: the A-nationality producing sectors; the B-nationality producing sectors; the A-nationality buyers of final goods; the B-nationality final buyers.

These eight groups are further subdivided according to the type of product or service. The producing sectors for each nationality are divided as follows: two consumer goods (C_1 and C_2); one raw material (R); one capital good (K); one sector that produces "components" (N); and one that produces services (S). The factors of production for each national group are: labor (L); profits (π), assumed to be payment for entrepreneurial services and to go only to the national group controlling an enterprise; three types of rent, for the use of money (i), for the use of land (R_n), for the use of all other types of property (R_o); taxes (T). The "final buyers" and their nationality can be divided among purchasers of consumer goods and purchasers of capital goods.

The value of the sales by the factors of production of any nationality is that nation's national income. Two of these factors require comment. Dividends received by any national group from ownership of stock in the corporation of another national group are considered a form of interest (i). The tax receipts (T) received by one government from nationals of the other country are considered income to the taxing country.

The four groups of sellers and the four groups of buyers can result in sixteen types of transactions: A producing sectors selling to A producing sectors; A producing sectors selling to B producing sectors; A producing sectors selling to A buyers of final goods, and so forth. However, four of these transactions are inoperative, if we assume that productive factors sell only to the producing sectors and not to the final users. Thus there are only twelve operative classes of transac-

Table 6.2 Transnational Transaction Matrix

Buyers\Sellers	PRODUCING SECTORS A Nationality $C_1 C_2 \ldots S$	B Nationality $C_1 C_2 \ldots S$	PURCHASERS OF FINAL GOODS A Buyers	B Buyers
PRODUCING SECTORS A Nationality Consumer Product—C_1 Consumer Product—C_2 Raw Material—R Capital Good—K Components—N Personal Services—S	I	II	III	IV
B Nationality C_1 C_2 R K N S	V	VI	VII	VIII
FACTORS OF PRODUCTION A Nationality Labor—L Profit—π Interest Rent—i Land Rent—R_n Other Rent—R_o Taxes—T	IX	X		
B Nationality L π i R_n R_o T	XI	XII		

tions, which for reference purposes are designated by roman numerals. Any element in the matrix represents the value of the transactions during some time period between the selling group designated in the row and the buying group in the designated column.

Several identities should be noted. First, for any producing sector, the sales taking place during some period of time must equal that sector's purchases for that same time period, where these "purchases" include profits. Thus, for each producing sector, its row total must equal its column total. Second, each nation's national income per time period will be the sum of the value of the sales of its productive factors. Thus, quadrants IX and X, when summed, become the national income for A, while quadrants XI and XII become the national income for B. There is no reason that the value of the final goods purchased by any national group must equal its national income. This would be an identity in a closed economy, but not in an open economy in which trade imbalances are possible. Thus quadrants III plus VII do not have to equal quadrants IX plus X; nor do quadrants IV and VIII have to equal quadrants XI and XII. But the *world* income has to equal the *world* purchases of final goods: that is, IX plus X plus XI plus XII must equal III plus IV plus VII plus VIII.

We can now investigate how various types of economic relations between As and Bs make certain types of transactions possible. The nature of the transactions may also affect the extent to which national productive factors are purchased, and hence can affect the income of the two national groups.

Let us begin with the nonexistence of economic relations between As and Bs—that is, both countries have closed economies. Then for A, quadrants I, III, and IX represent the only types of transactions that can take place, which must be among its own nationals. The value of A's output of final goods, quadrant III, is A's gross national product. This must equal the value of all payments to A productive factors, quadrant IX, which is A's gross national income. Quadrant I is Leontief's "interindustry" matrix. B's transactions are limited to quadrants VI, VIII, and XII, with similar interpretations.

Let us now introduce trade, but only for transportable products—so that all products except services (which require proximity of buyer and seller) can be sold from one national group to another over international boundaries. As a result (except for services) transactions in quadrants II and IV become possible, with A producing sectors selling goods to either B producing sectors or B buyers of final goods. Since the A producing sectors as yet can buy only A productive factors, the value of the transactions in quadrants II and IV will generate that amount of income in quadrant IX. Similarly, quadrants V and VII become possible transactions that generate income for Bs in quadrant XII.

If trade were limited to final goods—C_1, C_2, K—any sale by an A producing sector would generate income only for As. But when there is trade in intermediate goods as well (raw materials and components), any sale of final goods could generate income for productive factors of both countries. Thus, if the C_1 sector of A buys raw materials from B (quadrant VI) and then sells its output to either As or Bs (quadrants III and IV), these final goods generate income for As and Bs. The income to Bs would be the value of the raw materials purchased by the C_1 sector in A from Bs: the income generated by this sector to As would be the value of the C_1 goods sold minus the value of the imported raw materials.

If we introduce the possibility that individual nationals of one country are located in the other, so that there is physical proximity of As and Bs, personal and business services can now be sold from one national group to another. Then the "S" lines in quadrants IV and VII can have values. Income, of course, is generated for the national productive factors of the country providing the services.

Two quadrants—X and XI—which reflect the sales of productive factors of one nation to the producing sectors of the other nation, do not as yet have any transactions. For transactions of these types to take place, foreign investment is necessary. When international loans are introduced, row "i" (interest payments) in quadrants X and XI can also have values, with a similar generation of income for those doing the selling.

With direct foreign investment, the "labor" and "land rent" lines of quadrants X and XI become possible. The labor lines of X and XI also become possible transactions if, as in the case of the "guest worker" programs in Europe, or Mexicans in the United States, the workers of one country can work in another. Ignoring this last possibility, direct foreign investment of A in B will be required if the L and R_n lines of quadrant XI have non-zero values, and these transactions generate income for Bs. Similarly, direct foreign investment of B in A makes possible the L and R_n transactions of quadrant X, which generate income for As. It will be noted that only the host country's income can benefit from these types of transactions—if we again leave out the possibility of "guest workers."

It is also important to realize that all taxes paid by a foreign-owned firm to the host government are a form of income to the host country —and can be viewed as a payment for government services. It should be appreciated that taxes collected by a government from foreigners are a source of income, while those collected from its own citizens usually amount only to an intranational transfer of income.

Under transnational accounting, the profit lines of quadrants X and XI cannot have transactions. This is because we have associated the nationality of an organization with the nationality of those who own and control it. Thus, entrepreneurial services, for which profit is paid, are the one productive factor that cannot be sold directly to an organization of another nationality.

Direct foreign investment may also enable sales of services in quadrants II, IV, V, and VII, in which the physical proximity of buyer and seller is necessary. In this respect, direct foreign investment is similar to tourism—both enable the physical proximity necessary for one national group to sell nontransportable services to the other.

This matrix, as we have developed it, shows only the primary impacts of transactions upon incomes. These transactions, of course, can also have secondary (but not less important) impacts upon income, and these will concern us in later chapters.

CHAPTER SEVEN

Theories Explaining
Direct Foreign Investment

We turn to the question of why firms and individuals choose to locate abroad as an alternative to investing domestically. Several existing theories will be outlined and discussed, and toward the end of this chapter we offer still another theory. On one level it is very easy to explain direct foreign investment. Taking into account different degrees of risk, investors should be expected to locate wherever the returns to capital are higher. Once this underlying motive is accepted, the interesting question becomes: why do the rates of returns on investments vary between nations?

Several theses have been proposed to answer these questions, but they are, for the most part, inadequate, and a number of rather obvious explanations of direct foreign investment have been largely ignored. The reasons for some of these failures, I believe, lie with the use of the Heckscher-Ohlin trade model as a starting point for explaining investment, and with a reliance on price ratios rather than monetary prices. The shortcoming of the Heckscher-Ohlin model is not that it is formally incorrect, but rather that it focuses only on a single variable to explain trade—differences in factor prices—while ignoring or conveniently assuming away the existence of many other variables. The trade model developed in chapter 3, because it attributes trade to the many forces that can explain international pretrade price differentials, is much less restrictive in its assumptions and can therefore provide a broader framework.

For the most part, private individuals and firms make the actual decisions concerning where to invest. These decisions are not made in a public policy vacuum, however. Governments adopt numerous policies which either purposefully or inadvertently affect incentives for firms to locate in certain countries or for individuals to invest in one country rather than in another. On one level it is therefore possible to focus on these policies. In this chapter, however, we will not attempt to explain why governments adopt certain policies. Rather, we assume the existence of a "regime" of public policies, and focus our attention on the firm or individual.

It is necessary to begin this chapter with a section not on a theory to explain foreign investment, but on a theory that purports to explain why foreign investment should *not* take place. This theory, a deduction from the widely accepted Heckscher-Ohlin trade model, concludes that free trade should lead to an equalization of wage rates and returns on capital—indeed of all factor prices—in the trading countries. If this theory is both true and relevant—a question we closely examine—then with free trade there should be no incentives for foreign investment, or for the international mobility of labor. Since this factor-price equalization theorem is widely accepted by economists, explanations of the observed international investment that has taken place have tended to begin by implicitly asking: which necessary conditions for factor-price equalization are not fulfilled?

A. THE FACTOR-PRICE EQUALIZATION THEOREM

Given the complexity of economic phenomena, nobody can deny the necessity of constructing simplified models that can help us understand the very complex real world. All models require the use of abstractions and assumptions, if they are to be simple enough to be tractable and yield useful insights. The extent to which abstractions and assumptions are removed from reality will, of course, limit the applicability of any model—and if the assumptions in particular are too "strong," a model could be irrelevant even though interesting as an exercise in deductive logic. In some models, the line of deductive reasoning from assumptions to conclusions can be quite complex, evoking a degree of admiration even from those who, on either intuitive or empirical grounds, reject the conclusions of the model. Sometimes, perhaps out of a combination of admiration for the feats of model-builders and a lack of alternative models, we tend to forget the necessary abstractions and assumptions, and focus completely on the conclusions, taking the latter as "proved."

The factor-price equalization theorem is an excellent and important example of the hold deductive models can have on economists. The line of reasoning, which argues essentially that free trade will result in equal factor prices in the trading countries, is both complex and subtle, and can even be called brilliant. To be sure, many economists have rejected the main conclusions—somewhat unhappily, because they have been unable to discover the flaws in the logic. Other economists, however, because there seem to be no flaws, have accepted the conclusions as valid—and among this group are many leading theoretical economists of today. It can be asserted that the high degree of acceptance of the factor-price theorem has obstructed our understanding of direct foreign investment.

The factor-price equalization theorem is based on the Heckscher-Ohlin model of trade, in which trade is explained by differences in the factor intensities used in the production of various products, together with differences in relative factor scarcities in the trading nations. The theorem itself has been deduced from the underlying Heckscher-Ohlin model by a number of prominent economists, among them Paul Samuelson, Harry Johnson, Roy Harrod, and Kelvin Lancaster. The reasoning is highly abstract, and argued in terms of relative price ratios rather than monetary prices. The argument is much too complex to reproduce here, and has been ably presented elsewhere.[1] But the essence of the argument is as follows: trade equalizes relative commodity prices in the (two) trading countries; changes in output brought on by trade in each of the countries result in changing demands for the (two) factors; the factor prices will be in the same proportion to each other in both countries; the relative factor prices must reflect the marginal products of these factors in both countries; if technology is the same in both countries—a key assumption—the marginal products will be the same in both countries; hence, the factor prices will be the same.

Because of the complexity of the reasoning, and also because of the desire to use graphic methods as much as possible, the deduction of the theorem is usually limited to the simplest case: two countries; two factors of production (labor and capital); two commodities, both of which are tradeable. Samuelson, however, by the use of nongraphic mathematics, has been able to extend the analysis to any number of countries, commodities, and factors of production—arguing that factor-price equalization will still hold.[2] Of course, the reasoning has to make many assumptions—unimpeded free trade, perfectly competitive markets, perfect knowledge, identical technology, the number of commodities greater than or equal to the number of productive factors, incomplete specialization of both countries after trade, constant returns to scale. These assumptions will be examined at a later point in this section.

Those who have provided proofs for the factor-price equalization theorem have made some effort to limit its applicability to the real world. Harrod referred to it as a "curiosum in international trade theory."[3] Samuelson cautions that the derivation of the theorem is an exercise in pure logic: if certain assumptions are given, can a certain conclusion be drawn? He points out that the assumptions or conclusions may not be valid empirical generalizations.[4] Clement, Pfister, and Rothwell state: "the derivation and discussion of the factor-price equalization theorem vividly displays [sic] the power and elegance of a priori analysis: they illustrate as well the severe limitation of some kinds of pure theoretical work."[5]

Let us turn to some of the puzzles that this theorem has helped create. According to this theorem, free trade will lead to factor-price equalization. Since the factors of production presumably move from one country to another in response to differentials in factor prices, it is a short step to the conclusion that free trade should mean there will be no international movements of productive factors, or that with freer trade there should be a decrease in the international movement of productive factors.

There is an important corollary to this conclusion which has not received as much attention. If there are free flows of the factors of production internationally, then there should be no international trade. A free flow of the factors of production should also equalize factor prices in the various nations. The Heckscher-Ohlin thesis, it will be recalled, has, as one of the conditions necessary for trade, pre-trade factor prices that differ in the trading countries. If these differences did not exist, the cost of production and the internal price of any product would be the same in all countries, and, as a consequence, there would be no basis for trade.

It is clear then that free trade in commodities and the free movement of the factors of production are antithetical to each other, at least according to this theory. If there is free trade in commodities, there is then no economic basis for the movement of the factors of production. And if there is free movement of the factors of production, there is no underlying basis for trade in commodities. (For this conclusion, however, we could have to ignore the time necessary for full adjustment to take place.) This antithesis between trade and factor movements leads to some interesting puzzles. What if there are no impediments either to commodity trade or to factor movements? Could we get both? Or should we get trade without factor movements, or factor movements without trade? These questions have not received much attention in the literature. Ricardo, however, faced it many years ago and "solved" it by arguing that the factors of production could be *assumed* to prefer to remain in their native lands.

At any rate, we should not expect both trade and factor movements to increase as impediments to both are reduced. But even the most casual empiricism has not been kind to the conclusion that trade and factor movements are antithetical to each other. In the United States, for example, where there are virtually no legal impediments either to geographic trade or to factor movements, it is readily observed that both take place simultaneously. For much of the world, the postwar period has seen a major reduction of impediments to both trade and investment—at least among the industrialized nations—and *both* have grown dramatically. And if one searches history, there is evidence that trade and investment seem to rise and fall together. The United States, for example, both trades with and invests in Canada more heavily than with any other country. The European Common Market is also instructive. Not only have trade barriers been reduced among these countries, but there have also been reductions in barriers to the movement of both capital and labor. What, one may ask, is the point to reducing barriers to factor movements if free trade by itself could accomplish everything in the way of improved welfare for the common market nations?

The factor-price equalization theorem also appears to contradict the teachings of another field of economics, developmental economics, and this has led to attacks on this theorem from developmental economists such as Gunnar Myrdal.[6] A major claim of developmental economists is that incomes of workers in the poorer countries can only be increased by increasing the productivity of labor, which in turn can mainly be accomplished through increased capital formation. But, if the factor-price equalization theorem is taken seriously, it implies that labor wage rates in poor countries could be the same as those in rich countries merely through free trade. The only difference in incomes of the two types of countries would be for the capitalist classes, and this would not occur because of differences in rates of return but rather because the capitalists in the rich countries presumably own more units of capital. If this were the case, the poorer countries must be oblivious to their interests for not carrying the free trade flag in the march toward trade liberalization.

The assumptions underlying the factor-price equalization theorem have been stated clearly and fairly, and it certainly cannot be said that those who have helped in the development of this theorem have in any way tried to hide these underpinnings from attack. But this openness does not, of course, mean that these assumptions should not be evaluated for their reasonableness—a task to which we now turn.

One major assumption of the factor-price equalization theorem is the existence of perfectly competitive markets everywhere. This assumption has been so vigorously attacked by Edward Chamberlin, Joan Robinson, Keynes, and countless others that one can only wonder why a theorem so dependent on it should still be taken so seriously. There are many other assumptions open to question. The assumptions of identical managerial capabilities, technologies, and labor skills among the trading countries are difficult to take seriously as reflections of reality. Another assumption, that of constant returns to scale, is generally considered reasonable. But "constant returns to scale" is often confused with "economies of size"—the latter a relation between scale of plant and average production costs—and economies of size can occur with constant returns to scale.[7]

Perhaps even more important are the assumptions concerning the sectors of the economy and what could be traded. The theorem explicitly assumes that all output of the trading countries can be traded. This by itself is a fatal weakness, since it is obvious that large portions of all economies are devoted to nontradeable goods and services. Furthermore, the theorem assumes only consumer goods are traded: it cannot readily encompass trade in raw materials, capital goods, or intermediate components.[8]

One more point illustrates how arbitrary abstractions can be in model building. One assumption underlying the theorem is that there be at least as many different types of commodities produced as there are different types of productive factors. Samuelson writes: "when we add a third productive factor and retain but two commodities, the whole presumption towards factor price equalization disappears."[9] This is so, because the third productive factor, if present in different quantities in the trading countries, will cause the marginal products of other factors to be higher in the country in which this third factor is more abundant.

This limitation has not been given the attention it deserves. Economists tend to treat the factors of production as limited to a small number—labor, land, and capital—and furthermore generally treat each factor as completely homogeneous. On the other hand, there is no limit to the number of commodities that can be produced, according to the usual treatment. For these reasons, Samuelson's caveat has not been accorded much weight: it appears to many self-evident that there are always more commodities than factors of production.

But our treatment of the factors of production as being limited in number and homogeneous for any classification is surely just a convenient abstraction. There are actually many kinds of labor, many types of capital, many types and qualities of land. There is no a priori reason why in any country the number of productive factors must be less than the number of commodities. How many there are of each is purely a matter of definition, classification, and convenience—depending upon how we choose to group both productive factors and commodities that vary slightly in their physical characteristics. Since there is little question that there is a considerable element of arbitrariness in classification schemes, the validity of the factor-price equalization theorem is itself dependent on somewhat arbitrary and convenient matters of definition and classification.

From this discussion, it is clear that a large number of conditions must be fulfilled if the assumptions underlying the factor-price equalization theorem are to be reasonably realistic. Since many of these conditions are not met in the real world, the factor-price equalization theorem cannot be relevant to an understanding of international factor movements—or, at best, it can be used only as a starting point.

B. THE TRADE
IMPEDIMENT THESIS

If one accepts the factor-price equalization theorem and abstracts, as is usually done, from the time necessary for adjustment, there are then no incentives for international capital and other factor movements if free trade exists. It therefore seems to be a natural extension of this theorem to explain observed factor movements, capital in particular, in terms of impediments to trade. The corollary can also be effectively argued, namely that impediments to factor movements create incentives for trade.

Robert Mundell published a paper on the relation between trade and factor movements which appears to have been influential and probably reflects the thinking of many on the subject.[10] He argues both that trade impediments create incentives that lead to factor movements, and that impediments to factor movements create trade. Implicit in his paper is the corollary: lack of impediments to trade discourages factor movements, and lack of impediments to factor movements discourages trade. There is evidently an appealing symmetry in these arguments, and they clearly lead to the conclusion that trade and factor movements are alternatives to each other and hence substitutes.

A rather convincing case can be made for the first proposition: that trade barriers create incentives for capital in particular to locate abroad. Assume that A is the relatively capital-abundant country and is exporting a capital-intensive product. Let us say that trade has moved factor prices in the two countries closer to each other; we do not have to accept the stronger thesis that these prices be fully equalized. Let us now say that B imposes a tariff or import quota on A's exported good. Two important results should follow the obvious result that trade will be reduced. First, the price of the capital-intensive product would be considerably higher in B than in A. Second, wage rates should fall in B relative to wage rates in A. There are now two types of incentives created for As to locate plants producing the capital-intensive product in B. One is that the product can be sold at a higher price, assuming it is sold to the Bs, than it could be sold at if territorially exported from A to B. The second is that, because of the lower wage rate in B, the product can be produced more cheaply in B. Both, of course, will tend to increase the rate of return on capital to a plant located in B rather than in A.

This argument is not only persuasive in terms of a deduction from a formal theoretical model, but also has appeal from casual observation. Various nations have used "tariff walls" successfully as incentives to induce foreign investors to locate in their countries. Multinational firms are quite naturally eager to locate in countries with a protected market—that is, a market insulated from competition from outside by import barriers.

The supposedly symmetrical argument—that unimpeded factor movements reduce trade—has many flaws. One can, in fact, argue that the reverse is true, that factor movements *create* trade. Consider first the case of indirect international investment. Let us say that the As loan A money to the Bs, by buying securities issued by the latter. If the so-called transfer mechanism is working properly, there should be an increased amount of exports from A to B. Indeed the whole point of the loan is to enable B to increase its imports. (The transfer mechanism, however, could also conceivably serve to reduce B's exports to A.) Furthermore, when the Bs service and repay the loans, exports should increase from B to A. It is then obviously fallacious to even suggest that unimpeded flows of money should reduce trade: the result should be exactly opposite. How can prominent economists make such an error? The answer, it seems to me, is that they focus completely on *relative* factor prices as explanations of trade while completely neglecting the level of actual monetary prices—this is the accepted procedure of "pure" trade theory. Thus the effect of money transfers on the absolute money levels of prices—and loans should affect these levels—is completely missed in the analysis.

Could it be claimed that *direct* foreign investment reduces trade? If we view trade as trans*national* transactions, as we maintain should be done, it is clear that direct foreign investment can vastly increase at least transnational trade. A major purpose of companies locating abroad is to enable them to purchase labor and other nonexportable services and items, such as the use of land. And obviously transnational trade in commodities between the firm and local purchasers should be enhanced.

This argument, however, though correct in the eyes of this writer, may not be a valid refutation of Mundell's point, because he considered only transterritorial trade. But even accepting this more usual definition of trade, the argument that factor movements reduce trade still has serious flaws. The company located abroad will, first of all, but inclined to import into the country of location such items as machinery, components, and the like, all of which constitute trade in the usual sense. Second, the firm located abroad may not have been able to compete with rivals in the country of location if that firm were located in its own country: hence no exports will have been displaced by location abroad. Third, the firm presumably earns the foreign exchange of the country in which it is located: and these earnings should become transformed into exports from the host to the investing country.

Important as these points may be, they do not constitute the major refutation of the thesis that foreign investment reduces trade—and we now turn to perhaps the most important point. Mundell, with many other economists, implicitly assumes that firms owned by one country but located abroad sell all their output in the country in which they are located. But there is neither theoretical nor empirical justification for this assumption. If an item can be produced more cheaply in B than in A, it makes perfectly good sense for an A firm to locate and produce in B, and sell to A, or to B—or to other countries. That this has happened in the past, and is happening now—and on a vast scale —is so evident that we need marshall only a few observations to make its truth apparent. The most obvious case is in raw materials; American, British, and the firms of other countries surely produce minerals, agricultural products, and other raw materials not to be sold in the country of location, but to be exported back to the home country or to other countries. American firms locate manufacturing facilities in Mexico, Hong Kong, Malaysia, and elsewhere abroad mainly to produce goods to be sold in the United States. Many companies designate certain countries as "export bases," where production is carried on almost entirely for export. In colonial times, traders and producers from the mother countries located abroad virtually expressly for the purpose of obtaining goods to be exported back to the mother country.

This is not to say that firms never locate abroad to sell to the domestic market, but the implicit assumption that this is always the case is surely unwarranted. We must, therefore, accept the conclusion that factor movements are much more likely to create transterritorial trade than to reduce it. If trade is defined as transnational transactions, there is absolutely no question that factor movements create this type of trade. Indeed, all international loans were by themselves considered transnational trade in the previous chapter.

Not only can movements of production factors create trade, but it can also be persuasively argued that the elimination of trade barriers should *increase* direct foreign investment. The argument is simple. With trade barriers, firms from different countries are not in direct competition with one another. But when these barriers are reduced or eliminated, the competition between firms from different countries becomes sharpened. It therefore becomes more necessary for firms in high-wage countries to locate production facilities in low-wage countries—just to remain competitive. Furthermore, freer trade makes it more feasible to locate production facilities in one country but to sell to other countries. We should therefore not be surprised that both international trade and international investment have increased simultaneously.

C. DIRECT FOREIGN INVESTMENT: LOCATION-SPECIFIC ACTIVITIES

A decision by a firm to locate productive facilities abroad can be conceived as one in which a choice is made between location at home or location in a foreign country. Even when the option for a location abroad is selected, there still remains the question as to which country is to be selected for the productive facility.

For some types of economic activities, once the decision is made to engage in that activity, the choice is almost self-evident. This is because some types of activities—which we will call location-specific activities—can be carried out only by locating in certain areas. Among these are mining, some types of agriculture, retailing, banking (in the deposit line), construction. If, for example, an American firm wishes to grow bananas, there is no effective choice between growing them in the United States or growing them abroad—the firm has to locate in countries that have the special climate and soil suitable to growing bananas. There is no question of location here. The only question is one between producing bananas abroad, or buying them from others. If we want to understand why such a firm chooses to locate abroad, we must only ask why it prefers to produce rather than purchase.

The important activity of manufacturing is not as closely tied to specific locations, although one location may, because of cost differentials, be preferable to an alternative. The key aspect of manufacturing is that it can be carried on at almost any location in which there is a labor force. Inputs other than labor (and a few others) can usually be transported significant distances to the plant, and all outputs can be transported virtually anywhere to buyers at some cost. Thus there is usually an effective set of feasible choices as to where a firm may locate. A theory to explain manufacturers' locating abroad rather than at home must, therefore, consider variables in addition to those in which the activity can only be carried on abroad.

Historically, the great bulk of location-specific direct foreign investment has been in the production of raw materials. For some types of raw materials, there may be no effective home alternative. Whether or not there exists a feasible alternative at home will, of course, vary from one country to the next. There is one group of raw materials that the industrialized countries are almost completely unable to produce domestically—the "tropical" products: cane sugar, coffee, tea, rubber, cocoa, jute, cotton (to a limited extent), tin, hemp, various types of fruit, and so forth.

How can one explain the decision by firms from the more industrialized countries to locate abroad to produce these products? Of course, there would seem to have been strong profit motivations on the part of the firm. Since these products were not produced at home, there would have been no domestic competition for them and profits would, initially at least, have been high. All that really has to be explained is why producers indigenous to the tropical areas gave way to firms from the industrialized countries. Probably the most important reasons were that substantial amounts of capital, knowledge of markets in the industrialized countries, enterprises sufficiently large to take on risks, and transportation and warehousing facilities were required for the commercial production and marketing of such crops and minerals. In all these matters, the developed industrialized nations would have had considerable advantages over indigenous producers. Also, the weak political position of the tropical countries vis-à-vis the developed countries, including a history of outright colonialism, also played an important role.

Other types of raw materials may or may not be capable of production in the industrialized countries. But even if such materials can be produced domestically, firms have not been deterred from seeking these raw materials abroad; American exploration for oil is the most prominent example. The reasons firms of countries that have similar raw materials choose to produce abroad are readily shown—especially for depletable raw materials. The natural tendency of any nation is to exploit its lower-cost sources of raw materials first. As these become depleted, only the higher-cost sources become available for exploitation. Thus, with time, the difference in the costs of producing raw materials at home as opposed to obtaining these materials from "virgin" lands becomes greater, and this provides strong incentives to search for and produce raw materials abroad. This explanation also holds for agricultural products, since the developed highly populated country will also have to put marginal land into production. This explains why firms from industrialized countries where raw materials are more played out (Western Europe, the United States, Japan) are much more likely to seek raw materials abroad than are firms from developed countries still possessing cheap sources of raw materials, such as Canada and Australia. This explanation holds true more for non-renewable raw materials than for agricultural products.

D. DIRECT FOREIGN INVESTMENT IN MANUFACTURING: THE SPECIAL ADVANTAGE THESIS

Since manufacturing generally has a choice of effective locations, we can ask why a firm may choose to locate and produce abroad when a domestic location is feasible. One theory purporting to explain the choice of the option of locating abroad can be called the "special advantages" thesis. This thesis has been prominently developed by Richard Caves, Stephen Hymer and Charles Kindleberger, although others have also written along these lines.[11] They reject the notion that direct foreign investment is to be explained by such traditional variables as differences in relative factor prices. Rather, they argue that the explanation of direct foreign investment in manufacturing is to be found in the field of industrial organization, which deals with such matters as degrees of control of markets, differentiation of products, vertical and horizontal integration of firms, relative advantages of firms, and the like—all of which could be placed under the rubric of "market imperfections." This view is colored by a number of empirical facts. First, most foreign investment is carried on by large dominant firms. Second, a great deal of this investment, especially by American firms, has been carried on in industries in which there is new technology or product differentiation.

The "special advantage" thesis begins by posing a question: why can a foreign firm be successful in competing with domestic firms in the country of location? To put the question in terms of our two-country model, why should an A organization located in B be able to compete with B organizations also located in B in selling to the B market? If the A/B and B/B firms produce the same product, use the same technology, pay the same for inputs, and sell all output in the B market, it would seem that all the competitive advantages lie with the B/B firms. The B/B firms presumably know the market better, have less problems with communications, have better political and banking connections, speak the same language as their customers, and presumably buyers would rather buy from a firm of their own nationality than from a foreign-owned firm.

Once this question is posed, the only apparent answer, which is also the theory, is that the A/B and B/B firms cannot be exactly alike. The A/B firm, if it is to be successful in its competition with B/B firms, must have some unique special advantage that can compensate for its inherent disadvantage of being foreign. There are a number of sources of such special advantages. First, the A/B firm's product may be differentiated from, and superior to, the products of its B/B competitors. Second, the A/B firm may possess superior technology, enabling it either to produce a superior product or to produce a similar product more cheaply. Third, the A/B firm may have better marketing skills, which can be particularly important for consumer goods. Fourth, the A/B firm may be larger, which may enable it to produce at lower costs, undertake advertising campaigns, conduct expensive research, make better use of specialists, assume greater risks, and so forth. Finally, the A/B firm may be able to acquire capital on better terms than can its B/B rivals. The last possibility is not given great weight by Kindleberger and Caves, who see a fairly perfect international capital market in which all large firms can obtain capital on comparable terms.

Caves chooses to emphasize the importance of superior knowledge on the part of the A/B firm. This can be in product design, production efficiencies, or marketing skills. Superior knowledge varies in importance among different types of industries. It will certainly be more important in high-technology industries, such as computers, drugs, scientific instruments; in fairly sophisticated consumer products such as automobiles, tires; and in mass market consumer products requiring very special marketing skills, such as detergents, razor blades. The unifying threads among such products are that they are differentiable, they require rapidly-changing technologies (including marketing), and they require substantial and expensive research to develop the superior knowledge needed in their production and marketing. In other industries—steel, paper, basic chemicals, aluminum, simple textiles—the technology is well known and settled, the products are standardized, marketing skills are not vital, and the amount of research done is comparatively small.

It is, of course the "high-knowledge" firms with their special advantages that should be able to compete successfully in foreign countries with domestic producers. Caves, using American multinational firm data, cites empirical evidence to support the thesis that it is the high-knowledge firms that locate abroad. He notes that the bulk of American direct foreign investment is in such industries as autos, machinery, other consumer durables, scientific instruments, specialty chemicals, rubber (tires mainly)—all industries in which product differentiation, marketing skills, new technologies, are important. On the other hand, there is a decided lack of American direct foreign investment in steel, aluminum, basic textiles—industries with undifferentiated products and settled technology.

The "special advantage" thesis has a number of problems. Granted that, say, an American firm has special advantages vis-à-vis its foreign competitors; it is still not clear why that firm has to locate abroad to compete with these firms in the latter's domestic markets. The American firm's advantage should still hold through exports from its home location, and in fact several articles have shown it is just such "special advantage" products that are exported from the United States. Caves considers this, and then cites import barriers and transport costs as the reasons to locate abroad. But of course, in so doing, he wanders away from the "special advantage" thesis. These explanations become even less tenable when viewed against the background of postwar reductions in trade barriers and the fact that it is the high technology products that are best able to bear transport costs.

Another interesting problem is that in which firms producing similar but differentiated products cross-locate in each other's countries, such as the British Unilever locating in the United States while the American Procter and Gamble located in England. It would obviously not make much sense to argue that Unilever has an advantage over P&G in the American market and the latter has an advantage over Unilever in the English market. Perhaps the explanation is that a firm can locate anywhere so long as it faces no special *dis*advantages.

These problems aside, the "special advantage" thesis has a more fundamental weakness, one which it shares with the "trade impediment" thesis. This is its premise that a firm locates abroad to sell its output only in the country in which it is located. Thus, it assumes an A/B firm competes only with B/B firms on product markets in B, in which case the A/B firm may indeed require a special advantage. But the premise that the A/B firm will always sell just to the B market is most unreasonable. It could also sell to the A market or to third countries. With these possibilities, the A/B firm requires no special advantage vis-à-vis the B/B firm to locate in B; rather, it may locate in B primarily to *obtain* special advantages relative to the A/A firms in selling to the A market or to any other market. A most important advantage obtained by the A/B firm relative to the A/A firm would often be lower production costs in the B location.

E. "DEFENSIVE" COST REDUCTION

Once we are no longer intellectually committed to the factor-price equalization theorem, another rather simple explanation of direct foreign investment in manufacturing comes immediately to the fore: firms locate in foreign countries mainly to reduce costs, primarily production costs, but also possibly marketing and transport costs. Once factor mobility is introduced into the Heckscher-Ohlin model, then direct foreign investment becomes a very *natural* phenomenon. If capital is relatively cheap in A and labor is relatively cheap in B, it would be surprising indeed if A firms did *not* locate in B to take advantage of the lower labor costs. The A firm could have the best of all worlds—the cheap capital of A and the cheap labor of B. This quite obvious thesis has been proposed by many, but it has been somewhat clouded by claims that firms go abroad to *defend* their positions —not simply to take advantage of cheaper labor.

Perhaps the best-known explanation of overseas locations by American firms (and, to a lesser extent, by firms from other advanced countries) is the "product life cycle" thesis so closely associated with Raymond Vernon and Louis Wells.[12] As will be seen, this thesis is in no way posited on the factor-price equalization theorem (in fact, it implicitly rejects this theorem) and avoids the pitfall of assuming that a foreign-located firm sells all of its output in the country of location.

The "product life cycle" thesis proceeds along the following lines. New products and technologies are developed in the advanced countries, which have the technological base and markets to support such innovations. Because of the supposed superiority of these new products to existing products, American (for example) firms can profitably export them from a United States location. However, with the passage of time and the maturation of these products, the new technologies will be learned by firms in other countries, who will develop similar products that, because of lower labor costs, they will be able to produce more cheaply than the American innovators. Thus, if the American firms are to protect their market positions, in the United States as well as in other countries, they are compelled to locate abroad to reduce production costs. Cost reduction thus becomes the major motive to locate abroad, an explanation completely consistent with the fact that direct foreign investment by the advanced countries increased during a period when trade barriers were reduced.

The really interesting question is not so much why firms locate abroad, but rather: why are production costs lower abroad? Of course, the higher labor costs in the United States would seem to be the obvious answer to this question. But it has been argued for many decades that the disadvantages in these higher labor costs are offset by American advantages in superior technology and management and in cheaper capital. However, because developments increased the international mobility of those factors of production that accorded the United States its advantages, the United States was left with the disadvantage of higher-priced labor. Technology and management became internationalized in many ways: through international education and conferences, better communication, exports of high-technology machinery, licensing of patents. Financial capital became more mobile through an international banking system, fixed exchange rates, better communication, safeguards for the protection of capital. Technology, management, and financial capital thus became available to non-Americans on almost the same terms as to Americans. These developments by themselves can account for the lower production costs abroad, and hence the underlying incentives for American firms, and firms from other advanced nations, to locate abroad. It would seem, on close reflection, that an explanation of why more American firms have not located abroad poses more of a challenge to economic theory than why some have chosen to do so. Richard Robinson is one economist who did deal with this problem, and to explain it he had to bring in such nontraditional (to economics) variables as personnel problems and modes of organizational behavior.[13]

The Vernon-Wells thesis has some important implications for the ability of U.S.-based manufacturers to compete against foreign-based manufacturers, so long as the American wage rate remains above those in other countries. The U.S.-based firms would be able to compete only if they could maintain a technological edge, develop new products, obtain legally protected positions (as in patents), or perhaps have lower risks.

Although the Vernon-Wells thesis that American firms locate abroad to reduce production costs is both clear and eminently reasonable, it has been clouded by attempts to infer other motives on the part of these firms. As background to such attempts, it should be noted that charges have often been made that the location of American firms abroad has increased American imports and reduced American exports of manufactures, and has reduced the number of American jobs in the manufacturing sector.[14] In the light of these charges, the inference has been made that American firms locate abroad to *defend* market positions (a reluctant facing of the facts of economic life) rather than for the less-noble motive of simply increasing profits. Note the following statement before the United States Congress by Eldridge Haynes, a spokesman for American multinationals:[15]

> Now, the important thing is, and I would like to register this with all the strength I can, that I know of no company, not a single one, that has invested abroad in production facilities when there was a reasonable chance of winning a significant share of that market by exporting.

F. BARGAINING LEVERAGE: GOVERNMENT AND UNIONS

Any owner of a factor of production, in his negotiations with other factors of production and other entities, has a bargaining advantage with regard to his negotiating opposites to the extent that he has more alternatives than the other parties. The capability of capital in particular to locate in different areas and different countries should therefore give it bargaining advantages in dealing with entities restricted to geographical locations. The most important geographically restricted entities are government and labor, although other organizations, such as public utilities and railroads, with heavy fixed commitments to certain geographical locations, can also be at a disadvantage in dealing with some mobile entities. These bargaining advantages could be important motives of firms in locating in many countries, and could also help explain the pattern of direct foreign investment.

The implicit or explicit threat to relocate has provided firms in the United States with bargaining levers since the early post–Civil War days, during which the "large firm" began. In the 1870s there was very little federal regulation of corporations, with most regulation carried on by the individual states. The increased mobility of firms led, however, to competition among the states for legislation favorable to firms, which is evidenced most clearly in the extent to which state laws became less and less restrictive on corporations, the favored form of the large firm. The result, of course, was a loss of social control over firms by the states. But this loss of control by the states set in motion demands that the federal government become more active in the social control of industry, and these demands resulted in such federal legislation as the Interstate Commerce Act, the Sherman Antitrust Act, the Pure Food and Drug Act. Following these initial laws, the whole thrust of American economic policy toward firms has been for federal legislation to replace the increasingly ineffective laws of the states.

The multinational corporation, with its capability of locating production facilities in different countries, has obtained much the same bargaining leverage with national governments as the large multilocational firms had with state governments in the United States.[16] Multinational corporations are thus in a position to exploit differences in taxation policies, subsidizations, labor laws, antipollution laws, and the like among the various nations. Furthermore, they are often able to obtain special concessions from national governments through the implied threat to locate elsewhere. Taxes have been an especially important item in which multinational locations have benefited large firms: it is well known that these firms, through intrafirm transfers of goods across national boundaries at prices determined by the firms, can "show" their profits in whichever country has the lowest corporate tax rates. These possibilities associated with multinational locations have, of course, provided motives for firms to locate in different countries.

The threats the multinational firm can mount with respect to national governments are not without their limits. Once the firm has made its commitment of capital in a given nation, the power to extract concessions can shift to the national government having jurisdiction of the territory of location. The firm may then be pressured with regard to taxes, exports or imports, wage rates, the hiring of local managers, expansion, and so forth. There can be great temptation on the part of the host government to exert such pressures, which is precisely why the governments of the investing firms seek treaties assuring that "their" firms will be accorded "national" (nondiscriminatory) treatment by the host-country government, or at least that the treatment promised upon entry (if there is an entry agreement) will be adhered to over a number of years into the future.

Potential threats by host-country governments, including the ultimate threat of expropriation, have played major roles in the nature of direct foreign investment. Because of these threats, expropriation in particular, the investing firm naturally prefers its assets located abroad to be of those types whose expropriation will be of limited value to the host country or which can be rather easily relocated to another country. Thus, a large manufacturing firm, such as General Motors, might have a strategy of producing different parts for an automobile in different countries: the expropriation of a specialized transmission factory would be of little value to the host nation, and in the event of discriminatory taxation, for example, much of the machinery used in production could be relocated in another country—assuming this is not prohibited.[17] In fact, almost any productive asset used in the production of a "branded" ("differentiated") product will be of little value to host countries. This can be contrasted with, say, a steel mill, which produces items not specifically useful only to certain firms, and whose production facilities could hardly be relocated to another country. The possibility of threats by host-country governments can help explain the pattern of foreign investment in manufactures that Caves found. Investments in "high-knowledge" assets, which Caves found to be the preponderant type of American investment abroad, are precisely those most immune to expropriation and discriminatory treatment.

The bargaining advantages accorded capital by its international mobility in dealing with domestic labor unions are well known and obvious. What could be a better bargaining lever for the firm than the very credible threat it will close down or reduce its domestic operations in favor of its foreign operations? And, we may add, what may better induce labor to politically seek means to regain their bargaining advantages?

G. DEALING WITH FOREIGN COMPETITION

The railroad-building boom in the United States in the 1870s has been offered as an explanation of why American firms began to restrict competition among themselves, by means such as pools, trusts, and mergers. The railroads, by reducing transport costs, broadened markets and broke down geographic monopolies, thereby eliciting the reactions noted above.[18]

In the postwar period (WW II), much the same type of competition has emerged between firms in different countries. This, of course, has come about because of reductions in trade barriers and transport costs, better communications, and so forth. Again the natural reaction by firms would be an attempt to suppress competition. One way this could be done would be through the acquisition of foreign firms, which in fact has been the case. (This is now slowing down, partly because of opposition by host-country governments, but also because of the falling value of the dollar, so far as American acquisitions are concerned.) Another way to reduce competition is to pose threats to potential price-cutters, by gaining control over raw materials and by locating where retaliation can be made in the home markets of price-cutters. And, of course, locations abroad by American firms may enable them to operate under much less potent antitrust laws than those of the United States even though the latter have some extraterritorial reach.[19]

H. EXCHANGE RATES

One important element in the explanation of direct foreign investment, the exchange rate, has been almost completely overlooked. Yet the importance of the exchange rate is so apparent that one can only express puzzlement over its neglect.

Robert Aliber appears to be the only American economist who has prominently introduced the exchange rate as an explanation of direct foreign investment—although his thesis differs from that offered below.[20] Aliber emphasizes not the levels of exchange rates, but rather the possibility that exchange rates in the future may change. When this possibility is introduced, it can be shown that firms issuing securities in which payments are denominated in a currency expected to appreciate can borrow more cheaply in the international money market than can other firms. The currency of denomination is usually related to the nationality of the borrowing firm, because that firm, if it has a strong market position at home, will have much of its earnings in that currency. Firms from countries with strong currencies will, because of their ability to borrow more cheaply than firms from other countries, therefore have a significant competitive advantage over their foreign rivals.

Yet, although Aliber's thesis is plausible and probably correct, there is a much simpler explanation of the effect of exchange rates on direct foreign investment that is immediately apparent once the notion of transnational transactions is grasped and acknowledgement is made that firms often locate abroad to reduce production costs. This explanation is as follows: the higher the value of a country's currency, the cheaper will appear *anything* purchased by that country's firms from other countries. But, as we have shown, the only feasible way these firms can purchase nontransportable items such as labor is to locate production facilities abroad. Thus, when the dollar was more highly valued, foreign labor, and even foreign firms, appeared relatively cheap to American firms, and surely provided a major motive to locate abroad.

Why have economists paid so little attention to the effect of the exchange rate upon direct foreign investment? The reason, I believe, is a fixation on the thesis that firms locate abroad only in order to sell to the host country, while the fact that these firms also purchase host-country inputs is, for the most part, ignored. But once purchasing activities are properly taken into account, the importance of the exchange rate becomes self-evident.

There is evidence to support the view that a country whose currency appreciates in value will increase its direct foreign investment, and conversely that a country whose currency depreciates in value will become a host country. The July 14, 1975 issue of *Business Week* presented figures on direct foreign investment for five countries: the United States, England, West Germany, Japan, and Switzerland. In the late 1960s and early 70s, the value of the West German, Japanese, and Swiss currencies had appreciated and these countries showed the largest recent increases in direct foreign investment. In contrast, such investment by the United States and Great Britain—nations whose currencies had been devalued—was very moderate, and probably reflected reinvestments of earnings to a much greater extent than it did new investments. As more evidence, we can cite the recent increases of direct foreign investment *in* the United States that followed the devaluation of the dollar relative to other currencies.[21] In 1976, Volkswagen of Germany finally felt itself compelled to produce automobiles in the United States: the revaluation of the mark together with the devaluation of the dollar had clearly made Volkswagens produced in Germany uncompetitive in terms of price with cars produced in the United States.

I. GOVERNMENTAL POLICIES

In chapter 1, a number of measures designed to encourage American direct foreign investment were cited. Perhaps the word "encourage" is not quite correct: the official American position appears to be one of neutrality toward direct foreign investment, and the measures taken were merely meant to remove "artificial" barriers to such investment rather than to provide positive encouragement. (In the case of the less-developed countries, however, "encourage" is the proper term.) Despite the American stance of official neutrality toward direct foreign investment, it has been charged that two tax measures—the credit against American taxes for corporate taxes paid to foreign governments, and the nontaxation of unrepatriated profits —have given positive encouragement to direct foreign investment by American firms. These tax measures bear some consideration.[22]

Consider the tax credit. An American firm located abroad is allowed to deduct from its profits tax to be paid to the United States government those taxes on profits paid to the host-country government. If the foreign tax rate is close to that of the United States government, then of course the foreign government receives virtually all the taxes. The main reason often given for this tax credit—one that it would be difficult to quarrel with—is that it avoids the double taxation that would otherwise occur.

It is easy to show that the tax credit should be a neutral factor in the firm's motives to locate abroad—the firm still pays the same tax. The important impact of the tax credit, however, is not upon the motives of the firm, but upon the motives of the host-country government. The full tax credit is not the only way double taxation can be avoided. A very plausible alternative would be for the United States government to negotiate a split of the American firm's tax liabilities with the host-country government. But the current procedure cedes the lion's share of the taxes to the host-country government, which provides substantial incentives to that government to allow location in that country by American firms and to provide conditions under which they can operate profitably. One more point is worth considering. Since the host-country government receives most (if not all) of the taxes, it has the means as well as the incentives to offer special inducements to American firms to locate on its soil. (Firms, in their transfer pricing, have some discretion as to which countries their profits will appear in.

But I know of no evidence that this is used to increase the tax share obtained by the United States government.)

The nontaxation by the United States of any remaining profits of foreign-located American firms until repatriated to the United States obviously provides incentives for these firms to reinvest their profits abroad rather than repatriate them. The nontaxation of nonrepatriated profits and the tax credit not only encourage American direct foreign investment but also act to severely limit the foreign exchange earnings to the United States of such investment, at least in the short run.

J. THE INTERNATIONAL IMMOBILITY OF LABOR

Two important points made earlier are worth repeating. First, an important incentive for firms locating abroad, especially in manufacturing, is the reduction of its production costs when its foreign location enables it to purchase foreign labor that is presumably cheaper than labor at home. Second, firms do not always necessarily have to locate abroad in order to hire foreign labor: a possible alternative exists in importing this foreign labor to the home country. On this basis, we argued that direct foreign investment is often truly an alternative to the import of foreign labor or the inward migration of workers, as opposed to the more common view that such investment is an alternative to trade.

If this is so, then immigration policies must have an effect upon the pattern of direct foreign investment. To the extent a country restricts the entry of workers willing to work at wage rates lower than those currently existing in that country, incentives are created for firms to locate abroad to accomplish by an alternative means the same purpose, namely the hiring of lower-wage foreign labor. Immigration restrictions operate in two ways on those incentives: they make domestic wage rates higher than they would otherwise be, and foreign wage rates lower than they would otherwise be, thus leading to a large wage differential.

In support of this thesis, a few words on American immigration policy are in order. Until 1924, immigration into the United States was almost completely unrestricted. It had been, however, an issue in the United States for many decades before that date. Generally, proposals to restrict immigration were opposed by business interests, who quite correctly saw free immigration as a way to stem the growing power of labor unions. And, of course, much of the support for restrictions on immigration came from organized labor, and perhaps workers in general—and to this day organized labor is attempting to halt illegal immigration into the United States, mainly by Mexicans.[23] On the basis of these considerations, one might expect that American direct foreign investment would have increased substantially after 1924, which, if true, would be consistent with the thesis offered here. Perhaps the fact that American direct foreign investment before World War II was less than might have been expected can be attributed to the Great Depression and the unsettled political climate of the 1930s. On a long-term basis, however, the large amount of American direct foreign investment can be at least partly attributed to restrictions on immigration into the United States.

The "guest worker" programs in postwar Europe also have some bearing on this point. As is well known, large numbers of workers from the poorer countries of southern Europe have been working in the more prosperous countries in northern Europe, generally without being given citizenship in these latter countries. This has, of course, led to opposition by workers in the more prosperous countries and to problems that are just beginning to attract attention in the United States—although these problems have surely been attracting a great deal more attention in Europe. But the important point for our thesis is that, given the prosperity and limited size of these northern European countries, together with favorable movements in the values of many of their currencies, the amount of their direct foreign investment is perhaps considerably less than we might expect. If this is so—and it would take a good statistical study to prove it more convincingly than I am able to do here—this would lend additional weight to my contention that direct foreign investment is an alternative to the importation of foreign workers.

K. A COMPREHENSIVE
"LOCATIONAL" EXPLANATION

We have given a number of theories that attempt to explain why firms locate productive facilities in foreign countries, and have also discussed various factors that are likely to influence such a decision. All of them undoubtedly contain some elements of truth, and all of them can also be criticized on various grounds.

Criticizing most of these theories is not difficult, for the simple reason that they focus on just one explanatory variable. For so complex a topic as foreign investment it is surely a vain effort to search for the one magic explanation of why firms locate abroad. Books written from the viewpoint of advising the multinational firm typically list a fairly extensive number of factors that should be taken into consideration in such a location decision: production costs, transport costs, availability of inputs, nature of markets, commercial policies, attitudes of host governments, possibilities of exchange controls, and so on. For any firm, some of these are more important, others less important, with much depending upon the nature of the firm's activity and what its alternative options are in the way of a location at home.

Location theory may provide a useful framework with which to assess the forces underlying direct foreign investment.[24] Consider a firm in its locational choice, either within a country or between counties. First, there are "strategic" reasons for having a number of locations: bargaining leverage; the security obtained by diversification and increased options. In choosing among alternative sites, firms weigh a number of factors: transport costs; the availability and cost of nontransportable inputs; governmental policies; possible differences in output price. To the extent any of these considerations are less important, others become more important. Thus, if all transport costs and trade barriers were to disappear, so that prices of all transportable items are identical at all location sites, then the costs of nontransportable inputs, or perhaps government policies, become of greater importance.

In a country such as the United States, the advantages and risks attached to any site are limited by the fact that the United States is for all practical purposes a common market operating under a set of common laws and a single currency. As a result, wage rate differentials in different locations are limited by the internal mobility of labor, prices of goods typically vary only because of transport costs, and the power of local governments toward firms is constrained by the primacy of federal law on goods and services entering into interstate commerce. Nevertheless, although the advantages of any site may be limited, the nature of a common market and the competition it entails make it mandatory for firms in their location decisions to grasp any advantage they can.

For several reasons, the risks and rewards pertaining to a foreign versus a domestic location—as opposed to the choice within a nation—are often greater. International labor immobility and international differences in laws pertaining to labor, as well as relative factor abundance, lead to greater international wage differences than those within a country. Because of the sovereign powers to regulate international trade, prices of transportable goods can also vary greatly between countries. Laws pertaining to business also tend to vary much more between countries than, say, between two states in the United States. There can also be great international differences in the protection of private property and in the sanctity of contract. Finally, different currencies entail risks and rewards in the "international" location choice that have no parallel in a choice within a country.

If we can identify those postwar developments that either increased the rewards or reduced the risks of a foreign location, or in some way made that location more necessary, we then have an explanation of the growth of direct foreign investment in this period. Perhaps the most important factor was the reduction in trade barriers. This increased international competition and made it more necessary for firms to seek low-cost sites, generally where the wage rate is low. It also made it more feasible to produce in one country and sell in another. Improvements in transportation and communications had much the same effect. The increased activity of governments—in taxes, subsidies, pollution control, and so forth—also enlarged the differences among countries and thereby provided new possibilities for firms to take advantage of such differences. Efforts by the United States government to reduce risks of expropriation and discriminatory treatment also obviously encouraged direct foreign investment. Restrictions on immigration maintained international wage differentials, thereby making it profitable to locate in low-wage countries. Finally, the fixed exchange rate system reduced some risks to the foreign location, and the relatively high value of the dollar particularly encouraged American firms to locate abroad.

This locational framework has enabled us to draw together the varying motives and to identify developments that encouraged direct foreign investment. It also demonstrates that multicausality is at work. And it should convince us that direct foreign investment is a rather natural economic phenomenon, not to be explained by extraordinary events and policies.

CHAPTER EIGHT

Indirect Foreign Investment: Models and Impacts

This chapter first develops a model of indirect foreign investment, and then assesses its consequences for trade and capital formation. The following chapter goes into the welfare effects of indirect foreign investment for both the lending and the borrowing countries.

A. A MODEL OF INDIRECT FOREIGN INVESTMENT

In its essentials, the model of indirect foreign investment is the same as that for trade in goods. Whereas trade in goods takes place in response to differences in product prices, indirect foreign investment responds to differences in interest rates. International loans from, say, A to B can be in A money, B money, or gold. Interest payments and repayments of principal can be denominated in any currency—depending on the loan contract. The purchase of common stock is considered indirect foreign investment if the lending country does not obtain operating control of a productive entity.

1. The Domestic Capital Market

The domestic capital market is that in which households, or financial intermediaries such as banks or insurance companies, purchase newly issued financial securities. There are, of course, a wide variety

141

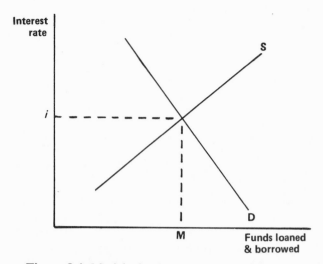

Figure 8.1 Model of a Domestic Capital Market

of securities, and the interest payments will vary among them to reflect differences in risk. Thus, there is no one interest rate, but rather a structure of interest rates. Having said this, we will nevertheless think of a single interest rate, which is a legitimate approach as long as all interest rates tend to move in the same direction.

Figure 8.1 provides a simplified model of the capital market. The position of the demand curve (the relation between funds demanded and the interest rate) is determined largely by the level of business activity and the profit prospects for long-term investments. Funds can also be demanded by governments (if deficits are not financed by the central bank), and by households. The position and shape of the supply curve of funds are dependent mainly on income levels, attitudes toward saving, and the faith of the investing public in financial institutions. The supply of funds can also in modern times be greatly influenced by the policies of the central bank. Some even view the supply curve as being whatever the central bank chooses it to be— although this choice would usually be made by assessing the effects of the supply of money and the interest rate upon employment, inflation, and capital formation. It is important to realize, however, that a central bank, through its monetary policy, can also affect a nation's international lending or borrowing.

2. Interest Rate Comparisons

Let us assume the risks of default to be the same for country A's and country B's securities, so that only interest rates determine international lending. We may now ask how an interest rate in B would be translated into a price equivalent by As. If exchange rates are guaranteed to be fixed, it is easily shown that the level of the exchange rate does not affect this interest rate: that is, the interest rate in B will always be the same interest rate to an A lender or an A borrower. But if the exchange rate can change *after* the loan is made, there can be an associated risk to either the borrower or the lender, depending upon the monetary denomination of the interest payment and repayment of principal.

Let us construct an example to demonstrate this point. First, assume the pound/dollar rate is *either* 1:2 or 1:4. Assume also that an American lender buys a 1,000 £ bond issued by a British borrower that pays interest of 100 £ per annum. If the exchange rate were 1:2, the American would pay $2,000 for the bond and receive $100 per annum. If the exchange rate were *instead* 1:4, the number of dollars both paid and received by the American lender would double, but clearly the interest rate is unaffected.

However, if the exchange rate changes *after* the loan is made, the effective rate will change for *either* the lender or the borrower, and which party will be affected will depend on the denomination of the loan and interest payments. Assume the pound/dollar rate changes after a loan from 1:2 to 1:4. If the loan and interest are denominated in dollars, and the American lender loaned $1,000 at $100 per year, his interest rate remains at 10 percent after the dollar devalues. But if the loan and interest are denominated in pounds, the pounds received by the American lender are worth twice as much in terms of dollars, while the dollars used to purchase the bond remain unchanged. The English borrower could also be affected by the postulated dollar devaluation, with his effective interest rate in pounds falling to 5 percent if the loan and interest were denominated in dollars, while he would be unaffected if these were denominated in pounds.

When changes in the exchange rate are possible, comparisons of interest rates must consider the risk of these possible changes. Thus, if an A lender can buy B securities, with interest payments (and repayment of principal) denominated in B currency, and if he thinks B currency might depreciate, he will lend to Bs only if the B interest rate is sufficiently higher than the A interest rate to compensate for the risk. Thus, an 8 percent interest rate on a B security may be the risk-adjusted equivalent of, say, a 6 percent interest rate on an A security.

3. A Model of the Integration of Capital Markets

Figure 8.2 is a model of the integration of two capital markets, and is constructed on the same principles as the model developed in chapter 3. It is assumed that A has the lower preloan interest rate and that exchange rates are fixed. The integration of the markets will equalize interest rates. In addition, loanable funds rise in A from Q_s to Q'_s while borrowings fall from Q_d to Q'_d—the reverse occurring in B. The amount Q'_s minus Q'_d is the periodic amount of indirect foreign investment.

Consider now the possibilities of exchange rate changes, and assume payments of interest and principal are to be in B currency. If B currency is expected to depreciate, A lenders will require the interest rate on B loans to be higher in order to be equivalent to the interest rate in A. Thus fewer funds will be supplied by A to B at each interest rate in B. The result will then be a higher postloan interest rate in B than in A. Of course, if B currency is expected to appreciate, then the postloan interest rate in B will be lower. If preloan interest rates are similar in both countries, one should expect foreign funds to flow to that country whose currency is expected to appreciate in value.

4. The Continuity of a Creditor/Debtor Relationship

So long as the preloan interest rate in A is lower than that in B, and there is no risk of exchange rate changes, there should be a peri-

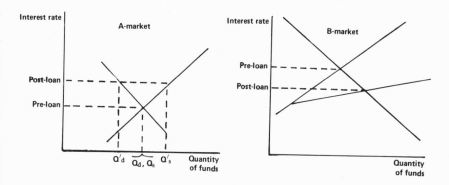

Figure 8.2 A Model of Indirect Foreign Investment

odic flow of loans from A to B. We may ask if there are any forces that would reduce this flow. The direct answer to this question depends upon the course of future preloan interest rates, but more fundamentally it depends on how productively the borrowing country uses the loans.

Assume that B uses its loans for consumption purposes rather than to finance new capital investments. Then the return flow of interest and principal from B to A should shift the supply curve of funds to the right in A, but to the left in B. This could widen further the preloan interest rates, and enlarge the monetary flows from A to B, with B becoming a perpetual debtor. If, however, the loans are used by B to raise output (and incomes), and if some portion of this incremental income is saved, the supply curve of funds in the B market should shift to the right. It is also possible that the higher interest rate in A will reduce capital formation and income in that country, with a consequent leftward shift of the supply curve of funds. Thus, preloan interest rates could become the same, and indirect foreign investment could disappear. It is even possible that the preloan interest rate could become lower in B, in which event the loan pattern would be reversed.

5. The Expected Pattern of International Lending

It is often assumed that the natural flow of international lending is from capital-abundant to capital-scarce countries. Since the capital-abundant countries tend to be the richer countries, this assumption is tantamount to expecting financial capital to flow from rich to poor nations. There are several reasons why this assumption has been maintained. The higher income of the richer country, together with the lower profit rate generally found in richer countries, should act to lower interest rates in that country. For the opposite reasons, interest rates should be higher in the poorer country.

Yet, for several reasons, this assumption may not always reflect reality. The wealthier country may have a higher growth rate in capital formation. The wealthier country may be a better risk in being able to repay the loan. Furthermore, if exchange rates change, it is usually the poorer rather than the richer country's currency that is in greatest danger of devaluing. Also, sometimes the governments in poorer countries artificially hold down the interest rate. For these reasons, loans may easily flow from the poor to the rich countries. An important reality of economic life is that money, like any other productive resource, does not flow to those who "need" it, but rather to those who can use it productively.

The assumption that funds will flow from the "rich" to the "poor" nations is based largely on the nineteenth-century experience in which massive funds flowed from such rich countries as England, France, and Holland to "underdeveloped" countries such as the United States, Canada, Australia, and the Latin American nations. But this nineteenth-century experience may not be very relevant to the twentieth century.[1] The recipient nations then were not really poor; they were truly undeveloped, but they had great potential. They also produced raw materials that could be easily exported, and they were thus able to repay the loans. Since exchange rates in the nineteenth century were largely fixed, the possibilities of devaluation created no great problem.

B. TRANSFER MECHANISMS

It would seem that from the viewpoint of B taken as a whole, the purpose of borrowing from A is to enable B to maintain a trade deficit —to import more than it exports. If the purpose of borrowing were only to reduce domestic interest rates, in modern times this could surely be easily and cheaply accomplished through domestic monetary policy, which avoids the costs of debt payments to foreigners.

Yet there is no simple mechanism whereby borrowings are transformed into trade deficits, and one can find examples of countries which, at the same time, are net borrowers and have trade surpluses. The B organizations who borrow from the As are not necessarily those who use these funds to increase their imports from A. They are presumably motivated to borrow from A only to reduce interest costs, and typically convert any A money received into B money by selling the A money to their central bank. Thus, there is no direct relation between foreign borrowing and imports, and one must ask whether mechanisms exist whereby a flow of money is transformed into a "real" flow of goods. These mechanisms are widely known as "transfer mechanisms." That the relation between the flow of money and the flow of goods is often referred to as the "transfer problem" suggests that these mechanisms have not always functioned well.[2]

One transfer mechanism works through the relation between money supplies and internal prices, and harks back to such early writers as David Hume and David Ricardo. A flow of money from A to B should lead to a rise in commodity prices in B and a reduction of such prices in A. These internal price changes then provide the incentives that should result in a "real" transfer of goods from A to B. When repayments are made from B to A, this mechanism should work in reverse.

Two important conditions must be present for this mechanism to function automatically, namely well-functioning commodity and labor markets and noninterference by central banks with the internal money supplies. If there are oligopolies and labor unions in A, it is of course quite likely that any reduction in the demand for goods in that country will result in unemployment rather than price reductions. And if unemployment existed in B prior to the loan, increased demand in B can result in higher employment rather than higher prices. Thus, malfunctioning markets can frustrate this mechanism. But even if internal prices *could* change, the central banks must *allow* these price changes to take place. The central bank of the lending country can frustrate this mechanism through a compensatory money policy—that is, by increasing the domestic money supply by the amount of the loans. The central bank of the borrowing country can, of course, do just the reverse. Thus, if the transfer of real goods is to work through this "internal price" mechanism, the central banks (and governmental authorities in general) will have to refrain from "correcting" a price inflation or deflation often considered undesirable.

The second mechanism, which *presumes* malfunctioning markets, works through changes in income and follows the Keynesian analysis. The flow of funds from A to B should raise interest rates in A and lower them in B. This should lead to higher investment, employment, and income in B, the opposite taking place in A. These income changes will increase B's demand for imports, but decrease A's demand for imports, which should then induce the real flow of goods from A to B. Once more, it can be easily seen that incentives and means are present which may frustrate this mechanism. Country A in particular would normally not be willing to suffer unemployment to induce an outflow of goods (which under some conditions may not even occur) and, as we have seen, has options available to counteract the unemployment.

The third mechanism, as the reader will surely have anticipated by now, operates through exchange rates. So far as the international money market goes, the demand by As for B securities is no different from that for B goods. Both will elicit an increased supply of A currency on this market, so that the loans should lead to a devaluation of A's currency relative to that of B. This change in exchange rates should then induce a trade surplus for A. Of course, this mechanism assumes that flexible exchange rates are permitted.

This third mechanism is surely the most acceptable of the three, since it does not entail any sacrifice of domestic stabilization goals. We must, therefore, mark up one more argument in favor of flexible exchange rates. Although flexible exchange rates may create problems of risk to private lenders and/or borrowers, they also provide the most acceptable means for transforming a flow of funds into a real flow of goods. Thus, an argument for fixed exchange rates on the grounds that by reducing risks they encourage an international flow of funds founders on the argument that they inhibit the real flow of goods, which, it would seem, is ultimately the social reason for the loans.

For different reasons none of these mechanisms may work effectively, in which case one may wonder what national purpose the loans may serve. In the absence of a real transfer, the lending country will at least be a gainer: the interest payments received will be income to it in the future, and a rather pleasant type of income entailing little sacrifice, especially so if monetary policy compensates for the rise in interest rates in the lending country that would otherwise take place. The real mystery is what the borrowing country may gain. It would seem to be paying for the right to hold and use someone else's money in domestic activity when it can easily print its own money— and in fact will do just this if the borrowed funds are converted into domestic currency. The burden for making the loans socially productive must clearly fall on the borrowing country.

C. INDIRECT FOREIGN INVESTMENT AND CAPITAL FORMATION

The transfer of funds from A to B, through its effects upon interest rates in both countries, should lead to changes in the rates of capital formation in both countries. In this section we discuss what these effects might be. The pattern of capital formation will then have long-term impacts on trade patterns that are to be distinguished from the real transfers of goods responding to the initial flow of funds from A to B. These long-run impacts on trade receive our attention in the following section.

Before proceeding, it is necessary to make explicit a very important assumption, which will be maintained until explicitly relaxed. We assume that neither the lending country nor the borrowing country will adopt a monetary policy designed to compensate for the effects of the international loans on domestic interest rates.

1. Interest Rates and Capital Formation

In a private enterprise economy, there should be a fairly fixed relationship between profit rates and fixed interest rates on loans in the long run, with the former higher to compensate for the risks of entrepreneurship. Indirect foreign investment, it was shown, would—if there were no compensating monetary policy—raise interest rates in A, the lending country, and lower them in B, the borrowing country. Thus profit rates become "too high" relative to interest rates in the borrowing country, and "too low" relative to interest rates in the lending country.[3] What forces should bring these two rates into their long-run fixed relationship in the two countries? In B, capital formation should tend to expand, which should tend to drive profit rates down to their former relationship to interest rates. But in A, capital formation should tend to be reduced, which would increase profit rates back to their preloan relation to the now higher interest rates. Thus the loans should have a favorable impact on capital formation in the borrowing country, with an unfavorable effect on capital formation in the lending country.

Although these are the first-order expectations of the response of capital formation to changes in interest rates, there are other forces to consider. These expectations are reasonable only if nothing other than the size of the capital stock of a country affects profit rates. There could, however, be other forces that affect the prices of items firms buy and sell, and hence the profit rates of these firms. To the extent these other forces are operative, capital formation may not respond entirely as anticipated.

2. Capital Formation in B, the Borrowing Country

The lower interest rates in B should stimulate greater capital formation, and higher consumption levels as well—and both of these can lead to inflation. If the real transfer mechanism works, B's imports rise and/or its exports fall, which will moderate the inflation. However, there is little assurance that B's trade deficit will exactly equal the increase in domestic demand, and, if the deficit is smaller, prices of both goods and labor may rise in B. If wage rates rise by more than the prices of goods, profit rates will fall and capital formation in B may not increase substantially despite the reduction in interest rates.

The movements of the prices of goods compared to the wage rate of labor can be crucial to whether capital formation in B is most successfully induced by the loans. The labor supply curve will largely determine the effect of the increased demand for goods upon wage rates. If the curve is highly wage-elastic, possibly because of negotiated wage rates and unemployment, then wage rates should not rise greatly, and this favors profit rates and capital formation. But if the labor supply curve is highly wage-inelastic, wage rates may rise a great deal. The nature of the imports from A could affect the prices of goods. To the extent these additional imports do not compete directly with the goods produced by B-firms, the output prices of these firms should also move in a way favorable to capital formation. Thus, a wage-elastic supply curve for labor and a complementary rather than competitive pattern of imports will tend to reinforce the favorable impact of the lower interest rates upon capital formation in B.

If we assume that conditions for increased capital formation in B are favorable, the next question is: which sectors will the capital formation take place in? To investigate this question, let us assume that the two major products produced in both countries are C_1 and C_2; C_1 is produced by capital-intensive means, and C_2 is produced by labor-intensive means; country A is the relatively capital-abundant country; before the capital formation in B, A exports C_1 and imports C_2; wage rates are higher in A than in B. The question can now be posed as follows: will B's capital formation take place in the C_1 or the C_2 sector? If the bulk of this capital formation is in C_2, then B's new investments will be complementary to A's economy. But if this capital formation is largely in C_1, then B's new investments are competitive with A's economy.

One important result of the flow of funds from A to B is that the rate of interest, or the cost of capital, becomes equal in both countries. Yet if the labor market malfunctions in either or both of these countries, the wage rate in A could remain higher than that in B. In such an event, at the existing exchange rate, B will have an absolute cost advantage in the production of *both* products—unless A is somehow able to maintain some compensating superiority in technology or management. In the absence of these possible offsets, Bs could profitably invest in either C_1 or C_2, or in both. Given B's lower wage rate, one might expect most of B's new capital formation to be in C_2, the labor-intensive product. But the case for this expectation is not exceptionally strong: future prospects for C_1 might be better; the B government may want its imports of C_1 reduced; the production of C_1 may have favorable externalities and thus be encouraged by the B government. The important point is that B, through the reduction in its cost of capital, is given an absolute cost advantage in both C_1 and C_2, and much of its capital formation may be in C_1.

There is, however, one development that can more reasonably assure that B's capital formation will be in C_2 rather than C_1. This is a devaluation of A's currency. Such devaluation will increase A's exports of C_1 to B, reduce the price of this product in B, and thus make investments by Bs in C_2 more attractive than in C_1. The devaluation in A currency will also convert the *absolute* monetary cost advantage B has in both products to a cost advantage only in C_2, in which B maintains a *comparative* advantage. Thus, the devaluation may be necessary to bring the law of comparative advantage into operation, and with it, two-way trade.

There is, however, no assurance that a devaluation of A's currency will always take place. First, there may be an international system of fixed exchange rates. Or A's currency may be pegged to gold. Or even if there is a completely free market in foreign exchange, the return flow of funds from B to A may hinder the devaluation of A's currency.

3. Capital Formation in A, the Lending Country

Prior to any loans, there should be in A also a more or less constant relation between profit rates and interest rates on securities bearing interest, with the former somewhat higher to reflect risk differentials. Loans from A to B will raise interest rates in A, perhaps even above profit rates, and will therefore upset the relation between interest rates and profit rates. But not only will interest rates rise: in addition, profit rates may fall. To the extent capital formation is successful in B, imports from B, which will be partly financed by the return flow of interest payments from B to A, may force down the prices of goods in A and thereby reduce profit rates.

A situation in which interest rates lie above profit rates is not stable, and forces will be set in motion to bring interest rates and profit rates back to their preloan relationship. The major mechanism to bring this about would be a decline in capital formation by the A-firms. This should reduce the demand for inputs, especially labor, thereby possibly reducing input prices to the A firms. The decline in capital formation may also raise the prices of goods produced by these firms. Changes in these two sets of prices should raise profit rates for A firms to their preloan relation to interest rates; but in the process of doing so, capital formation in A will have declined.

The extent to which the decline of capital formation affects changes in these input and output prices will greatly influence how great the decline in capital formation will be. But the decline in capital formation in A is not the only force that will influence these prices. Capital formation in B should affect trade and have still additional effects upon prices in A. To assess the full impact of the loans on capital formation in A, we therefore must ask how these two sets of forces —the decline in capital formation in A, and trade—will influence prices in A.

Let us turn first to the wage rate in A. Once we are past the short-run stimulative impact of the loans on the A economy, coming about because of the transfer mechanism, the long-run impact of the loans should have a depressing effect upon the demand for A labor. There are two main reasons for this expectation. First, the higher interest rates in A should reduce capital formation and consumption expenditures in A—and thereby the demand for A labor. Second, the interest payments and repayments of principal by B to A should lead to increased imports by A. These imports can reduce output prices in A (or the demand for goods from A oligopolists at some nonchanging price), which will also reduce the demand for A labor.

If wage rates fall, the reduction in capital formation by A firms will clearly be smaller. But monetary wage rates in A may not fall. This, of course, can be the result if the labor market in A is malfunctioning, in which event reductions in the demand for labor will lead to unemployment rather than a reduction in monetary wage rates. To the extent the A government has policies on minimum wage rates, unemployment payments, welfare, the likelihood that monetary wage rates will not fall is increased. The combination of higher interest rates, import competition from B, and a downward inflexible wage rate will therefore lead to greater reductions in capital formation in A than would have occurred had wage rates fallen. So long as interest rates remain above profit rates, businessmen in A not only will reduce capital formation, but will allow their existing capital stock to wear out, using any funds generated by these assets to loan abroad.

The course of output prices can also affect capital formation in A. With respect to these output prices, the pattern of capital formation in B can be crucial. If B's capital formation is in goods that are highly competitive with A's goods, there will be downward pressures on the output prices of A firms. This, together with a downward inflexible wage rate in A and the higher interest rates in that country, should lead to large reductions in capital formation in A. But a different picture emerges if B's capital formation is complementary to A's industries. If B increases its production of goods that require items supplied by A firms, then the output prices of A firms should rise, which will have a favorable effect on profit rates and capital formation in A. Or if B increases its production of items purchased by A firms, such as raw materials, thereby reducing the prices of inputs used by A firms, this too raises profit rates in A and has a favorable effect upon capital formation in A.

Allowing exchange rates to change can also influence capital formation in A. If B's pattern of capital formation is competitive with A's industries, and if B has the cost advantage because of lower wage rates, this advantage can be offset by a devaluation in A's currency. Such devaluation would mean that output prices would not fall in A, and that profit rates and capital formation in that country would be favorably affected.

If we adopt the assumption that no offsetting policies are enacted by the A government, we can now sum up the effect of indirect foreign investment on A's capital formation. Reductions in wage rates, a complementary pattern of capital formation in B, and possibly a devaluation in A's currency, can all minimize the adverse effects of the higher interest rates on A's capital formation. But if these conditions are not fulfilled, it is very likely indirect foreign investment will lead to large reductions in capital formation in the lending country. It is for this and other reasons that Keynes, among others, was so critical of the huge capital outflows from England in the early years of the twentieth century; these loans were running as high as 7 percent of England's gross national product.[4]

4. Monetary Policy as a Counterbalance

We have shown that international lending by A can have undesirable impacts on that country's level of capital formation, with much depending upon the nature of its labor market and the pattern of capital formation in B. This conclusion, however, rested upon the assumption that the monetary authorities in A do not respond to the higher interest rates by increasing the money supply to drive down the interest rate. Although such a policy runs some risk of inflation, it can stop the decline of capital formation in A that might otherwise take place. Keynes, one could suspect, may not have opposed British indirect foreign investment if he had fully realized the potential of the use of monetary policy as a means to restore preloan interest rates in England.

5. Capital Formation and Income-Earning Assets

Although indirect foreign investment should encourage capital formation in B, but lower it in A, it does not follow that A will have a
diminished ownership of income-earning assets while B will have
greater ownership of such assets. Ownership of such assets is linked
to savings, and the effect of indirect foreign investment will be to
increase savings in A and lower them in B. Thus, the amount of
income-earning assets held by As should rise. But these assets will
increase because of claims on the incomes of B organizations rather
than claims on A organizations—claims on the latter, in fact, should
fall. Much the opposite should occur in B.

D. POST-CAPITAL-FORMATION EFFECTS ON TRADE

Loans from A to B will have two sets of effects upon trade between
these countries. First, there will be the short-term effects of the work-
ings of the transfer mechanism—which, when operative, should result
in a trade surplus for A. Second, there will be the long-run effects
that come about after the impacts of the loans on capital formation
in the two countries. This second type of effects concerns us here.

In the long run, A should have a trade deficit in goods, with the
deficit made up by interest payments from B to A. There are two
reasons why this deficit should come about. First, interest payments
and any repayments of principal should tend to increase the demand
for goods in A and lower it in B. Second, higher capital formation
in B will shift the supply curves for goods to the right in that country,
while any reduction in capital formation in A will have the opposite
effect in that country. The result of these two sets of forces will then
raise "pretrade" prices in A, and lower them in B, which of course
should result in the trade deficit for A.

Country A will therefore become a rentier in the international economy, trading the use of its money, and any associated financial services, for its import surplus. However, there is some question as to how

long A can maintain this not unenviable position. Much will depend upon the course of the growth of income and savings in B. To the extent this growth is significant, new loans will not be made from A to B, and eventually the older loans will be repaid. If and when this occurs, A will no longer be a rentier. The same result will obtain, of course, if capital formation, and with it income and savings, falls in A.

If and when A loses its rentier position, the pattern of capital formation in B will largely determine whether A will have trade difficulties. If this pattern is complementary to A's output mix, then A may not have trade problems. But if the pattern of capital formation in B is essentially competitive with A's industries, and if we assume A's wage rates remain above those in B because of malfunctioning markets and governmental policy, then B will have an absolute cost advantage in the production of all products, and A will surely have trade deficits, along with the associated problems of unemployment. However, those dour prospects will occur only at some nonchanging exchange rate. Even with a competitive pattern of capital formation in B, A can still remain competitive in the international economy with a devaluation of its currency.

CHAPTER NINE

The Welfare Implications of Indirect Foreign Investment

In this chapter we ascertain the impacts of foreign lending and borrowing upon the welfare of the countries involved, continuing to use real national income as our measure of welfare. Indirect foreign investment can be thought to have both short-run and long-run effects, and this chapter is mainly organized on this basis. The short-run effects include all changes in real national income in the two countries attributable to the indirect foreign investment before the pattern of capital formation has become effective. The long-run effects, of course, are those attributable to the pattern of capital formation induced by the flow of financial capital. The short-run effects revolve mainly about macroeconomic stabilization, the long-run about capital formation and economic growth.

It can be anticipated that the welfare effects of indirect foreign investment will depend upon a host of forces: whether markets are well-functioning or malfunctioning; whether unemployment exists; whether or not exchange rates are fixed; whether countries react to monetary flows with compensatory changes in monetary policy; the pattern of capital formation; whether or not technology is the same in both countries. It is, of course, possible to make strong and precise assumptions about the various forces that may affect the extent to which indirect foreign investment influences real national income, in which event we can obtain precise results. The course chosen here, however, is to vary our assumptions about these forces, thereby exploring how alternative conditions and/or policies affect the impacts of indirect foreign investment on real national income. It is surely more important to identify the conditions and policies under which indirect foreign investment will prove beneficial than to arrive at a contrived "solution."

A. AN INTRODUCTORY VIEW

We have stressed the point that an international loan, say from A to B, is an export when viewed over the whole transaction, including interest payments and repayments of principal. A loan is a rental of money, and it is a most salient fact that the lender receives income from allowing the borrower to use his money, while the borrower must pay for this privilege.

Lending out money can be a most attractive way of earning income. An outright sale or rental of goods from A to B means that country A has less of those goods to use itself, so that there is a real sacrifice to the exporting country. This will also be true if the money were, say, gold. In this latter case, real resources were used to mine the gold—if that country had gold mines—or to produce and export goods to others in return for the gold. But today money can be costlessly created with the stroke of a pen by a loan officer of a bank. Thus, the lending of money *by itself* does not entail much sacrifice to the lending country in modern times.

In this regard, it might be useful to cite Adam Smith's views on international lending. Smith, in *The Wealth of Nations,* was of course greatly opposed to the mercantilist policies of trying to amass gold (and silver) holdings through export surpluses. To him, there was some "correct" amount of money needed to carry on domestic commerce, and any holdings above that amount were as senseless, to use his analogy, as a household acquiring more kitchen utensils than it needed: it tied up the nation's capital and prevented it from being used for more useful things. Thus, he advocated that all excess gold be loaned abroad. In this respect, the activities of commercial banks were of interest to him. These banks, by printing paper money to be used instead of gold, in effect meant that less of the nation's capital need be tied up in gold: hence, more gold could be available for foreign loans, or to purchase more useful commodities. If Smith were living today, when any amount of paper money can be created without cost, and when other countries are willing to borrow this paper, one can be quite certain he would advocate making these loans.

The loans themselves, then, entail no sacrifice by the lending country. But a loan of money does have one other important distinction from any other type of export. Whereas an export of anything else from A to B in return for money will impair B's claim on A's goods, an export of money at least temporarily enhances this claim. Any sacrifice by A, therefore, in the export of money arises not because of the loss of the money but because B may use this money to lay claim to A goods. These claims may not always be manifested. Country B may take steps to prohibit the operation of the transfer mechanism. Or country B may use the funds to buy goods from country C. In either of these cases, A makes virtually no sacrifice whatever. In regard to this point, there is sometimes consternation, by Americans in particular, that dollars loaned abroad do not "come back." But this should really be cause for American cheer: if others are willing to pay for the use of dollars that are then not used to bid away goods from Americans, from an American viewpoint this is surely to the good. In addition, the dollars actually do "come back"—but in the form of interest payments and repayments of principal (and a net gain in foreign exchange) rather than in payment for goods.

Even if the transfer mechanism works, the sacrifice to A in goods may not be great. This is usually so if A has unemployment, and thus unused productive capacity. The additional exports by A can then come not from any sacrifice in the purchase of goods by As, but rather from higher levels of output.

Although the loan of funds *may* not entail any real sacrifice for the lending country, there will *always* be a sacrifice to the borrowing country. Interest payments made on the loans represent a future claim on the output or existing goods of the borrower by the lender, and the lending country's net claims on the borrower's goods over the length of the loan are increased by international lending.

B. SHORT-RUN IMPACTS ON REAL NATIONAL INCOME: THE LENDING COUNTRY

We turn now to the short-run impacts upon A of loans from A to B. A number of conditions will affect these impacts. The most important are as follows:

(1) well-functioning markets
(2) malfunctioning markets
(3) full employment
(4) unemployment
(5) no compensatory monetary policy
(6) compensatory monetary policy
(7) transfer mechanism works
(8) transfer mechanism does not work

A few comments on these conditions are in order. First, the possibility of unemployment is conditional on malfunctioning markets. Second, compensatory monetary policy is defined as an attempt by the monetary authorities to take action to compensate for the foreign loans. For the lending country, this means trying to restore postloan domestic interest rates downward to their preloan levels. The transfer mechanism can be frustrated either by import barriers enacted by the borrower or by a compensating monetary policy on the borrower's part. The effect of the loans on A's real national income can now be analyzed by various combinations of those conditions that are not mutually exclusive. Our major organization in this section is by type of market.

1. Well-Functioning Markets

As long as A's markets are purely competitive, its loans to B cannot have much effect upon A's short-run real national income. Assuming neither country adopts compensating monetary policies, or attempts to interfere with the transfer mechanism, the higher interest rate in A should lead to smaller consumption and capital expenditures by As, while the lower interest rates in B should have the opposite effect in that country. If A's export surplus is just equal to the reduction in domestic expenditures, its real national income will be unaffected and its price level will remain the same. A, however, does make the usual sacrifice of a lender in lower consumption levels and less capital formation.

Consider now the possibility that A uses a compensatory monetary policy, increasing its domestic supply of money to make up for the loans. Now A's domestic expenditures do not fall, and to the extent B increases its imports from A, there will be price inflation in A— although without any change in real national income. The transfer mechanism, however, which under these conditions depended upon a reduction of A's pretrade prices, may not work to the full extent, in which event inflation in A will be lower. This use of compensating monetary policy by A under these circumstances may be regarded by B as an unsocial act. It is as if a lender who also supplies goods to a borrower takes steps after the loan to increase the prices for these goods. The borrower, who borrowed on the expectation of a given set of prices for these goods, then receives fewer goods or may even choose not to buy them at all.

Another possibility is that the B government acts to frustrate the real transfer of goods, either by reducing its money supply or by enacting import barriers. If, under these circumstances, A does not use a compensatory money policy, there will be a price deflation in A; if a compensatory monetary policy is used by A, the price level should remain constant. In either case, A's real national income does not change. A would be a complete gainer by such a policy by B: it obtains interest-earning securities without any sacrifice in current consumption or capital formation. If B wishes to use A money in its internal commerce or to buy from others—money that A could supply without cost to A—and if B is willing to pay for this use of A money, A should not find this objectionable.

2. Malfunctioning Markets

When the lending country's markets are malfunctioning, its loans can have a very significant impact upon its short-run real national income. Whether this impact is favorable or adverse will depend heavily on how that country uses monetary policy.

Consider first the case in which there is full employment in A, and neither country enacts policies that would interfere with the real transfer mechanism. Then if the reduction in domestic demand in A is exactly offset by its resulting trade surplus, real national income will not change. A sacrifices current consumption and capital formation for the future interest income. However, there is little assurance that the trade surplus will exactly equal the reduction in domestic demand. If the trade surplus is less than the reduction in domestic demand, A will have to increase its monetary supply to maintain its full employment and level of real national income. Of course, if the trade surplus is greater, a contractionary monetary policy is needed to avoid inflation.

If B acts to frustrate the transfer mechanism, or if the loans are used to purchase goods from C (and C does not increase its imports from A), there will be a reduction in aggregate demand for A's goods. If unemployment and a reduction in real national income are to be avoided, it is now mandatory that A increase its money supply to maintain domestic demand. With such a monetary policy, A would gain: it receives interest-earning securities without any sacrifice in consumption, capital formation, or short-run real national income.

When there is unemployment in A, loans to B provide golden opportunities for A. If the trade surplus exactly equals the reduction in domestic demand, A's real national income remains the same. But if A also uses compensating monetary policy to keep interest rates from rising, its exports to B may increase without a reduction in domestic demand. The trade surplus, operating through the Keynesian multiplier, can now result in a dramatic increase in real national income, and possibly full employment. It is clear that a country with unemployment should be eager to loan abroad when this is coupled with a compensating money policy. It is true that A can also simply increase its money supply to stimulate domestic demand, and thereby obtain the same increase in real national income without the loans. But increasing real national income through the loans and export surplus may be more attractive: A obtains foreign exchange that can be used in emergencies; A obtains income-earning securities. Furthermore, the use of monetary policy to raise internal demand often leads to a trade deficit, which is obviously avoided by the alternative stimulus of foreign loans.

This analysis demonstrates that the lending country must use monetary policy very deftly, especially when its markets malfunction: monetary policy decisions can make all the difference as to whether A's real national income falls or rises. However, in practice, the optimal use of monetary policy may not always be readily formulated. It will require an assessment of B's monetary policies, whether and to what extent exports will increase, and how much domestic demand will fall. Either the data or the tools of economic measurement may not be equal to the task.

C. SHORT-RUN IMPACTS ON REAL NATIONAL INCOME: THE BORROWING COUNTRY

There are a number of variable conditions that can also influence the effect of borrowing on B's real national income that are similar to those in the preceding section. First, there can be well-functioning or malfunctioning markets. Second, given the latter, there can be full employment or unemployment in B. The borrowing country too can use monetary policy to compensate for the inflow of foreign funds: such policy would be designed to prevent a reduction in the interest rate. Finally, B can frustrate the operation of the transfer mechanism, which can be done through monetary policy or import barriers. We divide this section on the basis of well-functioning and malfunctioning markets.

1. Well-Functioning Markets

As long as B has well-functioning markets, the borrowed funds will have little effect upon its short-run real national income. The borrowings will reduce interest rates, which in turn will stimulate domestic demand for both consumer and capital goods. Whether this increased demand leads to inflation will depend on whether B's imports increase sufficiently (or exports fall) to compensate for this increase in domestic demand.

Country B may take steps, perhaps inadvertently, that will make the transfer mechanism inoperable. If its central bank sets a target for interest rates—a common procedure—it might reduce B's money supply to keep interest rates from falling. Then there would be no inflation, no trade deficit, and no change in real national income. (We should note that there may still be a trade deficit—if as a result of the loans B's currency is allowed to appreciate in value.) Country B, in effect, simply has more A money and less B money for use in its domestic commerce. (More accurately, the A money will provide the base for part of the B money.) B may plausibly also react to its trade deficit with restrictions on imports or promotion of exports. Then there would be inflation.

Neither of these policies make much sense to B. The social purpose of its borrowings is to have a trade deficit, and if this does not come about B pays interest on the loans without any apparent benefits. If B does not wish lower interest rates or a trade deficit, the loans are not in its national interest—and these interests would be better served by prohibiting the loans themselves rather than by trying to compensate for the effects of the loans. (I am ignoring the case—a rather extreme one—in which a country may require loans in order to bring about some confidence in its currency. Such loans, of course, are only short-run solutions to such problems.)

2. Malfunctioning Markets

Even with malfunctioning markets there can be full employment. Under these circumstances, the reduction in interest rates attributable to the loan will stimulate domestic demand, but real national income will remain the same, and there will be no inflation, as long as the trade deficit equals the increase in domestic demand. If B acts to restrict imports or to promote exports as a response to the trade deficit, then the loans will be inflationary. If it uses compensating money policy, then the loans will have no effect upon trade, real national income, or the price level.

Now assume there is unemployment in B. The reduction in interest rates attributable to the loans should stimulate the B economy via higher domestic consumption and investment expenditures. But if the transfer mechanism is allowed to operate, the stimulation to B's economy from the lower interest rates will be reduced: in Keynesian parlance, the increased imports by B will be a "leakage" that will dull the effects of the consumption and investment multipliers in increasing employment. If B also uses compensating monetary policy, there will then be no effect by the loans on B's real national income. But this would make no sense to B: it would again amount to B using more A money and less B money, and paying interest to A for a loan that has no benefits.

One can make a very strong case that borrowing to B is adverse to its interests so long as there is unemployment in that country. B will in all events be incurring obligations to A, and thus a future claim on B's goods. But what does B gain in return? The reduced interest rates resulting from the borrowing will, it is true, stimulate B's economy. But B can accomplish the same goal simply by expanding its own money supply. Any increased imports attributable to the borrowing are likely to lead to additional unemployment. A country really needs additional imports of a type it can produce only when there is full employment and thus upward pressure on prices; an economy with unemployment does not usually face these problems. The only purpose foreign borrowing may serve for B, taken as a whole, is possibly to enable B to import necessary items that cannot be produced at home. A country with unemployment that can produce a full range of goods has no national interest in foreign borrowings—although, of course, private groups could gain.

3. The Optimal Flow of Funds: A World View

When full employment exists in all countries, a flow of indirect foreign investment from rich to poor countries has a great deal of merit—when seen strictly from a worldwide viewpoint. The wealthier country is presumably in a better position than the poorer to make the sacrifices in consumption necessary for capital formation. But when unemployment exists in some countries, the socially desirable flow can be quite different. It should in fact always be from the countries with unemployment to the countries with full employment. The countries with unemployment have excess productive capacity, and are thus in a position to finance and produce a flow of goods to the borrower without any sacrifices in its current consumption or capital formation. In fact, loans by the countries with unemployment will help to raise their real national incomes. The fully employed economies, on the other hand, are those that most require additional capital formation; yet, if this capital formation is financed from domestic sources, there would have to be a real sacrifice in current consumption. A flow of funds from the unemployed to the fully employed economies can lead to an enhancement of capital formation internationally and fuller employment in the lending country—all without any sacrifices in current consumption standards. (Note: My argument that the country with unemployment is in less need of capital formation may appear odd, since a shortage of capital expenditures is often associated with unemployment. But what the country with unemployment strictly requires is an increase in the aggregate demand for its outputs, which can come from consumption or export increases as well as capital expenditures. Also, it is the fully employed economy that more requires the capital formation, because this is the *only* way its real national income can rise.)

D. THE LONG-RUN WELFARE CONSEQUENCES FOR THE LENDING COUNTRY

We have shown that the short-run consequences of indirect foreign investment can be beneficial to the leading country, especially if two conditions are present: A (the lending country) has unemployment, and A uses compensating monetary policy. When these conditions are met, loans provide a way for A to increase its exports and its real national income without any sacrifice in consumption.

The long-run consequences of indirect foreign investment for A can be much less sanguine. On the plus side there will be an inflow of interest payments, which become part of A's real national income. But on the negative side, the outflow of funds may lead to a reduction in the rate of capital formation in A. Such a reduction in capital formation would result in a smaller output level, and thus a smaller real national income, for A. We may take it as highly unlikely that the interest receipts by A would offset its reduced level of output, so there exists a prima facie case that A's long-run real national income will be less than it would have been had there been no indirect foreign investment—at least in the absence of offsetting policies.

The last chapter argued that there is a strong likelihood that indirect foreign investment by A will lead to reductions in captial formation in A. This reduction is greater to the extent the following conditions hold: interest rates rise a great deal in A; wage rates remain higher in A than in B; B's pattern of capital formation is competitive rather than complementary to A's industries; A's currency cannot devalue. We may ask whether there is any combination of policies and/or circumstances that would counter this tendency for a reduction in capital formation in A.

One possibility is to try to make labor markets work better in A so that wage rates may fall. Of course, this would mean reducing the power of labor unions, reducing welfare payments, doing away with minimum wage laws, and so forth. Although not in the realm of the impossible, such policies would be difficult to enact in democratic countries. Along these lines, wage increases in B may be beneficial to A, and conceivably A can act to restrict capital flows to countries with high population growth rates and low labor standards.

A second method by which the reduction of capital formation can be avoided is the use of monetary policy—specifically, the use of monetary policy to keep interest rates from rising too high. This is essentially a policy that can be readily carried out without much difficulty, although there may be problems in recognizing why that policy is needed and also in calculating its appropriate timing. Such use of monetary policy, however, may not be beneficial in dealing with the competition in trade from the borrowing country—assuming that country has been able to transform its borrowings into capital formation successfully.

A third possibility through which to counter a possible reduction in capital formation is a devaluation of A's currency, which can compensate for B's cost advantage attributable to lower wage rates. Of course, such a devaluation has to be allowed—A, for example, cannot have its currency pegged to gold. A devaluation, furthermore, is not without its complications. As we have seen, expectations of devaluations in A currency may lead to further outflows of funds from A to B, which can reduce further A's capital formation and long-term growth.

Perhaps the most crucial factor affecting A's capital formation and long-term real national income is the pattern of capital formation in B. If this is competitive with A's industries, then A's long-term prospects are not good. But if B's capital formation is complementary, the profits of A-firms may rise and capital formation in A may increase despite a rise in domestic interest rates. If A is an industrialized country, an expansion of raw material production in B can most greatly benefit A's long-term real national income.

Country A, then, clearly has a very strong interest in how B uses its borrowed funds. To the extent possible, A should take steps to assure that these funds are invested in raw material production or in other items complementary to A's industries rather than in industries competitive with those of A. This may all smack of mercantilist philosophy, especially the "colonialism" many would infer in any attempt to induce B to produce raw materials. But it can also be considered elemental self-interest. No rational business firm would lend money to its competitors to enable them to better compete with it, and it is difficult to see why this common-sense principle should not apply to loans by countries. A rational businessman, however, would lend money to help the productivity of firms from whom it purchases or to whom it sells—and this mode of behavior, too, seems applicable to a nation in its loans.

Although the lending country may prefer that the borrowing country's capital formation be mainly in sectors not competitive with the lending country's sectors, the nature of indirect foreign investment is such that the lending country may not have much influence over the pattern of capital formation by the borrowing country. Even if the lending country were to prohibit loans by its citizens to sectors that are competitive with its own industries, this would merely free up financial resources in the borrowing country that could be used to create capital in the competitive sectors. Money is such a fungible item that, once it is transferred, the transferer typically has little to say about how the transferee will use the funds. In this respect, direct foreign investment may be preferable to indirect foreign investment, because in direct investment the investing country may be better able to control the pattern of capital formation in the capital-receiving country.

Of course in a many-country world, A may have little leverage over B in any respect. If the A government restricts indirect foreign investment by A lenders to B, or tries to influence how B's borrowed funds will be used, then B may instead borrow from country C. In this event, A can face the same disadvantages of higher wage costs, but without receiving at least the interest payments. It is then competition from other lending countries that ultimately defeats policies by any single lending country to restrict the use of indirect foreign investment by borrowers in an attempt by the lender to channel that investment into sectors consistent with the lender's own interests.

If capital formation in B is competitive rather than complementary with A's industries, A may have to fall back upon other means to compete with the lower-wage country. This may be done with technological superiority, product differentiation, tied services, the use of special credits to foster exports, and so forth. A high-wage country loaning its funds to a low-wage country, enabling the latter to compete with it more effectively, must, in short, use its wits to compensate for the cost disadvantages it has helped bring about.

E. ECONOMIC TRANSFORMATION:
THE LENDING COUNTRY

Indirect foreign investment will have several major impacts on the lending country. First, the lending country (country A in our example) will become a rentier country in the international economy, specializing in savings and in the provision of a variety of services, especially those of financial institutions, of course at the expense of industrial production. Second, in the international economy, country A will have to acquire special skills—new products, superior technology (particularly in capital goods), financing of exports, reputations for products, invisible exports—to compensate for its cost disadvantages. These compensations are more necessary to the extent that: A's wage rate remains above that in the borrowing country; A fails to use monetary policy properly; A's currency is not allowed to devalue; the borrowing country's capital formation is competitive with A's industries.

Internally, there should be a redistribution of income in favor of the "monied" classes, and against labor. The redundant labor (which would occur with a malfunctioning labor market) will strive to move into the "service" industries, and, if private demand cannot support these services, political pressures will be placed on the government to supply or subsidize them. Because of the cheaper imports, commodity prices will be low, and wage rates, although they may not fall, should also not rise. Although some types of institutions will flourish, mainly those dealing with finance, the goods-producing industries will be characterized by dilapidated plants.

One country more than any other fits this description, namely England. By the turn of the twentieth century, England was exporting tremendous amounts of financial capital. Much of this capital in earlier periods went to industries complementary to England, that is, to those industries which produced raw materials. Thus there were loans that helped to develop transport, power, agriculture, mining, in "new" countries, such as the United States, Canada, Australia, and much of Latin America. But toward the end of the nineteenth century, loans were made to countries that were to become competitors of England: Germany, Japan, the United States (to a lesser extent), and even India. England began to lose its competitive advantage in manufacturing, even to the point of importing textiles, its most traditional export, from India. England then began to live off her interest income, and, to a large extent, her wits. Competition from the newly emerging industrial powers also led to increasing demands in England for import protection and for the Commonwealth preference system—all this by the country that was the center of the free trade philosophy.

Although England was by far the major lender in the world by the end of the nineteenth century, the newly emerging industrial powers began to challenge England in this area—as Germany, the United States, Japan, France began to develop financial institutions that could amass funds for foreign investment. Thus England, so dependent upon its "invisible" exports, had to take special steps to advance its now-crucial international banking industry. One such step was to go on the gold standard in 1925, promising to pay all foreign holders of sterling in gold.[1] Going on the gold standard meant, of course, that any devaluation of the pound became difficult, and in this instance meant an appreciation of the pound. The loans, the decision to peg the pound to gold, the downward inflexibility of wage rates, and a lack of understanding at the time of the possibilities of monetary policy, all conspired to produce trade deficits, high unemployment, and bitter labor strife in England.

Yet England was a comfortable place, although mainly for the monied classes. Earning foreign exchange through lending money can be much more pleasant than by producing textiles or steel. And England might have been able to do well in the international economy through its invisible exports. But the Second World War forced England to sell much of its interest-earning securities. In the postwar period, shorn of its securities, saddled with a dilapidated production capacity, and depending upon an elite with a diminished capability for managing industrial enterprises, England faced more international economic problems than any other industrial country.

Some of the countries who borrowed heavily from England then became the new industrial powers. One can make the case that countries like the United States, Germany, and Japan would have succeeded even without loans from England, but these loans surely made their prominence come sooner. It is widely thought that England, when in 1846 it eliminated its tariffs on food imports, thereby sacrificed its agriculture on behalf of its manufacturing sector. When it started to make massive loans abroad, specifically to countries and sectors that were competitive with its own manufacturing industries, it may have sacrificed its manufacturing sector on behalf of its money-owning classes and financial institutions.

F. LONG-RUN CONSEQUENCES:
THE BORROWING COUNTRY

We pointed out earlier that there is no guarantee that borrowed funds will always lead to capital formation in country B, the borrower. When capital formation does not take place, the only gain for B, assuming the transfer mechanism operates, is a temporarily higher living standard. This may not always be wasteful, especially if natural disasters, such as droughts, have brought the living standards down to the point the social order is threatened. But there is little question that, in the absence of capital formation, B's real national income in the future will be diminished. In the calculations of real national income, the interest payments on the loans must be subtracted from the value of B's output, since some portion of this output generates income for the As. Clearly, if there is no additional capital formation, the Bs bear the burden.

For the borrowing country, the long-run problem of benefiting from indirect foreign investment is clear enough: how to transform these loans into increased capital formation? But though the objective is clear enough, the means of bringing it about may not be easy. Perhaps B may restrict its foreign borrowing only to those who import capital goods into B. Or perhaps the B-government can take action to increase domestic savings: without such action, and with a lower interest rate brought about by the loans, the result would be increased consumption and reduced savings. If the Bs are successful in transforming the loans into additional capital formation, the welfare criteria is simple enough—the value of the additional output must exceed the interest payments and repayments of principal to the As.

There is the question of whether the borrowing country should invest in sectors that are competitive, or complementary, to the most important products of the lending country. In the context of the loans moving from the industrialized to the developing nations, this comes down to the choice by the latter of primary products (and simple manufactures) versus the more sophisticated type of industrialization. It is quite natural that many in the developing countries cry out for industrialization, since this is the path that was apparently chosen by the wealthier nations. But an emphasis on industrialization may not always be the wise choice. Sophisticated manufactured products are sold on the basis of reputation as much as on price, and even with a cost advantage the developing countries may have difficulty in competing with the more established economies. Raw materials, on the other hand, can almost always find a market. It may be true that, over a long stretch of history, the demand rose faster for manufactured goods than for raw materials, and that the fewness of the manufacturing nations and the development of new lands resulted in terms of trade favorable to manufacturers. But this trend may well have run its course, and there is nothing in economic theory that says efficient producers of primary products cannot prosper.

Perhaps more important is the relationship between the pattern of capital formation by the borrowing country and the availability of loans. We have shown that competitive investments are inimical to the interests of the lenders while complementary investments are consistent with these interests. Thus, international harmony and a "natural" order are created by complementary investments. In a laissez-faire era, only private motives are important, and the borrowers can obtain funds to use as they wish. But as national interests are identified, and governments become more active in managing economies, there is every reason to expect that loans not used in a manner consistent with the interest of the lending countries may not be forthcoming.

G. THE NECESSITY FOR PUBLIC POLICY

From these discussions, it is clear that the welfare consequence of indirect foreign investment can be both complex and uncertain, with much depending upon economic circumstance and public policy. Of course, it follows from this assessment that such investment is not automatically desirable to either country. It also follows that public policy measures along the lines suggested, by both the lending and borrowing countries, are necessary if indirect foreign investment is to prove beneficial to their respective interests. With the proper policies, such investment can be especially attractive to the lending country because, under modern monetary conditions, a country can essentially earn foreign exchange by allowing others to use something that is costless to produce.

H. CONTROLS ON CAPITAL FLOWS

In theory it should be possible to regulate and control the international flow of money with the same tools used to regulate flows of goods, mainly through taxes, subsidies, and quantitative restrictions. But in practice it is much more difficult to control the flow of money. Goods, after all, do have to be physically transported and must enter or leave designated ports where they can be examined and taxed by customs authorities. Money, on the other hand, can easily avoid controls. Even when money took the form of gold, Adam Smith noted that various Crowns who had at one point tried to prohibit the export of gold were unable to enforce such laws. Nowadays, an international movement of money does not even mean the funds have to cross international boundaries. A bank, for example, makes an international loan merely by crediting some foreigner's account on its books.

Yet there have been recent attempts to regulate the inflow or outflow of funds. The United States, in the early 1960s, placed a tax—known as the "interest-equalization" tax—on loans by Americans to foreigners. More recently, some European countries have tried to discourage the borrowing of money, or more accurately, an inflow of funds. Thus, as Donald Hodgman reports, Switzerland and others at times prohibit their banks from paying interest on bank deposits of foreigners.[2] But although such programs may have enjoyed some success, by and large the controls on foreign lending and borrowing require a close sort of governmental supervision largely beyond the general powers of democratic governments. Perhaps controls can be exercised by borrowing countries through the refusal of their central banks to convert foreign currencies into domestic currencies—but in practice it would be difficult to distinguish foreign currencies obtained by loans from foreign currencies obtained by exports of goods.

If controls on international transfers of funds cannot be directly exercised, then the only option of governments seeking to influence these transfers is to manipulate the incentives for the loans. Thus, a country not wishing an outflow or inflow of funds may have to use its monetary policy to raise or lower its domestic interest rate to the level of that in other countries. But, although the manipulation of interest rates may serve the purpose of discouraging the outflow or inflow of funds, its use for these purposes will preclude its use for what may be more important purposes, such as domestic stabilization. We come once again to the problem that the free flow of funds internationally may interfere with the attainment of domestic goals.

CHAPTER TEN

Direct Foreign Investment: Models and Impacts

This chapter begins with a model for determining the amount of direct foreign investment by one country in another—continuing to use A as the investing country and B as the host country. We then go on to assess the impacts of direct foreign investment on trade, foreign exchange positions, capital formation, and other aspects of the economies of both countries.

A. THE AMOUNT OF DIRECT FOREIGN INVESTMENT

We can safely assume A firms will locate in B as long as the rate of return (appropriately discounted) per unit of capital invested is greater in the B location. The very process of direct foreign investment, however, will itself affect these rates of return in the alternative locations, and when these rates are equalized—the equilibrium condition—no further direct foreign investment should be forthcoming. Our problem is to identify the economic forces that can bring about this equilibrium. Much will depend upon why the rate of return is initially higher in B than in A.

1. Categories of Firms Locating Abroad

Let us first eliminate from our consideration taxes or subsidies, bargaining leverages, and oligopolistic maneuvers as motives for an

A firm to locate facilities in B. This then leaves two basic motives for the A firm to locate in B: to reduce production costs; to sell its output at a higher price.[1]

If there is free trade and if transport costs are negligible, then inputs tradeable and transportable over national boundaries should cost an A firm the same in B as in A. There is then only one basic reason why production costs may be lower in B than in A: the nontransportable inputs in B are either cheaper than or superior to those in A. The two most important nontransportable inputs will generally be land and labor. The land, of course, will be most important to producers of raw materials, and labor (including the skill mix) will be most important in manufacturing. Other inputs should have little bearing on the decision to locate in A or B. Since the A firm owns and controls the A/B facility, there is no reason for technology or management to differ in the two countries. There is also no reason for the scale of the plant to differ in the alternative locations: even if B is a small country with a small market, the output of an A/B plant can be sold outside B.

Turning now to a higher price in B as a possible motive for an A firm to locate in B, consider first the production of a transportable product. If there is free trade, the price of that product should be the same in both countries, and thus locating in B in order to sell to the B market cannot be the main motive. If, however, B imposes import barriers and/or transport costs are high, the B market will be a high-priced protected market, and A firms will locate there to take advantage of this higher price. Consider next firms producing nontransportable services—such as construction and public utility services. Since these items are not transterritorially traded, their prices may be higher in B than in A—whether or not there is free trade is irrelevant. With the higher price in B, A firms producing these services will be motivated to locate in B: this is the only means by which they can sell these services to the B market.

On the basis of this analysis, we can divide A/B firms into four groups characterized by motive. This division will be helpful when we seek the equilibrium conditions for the amount of direct foreign investment.

(*1*) *Producers of Raw Materials* These A firms locate in B primarily because of the special qualities of the land and natural resources in B. These firms will sell their output anywhere.

(*2*) *Manufacturers Responding to Lower Labor Costs* If there are no trade barriers and if transport costs are negligible, virtually the only motive such an A firm would have for locating in B is to purchase the less expensive B labor. There is no reason why the outputs of these firms would all be sold to the B market. With freer trade, the purchase of B labor becomes a more important motive for the A firm to locate in B.

(*3*) *Manufacturers Responding to Higher Output Prices in B* This will be a motive, as we argued, only if B is a protected market. One should expect these A/B firms to sell virtually all their output to the B market. To the extent there is greater free trade, this category of firms should become less important.

(*4*) *Producers of Nontransportable Outputs* These firms, typically in utilities, construction, newspapers, retailing, locate in B to sell to the B market.

Using each of these categories as a basis, we now turn to the determinants of the amount of direct foreign investment by A in B.

2. Raw Material Producers

If B land is superior to A land for the production of a given raw material, this will be reflected in fewer units of capital and labor needed to produce a unit of this raw material in B than in A. The difference in these production costs determines the maximum land rent the A/B firm is willing to pay B landowners, who may be private citizens or a collective entity represented by the B government. Alternatively, this maximum land rent can be calculated as the difference between the average cost of production, including a normal profit, and the output price. (The willingness to pay up to the maximum assumes an absence of special risks.) As long as the actual land rent paid is less than this maximum, A firms will continue to invest in B. Competition among A firms for the use of this land will, of course, tend to push the actual land rent toward this maximum. The equilibrium condition can now be stated: the A firms will locate in B up to the point the B landowners capture the full land rent attributable to B's superior land. If the landowners (usually with the help of the B government) set the maximum rent independently of market forces, the amount of direct foreign investment will be smaller, because the attracting feature is the differential between the actual and the maximum land rent. If somehow payment is made by As to Bs in lieu of some of the land rent —political support, bribes, special taxes, foreign aid—then direct foreign investment will be higher. Investment in depletable raw materials can obviously also be limited by the depletion of the raw materials.

3. Manufacturers Locating in B to Buy B Labor

For these firms, the key to the location decision is the comparison of A wage rates and B wage rates. If W^a is the A wage rate, W^b is the B wage rate expressed in B currency, and e is the exchange rate, A firms will locate in B as long as $(1/e)W^b<W^a$—assuming no special risk differentials. The equilibrium condition is obvious: A firms will locate in B up to the point that $(1/e)W^b = W^a$. (If there are differences in the quality of A labor and B labor, then W^a and W^b can be usefully defined as the wage costs per unit of output.)

If there are free uncontrolled labor markets in A and B, the location of A firms in B rather than in A will tend to reduce W^a and raise W^b, thus bringing about the equilibrium condition. The amount of direct foreign investment required to bring about wage equalization (measured in terms of A currency) will depend upon whether the investments are in labor-intensive or capital-intensive industries. To the extent these investments are in labor-intensive industries—and we should expect these to be the more attractive sectors—the amount of direct foreign investment will be smaller. Any forces that interfere with the movements of these wage rates should lead to higher levels of investment. Thus, if wage rates do not rise in B, because of high unemployment or high population growth, or if wage rates do not fall in A, because of labor unions, minimum wage laws, and so forth, the amount of direct foreign investment by A in B will be greater.

Given the extent to which labor markets malfunction in the real world, it is fortunate for A labor (and A in general) that the exchange rate also plays a role in the wage rate equalization process. Those A/B firms responding to lower wage rates in B transnationally import B labor, while their outputs can be sold anywhere. To the extent the output is sold in A, the operations of these firms tend to drain A's foreign exchange, which, with flexible exchange rates, can lead to a devaluation of A currency. Such a devaluation will then raise the relative wage rate of B workers in terms of A currency to the A/B firms even if internal wage rates do not change in either country. The devaluation of A currency will then help bring about the equilibrium condition of equal wage rates in both countries in terms of A currency.

It is well to recognize that the devaluation of A currency is not in the interests of those A/B firms already located in B. Such a devaluation raises the price of B labor to these firms—and being already committed to their location in B reduces their profits. It should be noted that the devaluation of A currency will help the A/B firm to the extent it sells to the B market—but even so, that firm would have higher profit if it sells to the B market from an A location. Thus a country's firms located abroad mainly to hire the host country's labor will normally be a vested interest group opposing a devaluation of its national currency.

4. A Manufacturers Locate in B in Response to a Tariff

Assume that B enacts an ad valorem tariff of t percent on some product. Then $(1/e)P^b$, the price of that product in B in terms of A currency, will be higher than P^a, the price of that product in A. Both A/A and A/B firms will thus be eager to sell to the B market. However, because the tariff is enacted (usually) only on transterritorial trade, only the A/B firm can obtain the price of $(1/e)P^b$. The A/A firm, having to pay the tariff, will only receive the net price of $[(1-t)/e]P^b$. If all other things are equal, the A firm will be motivated to locate in B in order to sell at a higher net price to the B market.

All other things, however, may not be equal. The A/A firm hires A labor, while the A/B firm hires B labor. Assuming labor is the only input, and that W^a and W^b are now the labor costs per unit of output, the net receipts per unit of output for both types of firms selling to the B market will be as follows:

$$[(1-t)/e]P^b - W^a \text{ for the A/A firm, and}$$
$$(1/e)P^b - (1/e)W^b \text{ for the A/B firm.}$$

There are now two conditions for the equilibrium level of direct foreign investment: the net receipts per unit of output in selling to the B market must be equal for A/A and A/B firms; the price in B must be above the price in A. These equilibrium conditions can be shown as follows:

$$(1/e)P^b - (1/e)W^b = [(1-t)/e]P^b - W^a \qquad (10.1)$$
$$(1/e)P^b > P^a \qquad (10.2)$$

We can now identify the forces that determine the amount of direct foreign investment. The higher the value of t (the tariff rate), the greater the amount of direct foreign investment. The greater the impact of the A/B firms in forcing down the value of P^b (the local price in local currency), the lower the level of direct foreign investment. The impact of the A/B firms on P^b will depend largely on the size of the B market for the product and the extent to which B/B firms reduce their output levels because of competition from the A/B firms. The greater the impact of the A/B firms in raising W^b (the wage cost in B per unit of output) and in lowering W^a, the lower will be the level of direct foreign investment.

The exchange rate requires some special attention. The A/A firms only sell to B. The A/B firms, however, both buy from and sell to B. But, since the A/B firms under these conditions presumably sell most or all of their output in the protected B market, the A/B firms will now earn foreign exchange for A. If exchange rates are allowed to change, the effect of the foreign exchange earnings should be an appreciation of A's currency. (This should be contrasted with the expected devaluation of A currency when A firms locate in B mainly to buy B labor.) The A/B firms will then find selling to the B market less attractive, but buying B labor more attractive. However, since these A/B firms are net exporters to the B market, the appreciation of A currency should tend to limit direct foreign investment.

5. A/B Firms Sell Nontransportable Outputs

An A firm producing a nontransportable service has only two options: to produce in A, or to produce in B. Using the same symbols, direct foreign investment should take place to the point net receipts per unit of output are equalized in A and B. Or:

$$(1/e)P^b - (1/e)W^b = P^a - W^a \qquad (10.3)$$

The greater the impact of direct foreign investment on output prices in B compared to A, the lower the level of direct foreign investment. The greater the impact on wage rates in A and B, the lower the level of direct foreign investment. Since the A/B firm both buys and sells in the B market, it earns foreign exchange for A (since sales should normally be greater than purchases), which will tend to appreciate A currency. Since A/B firms sell to Bs more than they buy from Bs, any appreciation of A currency will make direct foreign investment by A in B less attractive. Thus the activities of A/B firms in this category should tend, through the exchange rate, to limit the amount of direct foreign investment.

6. Other Forces Influencing Direct Foreign Investment

Other forces can be analyzed in terms of their effects on the equilibrium conditions discussed above. Say the risks are greater in B than in A for A's manufacturing firms who locate in B to hire cheaper labor. Then A firms will invest in B only as long as B wage rates are sufficiently lower than A wage rates to compensate for the risks. Thus, in equilibrium the B wage rate may be below the A rate—and of course direct foreign investment will be lower. It can be readily seen that any increase of risks in B penalizes the B labor force. Consider next a subsidy by the B government to A/B firms locating in B mainly to buy B labor. Now the equilibrium level of the B wage rate could be above the A wage rate—with the difference related to the size of the subsidy. Of course, with such a subsidy, the equilibrium level of direct foreign investment will be higher.

B. DIRECT FOREIGN INVESTMENT
AND TRADE

In studying the effects of direct foreign investment on trade, it is necessary to bear in mind our two categories of trade: transnational and transterritorial. An A firm located in B can have two types of transnational trade with the Bs. One of these is the purchase by A/B firms of various B inputs: labor, components, rentals of various types, power, transport, credit, even the services of governments. These are all transnational exports by B which, even though they are not reflected in transterritorial accounting systems, nevertheless directly generate foreign exchange and income for Bs. The second type of trade consists of sales by A/B firms of their output to Bs. These sales do not necessarily always take place, especially if the motive of the A/B firms in locating in B is primarily to reduce production costs. To the extent these sales do take place, they represent transnational exports from A to B—although they are not recorded as exports in transterritorial accounting. In this section we analyze the effects of direct foreign investment on both types of trade. Although it is our position that transnational trade is more relevant to a nation's welfare, we also consider the effects of direct foreign investment on transterritorial trade.

1. Purchase of Inputs

Let us assume a number of A firms are located in B. To the extent these A/B firms purchase inputs from B nationals, their demands will be added to the demands of B/B firms. These additional demands will affect prices, output supplied by Bs, and purchases by B/B firms, in addition to the trade itself. Here we analyze the effect of A/B firms on trade in labor—much the same methodology can be applied to any B input. When the A/B firms' demand for B labor is added to the B/B demand for B labor, we obtain all the relevant results, as in figure 10.1.

In figure 10.1, W and L are the wage rate and employment in B prior to A's direct foreign investment. The additional demand by the

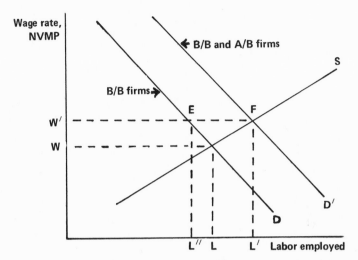

Figure 10.1 Impact of Direct Foreign Investment on the B Labor Market

A/B firms will raise the wage rate to W' and the employment level to L'. At this new wage rate, B/B firms hire only L" units of labor. The difference between L' and L" is then the amount of B labor transnationally imported by A from B. The foreign exchange earnings for B will then be L"EFL', and it must be stressed that these are as much foreign exchange earnings as any transterritorial export from B to A.

It is evident from this diagram that B labor is a beneficiary of A's direct foreign investment, since both wage rates and employment rise in B. The extent to which wage rates or employment are affected will depend upon the nature of the labor supply curve in B. If the supply curve is completely vertical and thus perfectly wage-inelastic—implying a fixed labor force that will work at any wage rate—then the full impact of direct foreign investment will be on wage rates. If, at the other extreme, the labor supply curve is completely horizontal (perfectly wage-elastic)—which could come about because of negotiated wage rates—and if there is unemployment in B, the whole impact of direct foreign investment will be only upon the employment level.

It can also be deduced that the more wage-elastic the supply curve, the smaller the reduction in the demand for B labor by B/B firms.

The A firms may invest in B by acquiring existing assets of B firms as an alternative to constructing new production facilities. With acquisitions, the aggregate demand curve of both A/B and B/B firms for B labor remains the same, but the B/B portion of this aggregate demand curve shifts to the left. Thus, acquisitions per se would not have the same favorable effect upon the B labor force as would new construction. The sales of B labor to the A/B firms would still constitute transnational exports by B, however.

2. Trade in Transportable Outputs

Even though the A/B firms are located in B, the outputs of these firms, until sold, belong to A nationals. There is no reason why these outputs must be sold to the Bs. They can just as easily be sold to other As or to third countries, and the choice of market will depend upon the prices of these goods in these countries. Trade barriers can influence the net prices received by A/B firms in alternative markets, and hence the sales pattern. We organize this section into two major subsections: in the first, there are no trade barriers; in the second, trade barriers are assumed to exist.

(*1*) *No Trade Barriers* Let us consider new investments by A firms in a product that A currently exports to B, with these new investments all located in B. These A/B firms also have a supply curve, and the quantities supplied can be thought to be in response to the price either in A or in B. It makes no difference which price we use, because with free trade the equilibrium price in A must be the same as that in B (considering, of course, the exchange rate). Since the outputs of the A/B firms are determined by As, the supply curve of the A/B firms can be added to that of the A/A firms as if the A/B firms were located in A.

Figure 10.2 displays the supply variation of the trade model developed in chapter 3 for this product. Prior to investments in B, the supply curve of the A firms is S in the A market (left frame). The

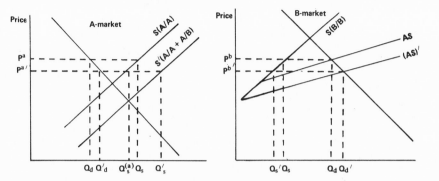

Figure 10.2 Effects of Direct Foreign Investment on
Trade

aggregate supply curve to the B market will be AS, as shown in that
market (right frame). The equilibrium price will be $P^a = (1/e)P^b$,
and A's exports to B will be Q_s minus Q_d, using the A market for
this purpose.

When the A/B plants are built, A's supply curve will be S', as
shown in the A market. This S' curve consists of output of both A/A
and A/B firms. With this new supply curve, a new aggregate supply
curve will result in B—shown as AS'. As one should expect, the equilibrium price falls to $P^{a'} = (1/e)P^{b'}$. The output of *all* A firms *rises*
to Q_s' (A market, left frame), but the output of the A/A firms *falls*
from Q_s to $Q_s^{(a)}$. ($Q_s^{(a)}$ is defined as the output of A firms produced
in A.)

The amount of exports from A to B depends on whether these exports are defined transnationally or transterritorially. On a transnational basis, A-firms (both A/A and A/B firms) increase their
exports from Q_s minus Q_d (left frame) to Q_s' minus Q_d'. But part of
these exports—Q_s' minus $Q_s^{(a)}$—will be supplied by A/B firms. And

only $Q_s^{(a)}$ minus Q_d' will be supplied by A/A firms. Thus, although A's transnational exports rise from Q_s minus Q_d to Q_s' minus Q_d', A's transterritorial exports fall from Q_s minus Q_d to $Q_s^{(a)}$ minus Q_d'.

The location of these A plants in B therefore reduces A's exports only on a transterritorial basis. But, whether we calculate these exports on the basis of the more correct transnational basis may not be too important. What really is important is that the A/A firms, in their exports, earn foreign exchange and income for As to the full value of the exports. The foreign exchange and income generated for As by the A/B plants, on the other hand, is only the difference between the value of their sales to Bs and their payments for B inputs.

Let us now assume that A firms locate plants in B to produce a product A currently imports from B. The supply curve of these A/B

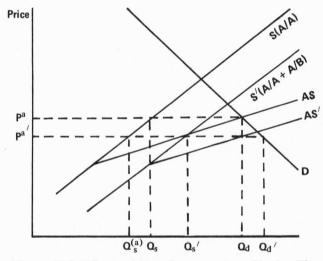

Figure 10.3 Effects of New Investment on Trade: The A Market

firms would still be added to the supply curve of the A/A firms to obtain the new supply curve for all A firms. Figure 10.3 shows the effects of these A/B investments on trade. We need only the A market for this purpose. Prior to the A/B investments, the supply curve of the A firms is that labeled S. When the supply of B/B firms to the A market is added to the supply curve of the As, the result is the AS curve. The equilibrium price is P^a, and A imports Q_d minus Q_s. With the new investments, the A supply curve (consisting of both A/A and A/B firms) is at S'. The new aggregate supply curve becomes AS'—this is obtained by adding the B supply curve to A to the S' curve rather than the S curve. The equilibrium price falls to $P^{a'}$. The output of *all* A firms rises to Q_s', but the output of the A/A firms falls from Q_s to $Q_s^{(a)}$.

The effect of the A/B firms on A's imports again depends on whether the transnational or the transterritorial definition of trade is used. On a transnational basis, A's imports fall to Q_d' minus Q_s', but on a transterritorial basis A's imports rise to Q_d' minus $Q_s^{(a)}$.

Again, there are foreign exchange and income implications. Prior to the investments abroad, A's foreign exchange bill for this product would be P^a (in terms of the equivalent in B currency) times Q_d minus Q_s in figure 10.3. But after these investments, this bill is reduced to $P^{a'}$ (in terms of B currency) times Q_d' minus Q_s', to which one must add all purchases of the A/B firms from Bs. And the portion of sales to As by B/B firms displaced by those by A/B firms will reduce the income of B productive factors from the full value of those B/B displaced sales to the payments of the A/B firms for the B inputs.

Transterritorial accounting evidently can give a misleading picture in both of our illustrations. In the first, in which the A/B firms are in A's export sector, territorial accounting gives the impression that A's exports have fallen, which is not so on a transnational accounting basis. And when the A/B firms are in A's import-competing sector, territorial accounting gives the impression that A's imports have risen, when they fall according to transnational accounting.

(2) *Trade Barriers* Assume B enacts an ad valorem tariff of t percent on a product A exports to B. For some price of that product in B —that is, P^b—its price equivalent in terms of A currency to an A/B

firm is $(1/e)P^b$, but is only $[(1-t)/e]P^b$ to an A/A firm. Since these two groups of firms respond differently to any value of P^b, we must think of two supply curves to the B market by A firms, one by A/A firms and one by A/B firms. To obtain the supply curve of the A/A firms, we use the technique of chapter 3. The A/B firms will supply their whole output to the B market as long as $(1/e)P^b$ exceeds the pretrade price in A. Since for any value of P^b the A/B firms attain the higher net price, the supply curve of the A/B firms will "start" at a lower value of P^b than will the supply curve of the A/A firms. These two supply curves can be horizontally added to obtain the combined supply curve of all A firms to the B market, as in figure 10.4.

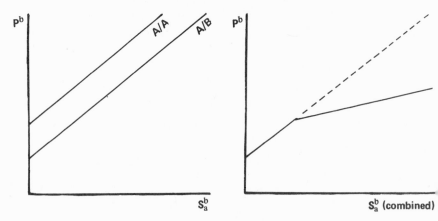

Figure 10.4 Supply Curve of A Firms to the B Market

Again using the basic procedure (the "market integration" trade model) developed in chapter 3, we arrive at the results shown in figure 10.5. It will be seen that there are three supply curves to the B market: one of the B/B firms, one of the B/B plus A/B firms, and the aggregate supply curve, which includes the supplies of A/A firms. On a transnational basis, B imports $Q_d - Q_s$ units from A. But these imports are divided into two portions: $S_{A/B} - Q_s$, the sales of the A/B firms to B; and $Q_d - S_{A/B}$, the sales of the A/A firms. Only the latter, $Q_d - S_{A/B}$, would be considered exports by A with territorially defined accounting.

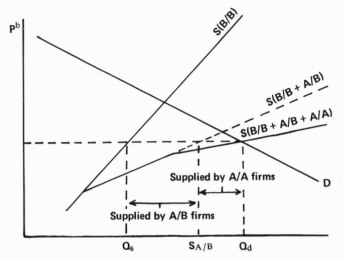

Figure 10.5 The B Market with Trade

C. FOREIGN EXCHANGE,
TERMS OF TRADE

In considering the impact of direct foreign investment on the foreign exchange positions of the two countries, we must bear in mind that A/B firms can both buy from and sell to B nationals. This type of trade can have both primary effects on the foreign exchange positions of A and B—that is, the effects of the operations of the A/B firms directly—and secondary effects, arising from how the trade of A/B firms affects other types of trade. We turn first to the primary effects.

Consider those A firms attracted to B in order to reduce production costs. If the outputs of these firms were all sold to As, then A's foreign exchange position would decline, and B's would rise, by the full extent of the purchase of B productive factors and any other items from Bs by the A/B firms. To the extent any of the output is sold to Bs or to other nations, any decline in A's foreign exchange holdings will be smaller.

Sometimes A firms locate in B primarily to sell to the B market—

generally in response to trade barriers and a protected market for manufactured goods, or for the production of some nontransportable service, such as construction. These firms will almost always contribute to A's foreign exchange holdings—the amount equal to the difference between sales to and purchases from Bs. Many economists have assumed that direct foreign investment is of this type—in which the output is sold mainly to the host country—from which it follows that the investing country always earns foreign exchange from the activities of its firms. But, as we have stressed, when A firms locate in B mainly to buy B inputs, then the A nation's foreign-located firms will often lead to a drain on its foreign exchange.

No matter what the motive of the A/B firms in their location decision—to reduce production costs or to sell in a protected market (or to sell a nontransportable product)—the B labor force will generally benefit, since the A/B firms will add to the demand for B labor. But the motive for foreign location will largely determine whether B's foreign exchange position improves or deteriorates as a result of the operations of the A/B firms. When the A/B firms respond to reduced production costs in B—often because of a low value of B currency—B's foreign exchange will improve. But when A/B firms are attracted by import barriers, in which event they can be expected to sell all their output to the Bs, country B's foreign exchange position will deteriorate. Thus, from the foreign exchange viewpoint, B would be well advised to attract A firms by a currency devaluation rather than by import barriers.

The A/B firms can also have secondary impacts on the foreign exchange positions of both countries, impacts which operate mainly through their effects upon the foreign trade of A/A and B/B firms. If the A/B firms sell to Bs items that displace similar sales by A/A firms, then A's foreign exchange earnings are reduced by the extent of the payments by A/B firms for purchases from Bs. If, however, the A/B firms sell items to As that displace sales to As by B/B firms, A's foreign exchange payments are reduced, from the payments for the goods from B/B firms to the payments of A/B firms to Bs for inputs.

The A/B firms also have implications for the terms of trade for both countries. On a transnational accounting basis, all purchases by A/B firms of B labor (and other B inputs) are imports to A and exports to B. Thus, to the extent B wage rates rise or fall—either because of a change in the internal wage rate or a change in the exchange rate—A's and B's terms of trade can either deteriorate or improve. The use of a tariff by B has some particularly interesting and somewhat ironic implications for the terms of trade. A tariff, it has been argued, should often turn the terms of trade in favor of the country enacting the tariff.[2] But with direct foreign investment, the impact of the tariff on the terms of trade can be completely reversed. When B enacts a tariff, it raises its domestic price. Since the A/B firms sell to the B market at this higher price, and since the sales of these A/B firms are part of A's exports, the tariff, when taken in conjunction with direct foreign investment by A in B, improves A's terms of trade.

D. CAPITAL FORMATION:
GENERAL CONSIDERATIONS

The effects of direct foreign investment upon the levels of capital formation *by* and *in* the various nations are important questions. Any locations of plants by As in B are of course themselves types of capital formation. But these A/B plants may have impacts on other types of capital formation. Will investments by A's in the A/B plants result in more, or less, capital formation by B/B firms? Will there be more, or less, capital formation by A's in both countries? Will capital formation *in* A rise, or fall? We assume in this section, for simplicity, that all savings are used only to finance private capital formation.

An empirical study conducted by Hufbauer and Adler provides a useful framework with which to begin.[3] They were not primarily interested in the impact of direct foreign investment on capital formation, but rather in the impact of American direct foreign investment on the United States' balance of payments. In the course of studying this problem, they developed a number of alternative assumptions about the relations between direct foreign investment and capital formation.

Their assumptions culminated in three "cases," which they called the "classical" case, the "reverse classical" case, and the "anti-classical" case. The classical case assumes that each country makes a fixed total amount of capital formation (no matter where located) in any time period. Thus any investments by As in B would mean that investments in A by As would be reduced by the same amount. In this case, then, foreign investment completely displaces domestic investment by the As. Investment by Bs in B, however, would remain the same, and the rise in investment in B would equal the fall of investment in A. In the reverse classical case, there would be a fixed amount of investment *in* each country. Thus, A investment in B would displace B investment in B, but A investment in A would not be affected. It will be noted that in both of these cases the total amount of capital formation by both countries taken together remains constant, but in the reverse classical case there is an overall displacement of B capital formation by A capital formation. The anti-classical case assumes that A investments made in B are in addition to investments by As *in* A and by Bs in B. From the viewpoint of increasing worldwide capital formation, this is the most desirable case.

The three cases used by Hufbauer and Adler imply further assumptions about the savings functions in both countries; that is, the relation between the interest rate and the amount of savings (or nonconsumption) that takes place. Thus, it is possible to assess the reasonableness of these three cases by the reasonableness of what they imply about the savings functions. In doing this, it should be borne in mind that interest rates will in the long run bear a rather constant relation to profit rates. We proceed only on the assumption of perfect markets.

The important fact about the classical case is that it implies that the savings of each country are completely insensitive to interest rates: that is, there is a fixed level of funds available for investment in each country no matter what the interest rate. This implies that the savings function in figure 8.1 is a vertical line. Evidently, under this assumption about savings, the capital formation by each country must be constant no matter where the productive assets are located, and any investments by A in B must displace investments in A. But the notion that savings in each country are completely unrelated to interest rates runs counter to much of modern economic theory, and hence the Hufbauer and Adler classical case should be rejected on the grounds that it requires much too strong an assumption about savings rates.

The reverse classical case states that direct foreign investment by A in B will raise A's *total* capital formation while lowering B's capital formation by the same amount. This implies more realistic assumptions about the savings function, namely that savings respond to changes in interest rates in both countries. The A firms, by investing in B, supposedly in response to higher profit rates in that country, will as a result have higher average profit rates. Thus, the A firms will increase their demands in the A capital market for funds, which will drive up the interest rate and thereby elicit more savings. The A/B firms, however, because of their competition with B/B firms, will tend to reduce the profit rates of B/B firms, and the result will be decreasing interest rates and decreasing savings in B. Thus, capital formation should fall *by* (but not *in*) that country. As a result, investments by A in B will tend to displace B investment in B. This model is based upon a plausible set of assumptions about savings rates, and will accordingly receive the bulk of our attention.

The anti-classical case states that A's total investment will rise while B's capital formation remains the same. What does this imply about the savings functions in the two countries? Clearly, if A's investment is to rise, A's savings must also rise, and this immediately implies that savings are responsive to higher interest rates. But what about B's savings rate? The A/B firms should reduce profits for the B/B firms, and, as a result, the demand for funds by B/B firms should fall. Interest rates in B should also fall. But if B's savings are to remain constant despite a reduction in interest rates, this would imply that B's savings rate is completely insensitive to interest rate. Thus, the anti-classical case implies completely different savings functions in the two countries, with savings responsive to interest rates in A but completely unresponsive to interest rates in B. It seems unreasonable to assume that such different savings functions in the two countries should exist; thus, the anti-classical case can also be rejected, now on the grounds of inconsistent assumptions.

The Hufbauer-Adler "reverse classical" case is clearly the most promising, since it rests upon plausible and consistent assumptions about savings rates in the two countries. But it does have one important problem connected with it: the assumption that the additional savings and investment by A must result in *exactly* the same reduction in savings and investment by B. If one tries hard enough, a set of conditions might be concocted in which the increased savings and investment by A would be equal to the decreased savings and investment by B. But the conditions one would have to assume about the reaction of the demand for funds in response to profit rates in the two countries, the nature of the savings functions in the two countries, and the sizes of their economies, would have to be unique for this to occur. Therefore, it is surely better to proceed on the supposition that direct foreign investment will raise A's capital formation and reduce B's capital formation, but that they need not offset each other completely.

There is still another problem to be considered. In tying the capital formation level and savings rate together for each country, we have implicitly assumed that the A firms only borrow from A savers, while B firms only borrow from B savers. But once the possibility of indirect foreign investment is introduced, the equality between a nation's savings rate and the level of capital formation by its firms need no longer hold. It is quite conceivable that when direct foreign investment reduces the average profit rate of B firms, while raising that of A firms, the savings rate of B's may not fall—because with indirect foreign investment, Bs could lend to As. Indeed the B's savings rate could rise if the increases in capital formation by A firms exceed the reduction of capital formation by B firms—since the net effect would be to raise the interest rtae (which with indirect foreign investment is the same in both countries) and thus induce higher levels of saving by Bs as well as by As. One must be careful now as to what is meant by a nation's capital formation. If A firms expand, and Bs partake in this expansion by loaning money to A firms, which country's capital formation is being expanded? Although other views are possible, we define capital formation for a country as productive assets *controlled* by its firms.

It is possible to construct a model that will help elucidate the conditions under which direct foreign investment would either raise or reduce the total amount of capital formation. To do this, we can combine the capital markets of the two countries into one diagram by making the assumption that indirect foreign investment is completely unrestricted. The resulting diagram is figure 10.6.

Consider first the savings functions in figure 10.6. The supply of funds by A's is labeled S^a, and the aggregate supply of funds by the two countries is labeled S^{a+b}. This aggregate supply-of-funds function is obtained by adding together the savings functions of the two countries. The line labeled D^a is the demand for funds by A firms, and we assume that firms borrow funds which are used only for capital formation. The D^{a+b} curve is constructed like the aggregate supply function: it is the aggregate demand for funds by both A and B firms.

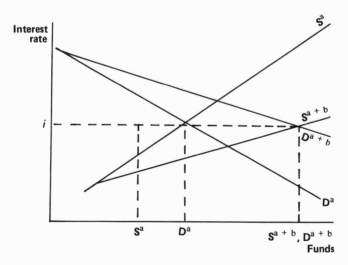

Figure 10.6 Worldwide Savings and Capital Formation

The intersection of the two aggregate curves determines the world-wide interest rate and the worldwide savings and investment levels, where the latter two must be equal. But, although aggregate savings and investment for the world must be equal, for any country one may exceed the other. Looking now only at the abscissa, we have S^a as the savings by A, $S^{a+b} - S^a$ as the savings by B, D^a as capital formation by A firms, and $D^{a+b} - D^a$ as capital formation by B firms. Also $D^a - S^a$ will be the borrowings of A firms from Bs.[4]

Can direct foreign investment change the level of worldwide capital formation? The demand for funds for investment, it will be recalled, is dependent on anticipated profit rates. Direct foreign investment by A in B should raise the A firms' profit rates and thus shift D^a to the right. But the profit rates of B firms should fall. Evidently, the aggregate capital formation can rise—that is, D^{a+b} can shift to the right—if the profit rates by A firms rise by more than the decline in profit rates of the B firms. Another possibility is that direct foreign investment will enlarge the incomes of the two countries. Then the supply curves in figure 10.6—or at least the aggregate supply curve —would shift to the right, and again worldwide capital formation could rise.

The main point here is that there is no reason for worldwide capital formation to remain constant as the result of direct foreign investment. This capital formation may rise, fall, or remain the same—and which will occur depends mainly on the impacts that direct foreign investment has on profit rates of both A and B firms, and also on the savings functions. Of course, with our emphasis on the welfare of nations as opposed to the welfare of the "world," we will be mainly concerned with the effect of direct foreign investment on the capital formation of each country.

E. CAPITAL FORMATION BY
THE HOST COUNTRY

Let us now explore the impact of A/B firms on capital formation by B/B firms. We assume an international capital market, so that

A/B and B/B firms can borrow at the same interest rate. Thus the capital formation of B/B firms depends mainly upon the impact of A/B firms on B/B profit rates. These profit rates, in turn, largely depend upon the course of prices of items bought and sold by B/B firms.

All A/B firms compete with B/B firms for B inputs, the most important of which we take to be B labor. To the extent that B wage rates rise because of entry into B of A/B firms, both the profit rates and the capital formation of B/B firms should be adversely affected. Whether and to what extent B wage rates rise will, however, depend upon the nature of the labor supply curve in B. If this labor supply curve is highly inelastic, then wage rates may rise a great deal and capital formation by B/B firms will fall a great deal. However, if the labor supply curve in B is highly elastic—particularly when there is unemployment at a negotiated wage rate—then wage rates may not rise in B and capital formation by B/B should not be adversely affected from this source. We may put this in the form of a general rule: the more elastic the supply curve of B labor, or in general the supply curve of any B input purchased by A/B firms, the less will be the adverse effects of direct foreign investment on capital formation by B/B firms.

Although the A/B firms always compete with B/B firms in B factor markets, they may or may not compete with them in product markets. The extent of the competition of these two groups of firms in product markets will largely depend on the motives of the A firms in locating in B: to reduce production costs, or to sell to the B market. When A firms enter B primarily to purchase less expensive B labor or B land, much of the output will be sold outside of B. Then the output prices of B/B firms should not fall greatly, and capital formation by B/B firms will depend mainly on the B labor supply curve. In this regard, the impact of A/B firms on the output prices of B/B firms will not differ much from what the impact would be if the As invested anywhere.

When A firms locate in B mainly to sell to the B market—usually either because that market is protected in the case of transportable goods or because the A firm produces nontransportable services—the impact of the A/B firms upon B/B firms' capital formation will be more serious. In these cases, the profits of B/B firms are doubly squeezed—both by higher input prices and by lower output prices—and accordingly we can expect a large decline in capital formation by B/B firms. The use of a tariff has ironic consequences. Whereas a tariff is often designed to protect the B/B firms, the entry of A/B firms motivated to sell to the protected B market will have just the opposite effect on the profits of the B/B firms.

Much of the impact of A/B firms on the capital formation of B/B firms can depend on the complementary/competitive relations of these two groups of firms. To the extent that A/B firms are complementary to B/B firms—selling items B/B firms purchase or buying items B/B firms produce—the adverse impacts of A/B firms will be minimal. If the degree of complementarity is great enough, it is even possible that the effect of A/B firms will be to raise profit rates of B/B firms.

To sum up, direct foreign investment by A in B will be least harmful—or perhaps even beneficial—to B's capital formation if one or more of the following conditions are fulfilled: factor supply curves in B are highly price-elastic; the A/B firms sell most of their output outside the B market; the products produced by the A/B firms are complementary to those produced by B/B firms. To the extent these conditions are not fulfilled, reductions in capital formation by B/B firms will be greater.

F. CAPITAL FORMATION IN THE INVESTING COUNTRY

When one turns to the effect of direct foreign investment on the capital formation of the investing country, there are two questions to consider. One is whether capital formation *by* A firms will rise or fall; the second is whether capital formation *in* A will rise or fall. It is, of course, quite possible for capital formation by A firms to rise even though capital formation in A falls.

1. Total Capital Formation by A Firms

Prior to direct foreign investment, we can suppose that profit rates and interest rates in A are in an equilibrium relation to each other, an equilibrium in which the difference between these two rates is just sufficient to compensate firms for the risks of entrepreneurship. When the possibility of direct foreign investment is introduced, and one assumes that profit rates of A/B firms are higher than those of A/A firms, direct foreign investment should increase the average profit rate of all A firms, at least in the short run. Thus one should expect capital formation by A firms to increase to the point that the average profit rate for all A firms is driven down to its long-term equilibrium relation to the interest rate.

It is clear that the behavior of interest rates will help determine the amount of additional capital formation by A firms. If interest rates rise, the profit rate that is in equilibrium with these interest rates will be higher, and, as a consequence, the additional amount of capital formation will be smaller. If we assume an international capital market, the behavior of interest rates depends not only on the savings rates in the two countries and capital formation by the A firms, but also on the capital formation by B firms, who are also in this market. To the extent that capital formation by B firms is reduced by competition from A/B firms, interest rates will be lower and the additional capital formation by A firms will be greater.

2. Capital Formation in A

There is a very strong presumption that direct foreign investment by A firms in B will cause capital formation in A to fall. This follows from the well-established economic principle that capital formation will be reduced in locations where the profit rate is below that in alternative locations. However, the extent of the reduction in capital formation in A may be affected by a number of factors, and it is even possible that under some circumstances capital formation in A will increase.

The behavior of wage rates in both countries as a response to direct foreign investment by A in B can have an important bearing on the extent to which capital formation in A falls, particularly in manufacturing. If wage rates rise in B and fall in A, the profit rates of A/A firms can be favorably affected and the decline in capital formation in A may be small. But if there is unemployment in B, or even if there is high population growth in that country, B wage rates may not increase by very much. Or, for reasons we have discussed, monetary wage rates in A may not fall. With such internal rigidities in wage rates, reductions in capital formation by A/A firms will be greater. However, a devaluation of A currency could compensate for internal wage rate rigidities and therefore temper the reduction in capital formation by A/A firms.

The effect of the activities of A/B firms on the output prices of A/A firms can also affect capital formation by the latter group. The most adverse circumstance is when A/B firms locate manufacturing facilities in B in response to lower B wage rates and sell much of their output on the A market. Then the competing A/A firms will have their profits reduced, and we should expect a larger reduction in their capital formation. But if A/B firms sell most of their output in the B market, the adverse consequences of direct foreign investment upon capital formation in A should be somewhat smaller.

A/B firms can also have complementary/competitive relations to A/A firms on output markets. To the extent that the relationship is complementary—the A/B firms produce items purchased by A/A firms but not produced by other A/A firms, or buy from A/A firms—capital formation in A should not fall a great deal, and may even expand. If A is an industrial country, the most important of these complementary products will generally be raw materials. Any reductions in raw material prices will not only raise profits and hence capital formation of A/A firms, but will also increase the demand for A labor.

If A is an industrialized country, it is doubtful if activities other than raw material production by A/B firms can have favorable complementarities for A/A firms. If the A/B firms are in manufacturing, they may be complementary to A/A firms in purchasing from the latter items such as machinery, components, and skilled labor. This argument has been used in defense of direct foreign investment by American firms and this type of complementarity may have been important. But over the long run, an industrialized country like the United States should not expect too much from this type of complementarity. Given the fact that the A/B firms bring with them technology and management, and given our presumption that B wage rates remain below A wage rates, there is really no reason why manufactured items that may in the initial stages of direct foreign investment be produced in A and sold to the A/B firms would not eventually also be produced by A/B firms.

We may now state the conditions that should govern the impact of direct foreign investment by A firms in B upon capital formation in A. The following conditions would have the most deleterious impact upon capital formation in A: wage rates in B fail to rise, and wage rates in A fail to fall (especially if exchange rates are fixed); the A/B firms sell most of their output (if competitive with those of A/A firms) in the A market; the outputs of the A/B firms are competitive with that of A/A firms. To the extent these conditions are not met, capital formation in A may not fall greatly, or at all. Unfortunately, the conditions most favorable to capital formation by A/A firms are not always those favorable to capital formation by B/B firms.

CHAPTER ELEVEN

Direct Foreign Investment: Welfare Implications

In this chapter we assess the impacts of direct foreign investment on the welfare of both the host and the investing nation. We continue to use real national income as the welfare criterion. It can be anticipated that the effects of direct foreign investment on real national income will depend on the existence or nonexistence of a number of conditions and economic relationships. Our aim will be not so much to ascertain the welfare impacts of direct foreign investment as to determine those conditions under which such investment is likely to be favorable or unfavorable to each nation's real national income.

A. THE INTERNATIONAL DISTRIBUTION OF INCOME

In chapter 6 we presented an international transactions matrix, and demonstrated how both indirect and direct foreign investment increased the possibilities of international transactions. These international transactions, it was shown, also affected the distribution of the income generated by production among the two national groups. We expand here on that model in order to clarify our welfare criteria.

If a nation does not trade at all, the value of its output of final goods determines the income of the various owners of its factors of production—and the output value and incomes must be equal. If a nation trades only final goods, its output mix will change, but the value of the final goods produced will still determine that nation's income.

It is only when international trade involves items other than final goods that the value of a nation's production of final goods may differ from its national income. In territorially defined trade, these traded items are limited to such intermediate goods as components and raw materials. Trade in intermediate goods means that the final goods produced by one country can generate income for the factors of production of another country. Put another way, when one nation contributes intermediate goods or services to the final goods produced by another nation, the revenues obtained by the sale of these final goods generates a like amount of income that is divided between both nations in proportion to the relative values of their productive contributions.

International investments make possible transactions in certain intermediate goods and services that are often not possible with territorially defined trade, and hence make possible new international divisions of income. Indirect foreign investment makes possible trades involving the use of money or credit, which can be considered intermediate services. Direct foreign investment makes possible (transnational) trade in a substantial number of types of intermediate services—generally those that are nontransportable, such as labor, the use of land, transport, power, the services of governments. To the extent that firms of one country buy such intermediate services from the other country, the value of their output generates incomes for both countries.

Evidently, the international division of income does not depend on the nationalities of the firms producing the final goods so much as it depends on the nationalities of those who contribute the productive services and intermediate goods used in the production of the final goods. Thus, just as the income generated by the final goods produced by a closed economy can be divided among the various classes of productive factors, the income generated by the final goods produced by the whole world can be divided in the form of income received among all national groups that contributed to the production of these goods. And, just as there can be a factoral distribution of income in any country, there can also be an international distribution of income.

For any nation, defined as a group of nationals rather than as a group of people living in a designated territory, its national income can be defined as follows:

    1. The value of all final goods produced by that national group (regardless of location)

  +2. The value of all intermediate goods and productive services sold to other national entities (regardless of location)

  −3. The value of all intermediate goods and productive services purchased from other nationals (regardless of location)

If the income of each national group were calculated this way, the aggregate of the national incomes for all nations would equal the value of the final goods produced throughout the whole world.

If we assume that the location of an A owned plant in B rather than in A has no secondary effects—it has no other effects on outputs, prices, or trade—then one important result immediately follows. To the extent this A/B plant purchases anything from Bs that would otherwise have been purchased from As had that plant been located in A, and if we assume these A factors or A goods would not have otherwise been employed or produced, the location of this A plant in B must always shift the international distribution of income in favor of B. Of course the location of this plant in B rather than in A can have many secondary effects, some of which may be difficult to determine. But it is nevertheless the salient fact that the primary impact of the location of this A plant in B rather than in A is an improvement in B's real national income at the expense of A's real national income. Anybody attempting to show that B's income falls as the result of this A/B plant, or that A's income increases, must bear the burden of demonstrating that the secondary impacts of the location in B overcome this primary impact.

We shall of course continue to study the impact of direct foreign investment on each nation's real national income to assess its desirability. However, others have argued that the welfare criterion should be that of the profitability of an investment. Thus, on the basis of this criterion, if an investment in B by an A firm leads to a higher level of profits than a similar investment in A, then the investment in B is desirable on the grounds that it is more productive in B than in A. This may be a valid conclusion if maximizing the world's income is the criterion of welfare, but it does not follow as a valid conclusion from the viewpoint of any individual nation's real national income.

B. THE HOST COUNTRY

In this section, we assess the long-run impacts of direct foreign investment on the host country's real national income. We also explore some other issues raised by such investment from the host country's viewpoint.

1. Direct Foreign Investment and Real National Income

The positive impacts of direct foreign investment upon B's real national income are fairly certain. The Bs can sell to As nontransportable productive factors and other services that cannot otherwise be directly sold to As in the absence of A/B firms. All these sales generate income for B. The Bs can also sell transportable intermediate goods to the A/B firms, which are also exports for B and generate income for that country. But such sales are not the most important consequence of direct foreign investment, since these types of goods can also be sold to A/A firms. Another source of income to the Bs is the taxes paid by the A/B firms to the B government—especially taxes on profits. If the A/B firms had no other impacts on the B economy, it is clear that B's real national income must increase.

There may, however, also be negative impacts of the A/B firms on B's real national income—which, it will be shown, are much less certain than the positive impacts. We showed in the last chapter that because of competition from the A/B firms, the capital formation of B/B firms may fall. More broadly, the output levels of B/B firms may fall and, to the extent this takes place, B's real national income from this source will be reduced. We can now easily state the conditions under which B's real national income will benefit from direct foreign investment: the sales of the Bs to A/B firms plus the taxes paid by A/B firms to the B government must exceed any reduction in the value of output by B/B firms.

Virtually the whole question about the benefits of direct foreign investment to B revolves about whether, and to what extent, the output of B/B firms will fall. The discussion in the last chapter pertaining to the effect of A/B firms on the capital formation of B/B firms holds in its entirety for the output levels of B/B firms. Thus, the negative impact on B's real national income from reductions in output of B/B firms will be smallest to the extent the following conditions hold: unemployment exists in B, or in general B's labor supply is highly elastic; the output of A/B firms is complementary to that of B/B firms; the output of the A/B firms is sold outside of B. To the extent these conditions hold, B's real national income is almost certain to be higher as a result of A's direct foreign investment—with much less certainty when these conditions are not fulfilled.

2. The Transformation of the B Economy

In what ways can direct foreign investment transform the B economy? Let us take first the case in which there is no unemployment in B and in which the A/B firms compete directly with B/B firms in the output markets. It is then likely that the B/B firms will do poorly, and they should become reduced in size and numbers. But other parts of the B economy may do very well. First, B labor is an obvious beneficiary, and B/B firms that cater to labor (retailing, services) should also benefit. Second, all firms and households in B that supply inputs to the A/B firms should also do well, and expand. These include transport, communications, power, public facilities of different types—what is often referred to as the infrastructure.

How can we describe this transformation? Very simply, the B economy will become specialized in the production and sale of nontransportable inputs, at the expense of the production of goods. Is this undesirable from B's viewpoint? It is true that B may lose some degree of "entrepreneurship," and some control over the composition of output produced in that country. But it is ultimately the purpose of any economy to use its productive factors—such as labor and land—to generate as high an income as possible. If B labor and B land-owners can earn more by supplying A/B firms at the expense of supplying B/B firms, this should benefit B as a whole, although some B firms will suffer. If the incomes of B productive factors can be increased through trade by selling their services directly to A firms rather than indirectly to As as embodied in goods produced and exported by B/B firms, it is difficult to see any disadvantages to the Bs.

What if the "ideal" conditions exist from B's viewpoint: unemployment, no trade barriers, and a complementary pattern of direct foreign investment? Then there will still be a transformation of the B economy in favor of the direct sale of productive services rather than the production of final goods, but without the penalty of less output by B/B firms. The B economy is still transformed, but by the expansion of certain activities without a reduction in other activities.

3. Merger/Acquisitions

Assume that an A firm acquires an existing B firm as an alternative to constructing new plants in B. If the A firm pays cash, then the acquisition itself should be considered an export by the Bs. If the A firm pays in financial securities, the acquisition would still be an export by B, but in addition there is indirect foreign investment of B in A. We have here the interesting case in which the same transaction results in direct foreign investment by A and indirect foreign investment by B.

Is B any the worse off by the A firm's acquisition as opposed to construction of new plants? First, the acquisition is an export by B that is likely to earn more foreign exchange than would the construction of new plants. The main drawbacks of the acquisition to the Bs are that they lose control of a productive organization (which may not be bad if it were a failing firm), and that competition is not enhanced in the B markets. But the Bs have received cash or securities of presumably equal value, and these can be used productively.

The main difference between the acquisition and new construction is that the former does not increase the net demand for B labor—assuming that the B sellers do not invest their funds in additional productive assets. But there are several advantages to B if the As rather than the Bs own the acquired plants. First, all sales of non-transportable or other inputs sold to an A/B plant generate foreign exchange for B—which may not be the case if the plant were owned by Bs. Offsetting this, however, is the *possibility* that the A/B firm will sell all of its output to Bs, in which event there will be a net drain on B's foreign exchange. Second, all taxes collected from A/B firms are income (and foreign exchange) to B, while taxes collected from B/B firms only amount to a transfer of income from some Bs to other Bs.

4. Technology Transfers

Any transfer of technology or managerial know-how accompanying direct foreign investment to the host country is of course beneficial to that country. But it must be clear that the mere presence of an A firm in B does not lead automatically to transfers of technology, in particular, to the Bs. Technology is expensive to acquire and valuable to firms—often the basis for their well-being. Thus, firms do not give away their technology, but they may sell it to the host country nationals. But the sale of technology could also be made from an A location. What the presence of the A firm in B is more likely to lead to is a transfer of managerial know-how and organization, which is usually acquired freely by host-country nationals. But for this type of transfer to occur, host-country nationals would usually have to have managerial and technical positions in the firm.[1]

5. Raw Materials

Host countries have been particularly sensitive to foreign-owned firms exploiting their raw materials, especially if these materials are depletable. It is quite understandable that any country would feel uneasy about its depletable raw materials disappearing, since its future income depends upon them, and it is always an uncertain economic calculation as to whether they should be left in the ground to fetch a higher price in the future. But this problem is not necessarily limited to the foreign-owned firm: it would exist for a nation even if all raw material exploitation were conducted by its own firms.

Leaving aside the emotional impacts on the host countries, there is no strong economic reason for a country to object to having its raw materials exploited by foreign-owned firms. If country B owns some mineral-bearing land which is exploited by A/B firms, the income generated by the raw materials will be divided between the B landowners and B labor and the A firms. If there is competition among firms for the right to use this land, the portion of income the firms receive should be just that necessary to cover expenses and yield a normal profit. The greater the competition, the greater is the assurance the landowner will receive the maximum rent. Also, to the extent the A/B firms have superior technology or can better market the product than can B firms, the higher should be the rent. One can cite a general economic principle here: the more and better the complementary inputs used with any factor of production, the greater will be that factor's income. The equipment and technology brought in by the A/B firms can be just as complementary to B land as it was shown to be to B labor, and thus can benefit B landowners in the same way it benefits B labor.

If the mineral-bearing land in B were all privately owned, and if competition prevailed, there is little doubt the host country would obtain the full rent value of the land. In many countries, however, the mineral rights are sold in the form of a "concession" by the government, ostensibly on the principle that all its citizens should benefit from the exploitation of its minerals. And often for various reasons there is insufficient competition. Given these two conditions, the values of the concessions are difficult to calculate, and with government officials doing the negotiating there is a great opportunity for bribery of one sort or another. It then becomes quite possible that the host country will not receive the full land-rent value. Or if B were politically dominated by A, the concession values could be below what they would have been were all parties free to act in their own interests. That bribery and political domination have taken place in the past, and probably still occur, cannot be doubted. But it does not follow that host countries cannot benefit from the exploitation of their raw materials by foreign-owned firms. Instead, the obvious problem is to avoid bribery and political domination, and to assure that competition is adequate.

6. Loss of Control

The argument is often made that, because of direct foreign investment, the host government loses some degree of control over its economy, and sometimes also loses some political control. Sometimes this loss of control is attributed to the fact that an A firm located in B is subject to the laws of both A and B, so that B is unable to exercise full legal control over firms operating on its soil. The loss of economic control can be attributed to the fact that an A/B firm operating in a number of countries has options not open to the B/B firm operating just in B.

So far as the legal control goes, one example is used ad nauseam to demonstrate the loss of control by the host country. This is the operation of the United States' "trading with the enemy" act, with which the United States has sometimes prohibited American-owned firms located on foreign soil from selling items of strategic value to communist countries. This, of course, has been blown up way out of proportion to its economic significance. But as a matter of principle, it is still an interesting question as to whether the host country should be able to *compel* a foreign-owned firm operating on its soil to do something it may not want to do.

There might also be some loss of control due to the extraterritorial reach of the laws of the investing country. Here the antitrust laws of the United States are most instructive. The United States will often take action against an American-owned (or even a foreign-owned) firm operating in a foreign country that engages in anticompetitive acts that could affect prices in the United States. Thus, collusion can be prohibited by American courts, even though it may be legal in the host country. The American courts, however, will not act in this extraterritorial manner if a court or legislature of the host country compelled rather than just allowed a certain type of behavior.[2] This being the most important example of extraterritorial reach of a country's laws, it can be seen that the United States has gone out of its way not to interfere with the laws of the host country.

Some arguments about the rights of the two governments are conditioned by incorrect views by the host country of the economic function of the foreign-owned firm. The host country may view the repatriation of profit by the foreign-owned firm as payments that the host country itself makes, and on this basis may conclude it has some rights in the operation and control of this firm. In this respect, the host country may view profit repatriations by foreign-owned firms as similar to payments on foreign loans, and, having the right to use these loans as it sees fit, may believe it has the same rights with regard to these firms. But there are really important differences in these two types of investments. In indirect foreign investment, the borrowing country takes on contractual responsibilities for payments—and since *it* has to make payments, it should indeed have control of the funds. But in direct foreign investment, there are no such contractual payments—except possibly to convert profits of firms into the investing country's currency. Consider also the question of risk. If the loans are unproductive, the borrow suffers the losses. But if the foreign-owned firm is unprofitable, the investing country suffers the consequences. By any test other than that of location—risk, obligation, payments—the foreign-owned firm cannot be considered the property of the host country. The host country appears to be little more than a landlord to the foreign-owned firm who, by the location of the firm, is able to sell its nontransportable productive factors. And the fact that the host country may have to provide foreign exchange for the repatriation of profits should not cloud the more important fact that the foreign-owned firm will often generate through its operations foreign exchange earnings for the host country.

There may also be some loss of control by the host-country government in guiding its economy. This comes about mainly because A/B firms typically will have many more options than B/B firms. Thus, A/B firms are as likely to respond to conditions in A as much, or even more so, than to conditions in B. A reduction in the interest rate, a change in taxes, a raising of labor standards, any of these is likely to elicit different responses from an A/B firm than from a B/B firm. But, in the end, the problems of economic control are no greater for the host country than for the investing country. As we have shown, once a country changes from being a closed economy to becoming, through foreign trade and investment, a part of an international economic system, it must pay the price of losing some autonomy and control. This holds as true for the investing country as for the host country. The basic question any country must always face is whether unregulated trade and investment are worth the loss of economic control that is bound to ensue.

A good case can be made that A/B firms may enhance the B government's control of its economy. An A/B firm, located as it is on B soil, and therefore ultimately subject to B law, can obviously be better controlled by the B government than an A/A firm; thus, on its face, direct foreign investment must expand the control available to the B government. In many ways, the B government can better control an A/B firm than a B/B firm. There are a number of reasons for this. First, the A/B firm is located in B supposedly because it can earn a higher rate of return there than in A. And to the extent that entry is restricted, the rate of return will remain higher in B than in A. Second, A/B firms are not as likely to have as strong a political base in B as have B/B firms. Third, any government today, if it chooses to do so, can take many actions that can be adverse to the interests of particular firms—and foreign-owned firms can be an inviting target. Thus, with A/B firms anxious to operate in B because of the higher profits in that country, yet heavily dependent upon the good-will of the B government, the B government has strong leverage with which to control, or at least guide, the policies of A/B firms.

Furthermore, the presence of A/B firms, or the threat that A firms will be permitted to locate in B, gives the B government some leverage over B/B firms. Modern governments often wish their firms to follow many policies with regard to prices, wages paid, output levels, investment, exports, and so forth. Yet these firms are often unwilling to abide by the government's wishes. What better threat could a government have, in negotiating with its own sometimes recalcitrant firms, than that it will allow into the country efficient foreign-owned firms to compete with them, especially when the foreign-owned firms would be amenable to the host government's desires?[3] The leverage that foreign-owned firms give a host government in dealing with its own firms can be a major reason so many governments welcome them.

The question of control is not always limited to that by governments. In many countries, a dominant role in the economic and political life is played by the leading business firms, or rather by those who control these firms. The entry of foreign-owned firms often poses a strong challenge to the business elite of the host country. As we have seen, A/B firms compete on many levels with B/B firms, and must necessarily undermine the power of the latter group. In fact, as Vernon has discussed, much opposition to the entry of foreign-owned firms in a country comes from that country's business elite, who quite correctly see their influence diluted and eroded.[4]

A few remarks are necessary on the possibility of political control being exercised by one government, through its firms located abroad, on the host-country government. A widely publicized example of this was the use by the United States government of American firms in Chile to try to overthrow the Marxist Allende government. There is little question that this case illustrates that a foreign-owned company can be a threat to a host-country government. But it should be recognized that expropriations of the American firms were already being undertaken, so that these firms had little to lose by allowing themselves to serve as a vehicle of the United States government. If the possibility of expropriation was still at issue, the American firms in Chile may well not have cooperated with the American government. One can even suggest that, *before* Chile's decision to expropriate, the American firms, out of fear of the possibility of expropriation as a retaliatory action, may have tried to inhibit American political action toward Chile.

7. The Issue of Exploitation of Labor

When A is an industrial country and B is a less-developed country, an A firm located in B is almost always able to pay a much lower wage to B workers than it would pay to A workers. Although the A/B firms often pay higher wages to B workers than do B/B firms, there are those who will compare only the wages paid in B with those paid in A by the A firms, and cry "exploitation!" This is to be expected from communist groups or their sympathizers in both the investing and host countries: after all, as Lenin put it, the business of revolutionaries is to make revolutions, and if this is their aim, economic arguments will be to no avail. But there are also many well-meaning people in the investing country as well as in the host country who also take up the chant of exploitation, and it is possible to reach them with well-reasoned economic arguments. We now ask whether this charge of exploitation has any basis.

As we have shown, many A/B firms locate in B primarily to purchase B labor. To the extent that A firms locate in B, this must improve conditions for B labor. The demand for B labor by A/B firms must either increase the wage rate or reduce unemployment in B. Firms are on no account to be considered benevolent organizations, but it is a strong economic principle that whenever and wherever a firm invests and produces, this by itself must increase real wage rates, and, not incidentally, reduce the general level of profit rates. This was long ago recognized by Adam Smith in *The Wealth of Nations*, who, in pleading for greater savings and investment, saw the beneficiaries as the working classes. Firms can never hurt the interests of workers by investing and producing, but only by *not* investing and producing. There would be a much more valid argument that A firms were aiding in the exploitation of B workers if they did *not* locate in B, or if they restricted their investments in B. Thus, although A/B firms may take advantage of low wages in B, they do not create those low wages; these firms, by their productive activities, can only improve these wages.

The party that should be blamed for the low wages in B is the B government, or, more broadly, B society. It is surely the responsibility of the B government, rather than of the A firms or A government, to bring about conditions under which B workers receive higher wages. To argue otherwise is to suggest that a "noblesse oblige" attitude is required by A in its dealings with B. This would imply that the Bs are not sovereign equals with the As, and puts the Bs in a relation as children or beggars to A, which is certainly no more a healthy basis for international than for interpersonal relations. If a nation is to be truly sovereign and independent, it, and only it, is responsible for the welfare of its citizens, and those who suggest otherwise are not helping that nation but casting it in a role of dependency.

Along these lines, we may comment upon the guest worker programs currently in operation in Europe. A Yugoslav, for example, working in Sweden will generally obtain only a menial, less well-paying job than those held by Swedes. This has led many, including Swedes, to try to obtain better positions and conditions for such workers—and one must applaud the basic goodwill of these individuals.[5] But which country is to be blamed for the plight of the Yugoslav working in Sweden: Sweden, which offered the Yugoslav a better job in Sweden than he could obtain in Yugoslavia; or Yugoslavia, which failed to provide economic opportunities for its workers equal to those in Sweden?

8. Summary

There is little doubt that direct foreign investment will almost always be of economic benefit (as defined here) to the host country—in fact, under most conditions, this country is much more likely to benefit than the investing country. This is immediately apparent once the principles of transnational accounting are grasped. The host country is in no sense "paying" profits to the foreign-owned firm; rather, the foreign-owned firm provides a vehicle whereby the host country can export the services of its labor force and other nontransportable services. To the extent that some portion of the host country's labor force is unemployed, and this of course is quite common, any sales of unemployed labor by the host country to the foreign-owned firm will generate both income and foreign exchange for the host country that may not be offset at all by decreases in output and income generated by the firms of the host country.

But one can suspect that governments of host countries are well aware of the economic benefits that accrue to them because of direct foreign investment on their soil. This is evidenced by their repeated willingness to offer special concessions to foreign-owned firms to induce them to locate in their countries. And, in 1976, when Chrysler in England incurred losses and contemplated closing its plant in that country, it is instructive to note that it was the British rather than the American government that offered financial aid to Chrysler in order to keep the plant in operation.

C. THE INVESTING COUNTRY

Using real national income as our welfare criterion, we found that direct foreign investment is almost certain to benefit the host country. But when we turn to the welfare of A, the investing country, we will find that such investment is often, but not always, adverse to its real national income.

1. Impact on A's Real National Income: Alternative Investments
   Located in A and B

Consider the alternatives of an A firm locating an identical production facility in A or in B, with management and technology the same in both facilities. The question for A's welfare is: which of these locations will generate the higher income for country A, taken as a group of nationals? If the A/A facility uses only A productive factors, its output generates income only for the As. But the A/B facility, which purchases B inputs and pays taxes to the B government, generates income for both countries. There seems to be, then, a strong prima facie case that the A/A facility will increase A's real national income to the greater extent. But there may be conditions under which the A/B plant is, from A's viewpoint, preferable, and it is our purpose to identify these conditions.

One consideration is that, although the A/A facility may generate income only for As, its use of A productive factors may result in the reduction of output by other A/A firms. These output reductions will reduce A's real national income by their value, so that we should subtract them from the value of output of the A/A facility under consideration to obtain that facility's *net* contribution to A's real national income. Allowing P^a and Q^a to represent the price and output level of that plant, its net contribution to A's income will be as follows:

$$P^aQ^a \text{ less: the value of output reductions} \\ \text{by other A/A firms} \qquad (11.1)$$

The A/B facility's contribution to A income will be its value of output minus all payments it makes to Bs. With $(1/e)P^b$ the output price of this facility in terms of A currency, and Q^b its output level, the net income generated by this facility for A will be:

$$(1/e)P^bQ^b \text{ less: all payments to Bs} \qquad (11.2)$$

For the B location to be preferable, the result of equation 11.2 will have to exceed that of equation 11.1. If $Q^b = Q^a$, and if $(1/e)P^b = P^a$, and if there is little or no reduction in output by other A/A firms, clearly the A/A facility will always generate the higher income for A. We therefore have to ask if there are circumstances under which these conditions may not hold.

Consider first the possibility that $Q^b > Q^a$. This possibility is most likely to occur in the production of raw materials. Since nature plays such an important role in raw material production, a more benign nature in B may lead to much higher output levels in B than in A for any level of investment. For other kinds of activities, such as manufacturing, it is much less likely that Q^b will exceed Q^a. Yet if B labor is more highly motivated than A labor, if the B wage rate is so much lower than the A wage rate that the A/B facility is utilized more intensively, or if the B government enacts fewer restrictions, it is still possible that Q^b could exceed Q^a.

Next, considering price, we ask if $(1/e)P^b$ can exceed P^a. If the output is transportable over national boundaries, and if there is free trade with negligible transport costs, then $(1/e)P^b$ should equal P^a. There are then only two conditions under which $(1/e)P^b$ can exceed P^a. One is—in the case of transportable products—if the B market is protected by import barriers or high transport costs. The other is when the outputs are nontransportable—such as construction services.

Consider next the possibility that the A/A facility may reduce the output of other A/A firms. If there is full employment in A, with a fixed labor force and well-functioning markets, the likelihood of this possibility should be considered high. Since traditional trade theory assumes these conditions, we have an explanation of why many economists have supported direct foreign investment. But if there is unemployment in A, or even if the A labor force expands in response to higher wage rates, the reductions in output by other firms will be small, if they occur at all. In fact, the A/A facility, through its generation of new income and expenditures, may, through the Keynesian multiplier, lead to *increases* in output by other A/A firms.

The value of the payments of the A/B facility to Bs can also be important. The lower the wage rates in B, the lower the taxes, the smaller the amount of purchases by the A/B facility from Bs, the more likely it is that the A/B facility will generate the higher income.

We can now summarize those conditions in which the B location may be preferable to the A location for A as a whole. One is a higher output level in B, which will generally occur most assuredly in raw material production. A second is when the A/B firm sells its output in B at a higher price than the A firms can sell in A, or to B from an A location. For this condition there must be trade barriers in the case of transportable products, or the production of a nontransportable service. Third, there should be full employment in A. Fourth, the payments to Bs should be small. It is not necessary that all these conditions exist for A to benefit from the B location.[6]

Of course, in the absence of these conditions, the A/A facility will generate higher income for A than will the A/B facility. By far the most adverse set of conditions for A's real national income is when the activity is in manufacturing; when there are no trade barriers; when there is substantial unemployment in A; when the payments to B, including taxes, are large.

There are also secondary impacts to be considered, which follow in large measure our discussion in the last chapter of the effect of direct foreign investment on A's capital formation. Direct foreign investment in raw material was shown to be beneficial to A's capital formation, the reverse being true for similar investment in manufacturing. The secondary impacts of direct foreign investment on A's real national income could be seen to reinforce the primary impacts.

Two questions can be raised concerning these assessments. The first is whether A can benefit, in terms of its real national income, if the cost of production of an A/B plant is lower than that of an A/A plant and if this reduces the prices of goods in A produced by the A/B plant. I do not think this would necessarily benefit A as a whole, since a nation's real national income is completely determined by the contribution of its productive factors to current production. Thus the only way the lower prices of the A/B plant can enlarge A's real national income is if they somehow raise either the volume and/or the value of the efforts of A's productive factors. However, this is not to say that some As could not benefit from these lower prices—but these benefits come about because of a redistribution rather than an increase of real income.

The other question is whether the location of the A firm in B rather than in A, in order to remain competitive, may not increase A's real national income above what it may otherwise have been. This rather complicated question will be considered in a later section.

2. Investment in B Compared to the Alternative of No Investment

In the preceding section, we assumed that any A plant located in B would otherwise have been located in A. But this may not always be a reasonable assumption. Essentially it rests on the classical model of Hufbauer and Adler, in which the capital formation of a country in any period is taken as fixed and essentially insensitive to interest rates. But we have chosen to reject this view, arguing instead that the level of capital formation is a variable, which depends upon the relation between profit rates and interest rates.

Can we specify the conditions under which an A investment in B would not have been made in A? The answer is yes. Let us say that the rate of capital formation in A is in long-run equilibrium. By this we mean that the differential between the average profit rate and the interest rate is just sufficient to compensate for the risks of entrepreneurship. Under these conditions A firms will increase their rate of capital formation only if plants can be located where the profit rate will be higher than in A. Thus, it is perfectly conceivable that if the A firms somehow cannot invest in B, these investments will not be made in A. Thus, the alternative to an A/B plant may be no additional capital formation.

When these conditions prevail, it is very likely that the A/B plant will have a favorable effect on A's real national income. If the profit rate of the A/B plant is sufficiently higher than the interest rate to the A firm, then the social benefits (the profits) to A must be greater than the social costs of the investment, which would be reflected in the interest rate. Thus, A would gain.

This constitutes one of the strongest arguments for direct foreign investment from A's viewpoint. But it must be stressed that a number of conditions must be fulfilled for this argument to be valid. First, the long-run equilibrium between profit rates and interest rates must exist, which is not always easy to demonstrate. Second, the A/B investment, to be beneficial to A, must yield a higher profit rate than *any* other investment that could have been made in A.

This last point requires some extended discussion. Large corporations, it is well known, do not generally pay out all of their profits in dividends, but instead retain a portion to use in their own lines of effort. Thus, some portion of the funds potentially available to finance capital formation are not available to the capital market to be allocated to firms and sectors on the basis of profits. As a result, a firm making a 10 percent rate of return, can, through control of its retained earnings, use these funds in its own business when other firms might be making a return of say 20 percent on new investments. This, clearly, is a misallocation of capital funds, which has been pointed out by many economists. Returning to our problem, this A firm may be willing to increase its rate of capital formation only if it can obtain a higher rate of return by locating in B. Thus, *for this firm,* the alternative to the investment in B may be no investment in A. But if the funds were available to the whole A economy through the A capital market, which requires that there be no retained earnings by corporations, there could be profitable alternative investments in A to the investment the firm made in B. Under these conditions, A would not benefit from that firm's investment in B as much as if the investments had been made by some firm in A. Thus, for the argument to be valid that investment by an A firm in B would not otherwise have been made in A, it must be shown that not only would a specific A firm not have made that investment in A, but that *no* A firm would have made an investment in A of that same amount.[7]

3. Direct Foreign Investment as a Necessity to Remain Competitive

We now turn to an analysis of one of the strongest arguments made for direct foreign investment from the investing country's viewpoint: the necessity to locate in low-wage countries in order to remain competitive in terms of production costs with other countries who may do so.[8] To investigate this argument, let us assume there is a third country, C, which, like A, is industrialized, has high wages, cheap capital, and superior technology and management. If C firms now locate in B to hire the cheaper B labor while A firms do not, it would seem that C firms can obtain an absolute cost advantage over A firms—and that the inability of the latter to compete will have unfortunate consequences for country A. Is it then in A's interest that its firms also locate in B to remain competitive with C/B firms even though by so doing the A/B plants would generate less income for As than would the alternative A/A plants?

Although on its face the argument that A firms have to locate in B may appear compelling, it does not stand up to careful analysis. To see why, it is only necessary to apply Ricardo's doctrine of comparative costs. In Ricardo's famous example, it will be recalled that Portugal, because of an assumed technological superiority, produced both cloth and wine more cheaply than did England. When trade was initially introduced, Portugal exported both wine and cloth to England. However, gold flowed from England to Portugal, internal prices rose in Portugal and fell in England—and at some point England was able to export cloth, the product in which it had a *comparative* advantage.

Ricardo's argument may have to be recast for modern times. In

Ricardo's model neither Portugal nor England had control of its money supply, and exchange rates, because currencies were usually tied to gold, were assumed to be fixed. But now the reverse conditions prevail: countries can control their money supplies, and exchange rates can change. Given these new conditions, the money-flow/internal-price mechanism cannot be depended upon to reduce Portugal's monetary cost advantage such that two-way trade can take place. But changes in exchange rates can also bring about two-way trade and the operation of the law of comparative advantage. Using Ricardo's example, the initial exports of both cloth and wine from Portugal to England would result in a devaluation of England's currency relative to Portugal's currency—and this should have brought about two-way trade with each country specializing in producing the product in which it had a comparative advantage.

Let us return now to country C locating in B to hire cheaper labor, thus giving C an absolute cost advantage in all products relative to A. We can think of country C as "Portugal" and country A as "England," and use Ricardo's examples of wine and cloth. The problem is really no different from the one Ricardo dealt with. Portugal again has an absolute cost advantage in both products, but now because it hires low-wage B labor rather than because of technological superiority. At first, there will again be one-way trade, with Portugal exporting both products to England. But, with exchange rate changes the trade adjustment mechanism, England's currency will devalue to the point England is able to export the product in which it has a comparative advantage. Thus, through the magic of changes in the exchange rate, the absolute cost advantage in both products accorded Portugal by its hiring of low-wage B workers disappears. Not only will there be balanced two-way trade, but, in terms of income, England will do much better than Portugal. All of England's output generates income only for Englishmen, while the income generated by Portugal's output must be shared with Bs.

There are also special interests vis-à-vis the general interests to be considered in this analysis. Assume at first that Portugal and England produce both wine and cloth at the same cost so that there is no trade. Now let us say that only Portuguese wine producers locate in B to reduce their costs—so that initially Portugal exports only wine to England while England exports nothing to Portugal. England's currency should then depreciate in value, and England will export cloth. It is possible now to see the conflict of interest between the English wine and cloth producers. If English wine producers do not also locate in B, they will fare poorly—but the English cloth producers will do well. If the English wine producers do locate in B, then they will be able to maintain their position, but the position of the English cloth producers will not improve.

From the viewpoint of national income, is England better off if its wine producers locate in B, or if they are not allowed to do so? If they are allowed to do so, England's wine production will be maintained—but some of the income generated by this production will go to the Bs. If they are not allowed to do so, then England's cloth production will be expanded—which generates income only for Englishmen. Thus the English wine producers who argue that they should be allowed to locate in B to remain competitive are really not advancing England's real national income, but are only a special interest group trying to deal with foreign competition.

The lesson of this analysis is clear with regard to the necessity to locate abroad in order to remain competitive. This is not necessary at all to the potential investing country, A, so long as its currency is permitted to devalue. It is, however, a valid argument under a regime of fixed exchange rates. But basically the argument advances the interests of those special producers having to compete with the C/B firms rather than the interests of the whole of A.

4. Loss of Control

It is obvious that with direct foreign investment the A government loses control over A firms and, as a result, over its own economy. When its firms can threaten to locate in B rather than in A, the power of the A government to enact legislation adverse to the interests of A firms must necessarily be diminished.

5. Foreign Exchange Earnings

We have demonstrated that direct foreign investment by A in B need not lead to foreign exchange earnings for A—in fact, A's foreign exchange position can deteriorate as a result. This deterioration is especially likely if the investment is in manufacturing and the A firms are motivated to locate in B to hire B labor rather than to sell to the B market. Largely because of liberalized trade, this type of direct foreign investment appears to have become increasingly important in recent years. The American devaluation in 1971 is instructive. After some sixty years of trade surpluses, and many, many billions of dollars of direct foreign investment by American firms—in which the latter supposedly earned foreign exchange for the United States—it is noteworthy that the dollar became weaker. Furthermore, the dollar never regained its status even though the inflation rate was higher in many other countries during the seventies. An important reason for the weakness of the dollar is surely that much American direct foreign investment did not earn foreign exchange—but rather lost foreign exchange for the United Stataes. This is completely consistent with our analysis that direct foreign investment will lead to a drain on the investing country's foreign exchange holdings when such investment is mainly in response to lower wage rates in other countries. And, quite consistently, direct foreign investment by England, which is second only to the United States in that area, has not seemed to help England's foreign exchange position, and has probably made this position worse.

6. Labor Problems

When A firms locate in B to reduce production costs in manufacturing—and this is surely a major reason for much of direct foreign investment—great problems are created for the A labor force. Without direct foreign investment or its alternative, the import of B workers into A, A labor and B labor are not in direct competition with each other, because A firms can only employ A labor and B firms can only employ B labor. These two labor forces do compete indirectly, through the sales of goods, but differences in the prices and qualities of other inputs, such as management, capital, and technology, limit the nature of the competition. Because of any superiorities of the inputs A firms may be able to provide relative to B firms, wage rates of the A labor force could remain above those of the B labor force. In effect, the superiority of A inputs that are complementary to A labor can compensate for the competitive disadvantage of A's higher wages. Those who have advocated free trade policies have for many years stressed the point that high wages are not a deterrent to a nation's competitiveness in trade *if* the other inputs (mainly capital) are cheaper and/or superior.

When direct foreign investment becomes a possibility, especially in manufacturing, and A firms have the option of buying either A labor or B labor, these two labor forces are put into direct competition with each other. Furthermore, since the B labor employed by A firms is able to enjoy the same superior technology, management, and capital as A labor, the latter group loses *all* competitive advantage vis-à-vis B labor. (This can be contrasted with indirect foreign investment of A to B, in which A labor only loses its advantage of cheaper capital.) If wage rates in the two countries are not equalized, A labor simply will not be able to compete with B labor. This must mean not only a reduction in territorially defined exports from A, but a loss of jobs and income for A, in favor of B.

In the initial phases of direct foreign investment, the lower-skilled industrial workers of A will be most harmed by the competition from B workers. But in the longer run, there is no reason the more highly skilled A workers—engineers, marketing and financial experts, accountants, middle management—will not also be thrown into competition with their B competitors. This is not mere speculation. Anybody familiar with American multinational corporations can attest to the fact that these firms have gradually replaced such highly skilled American workers with foreign workers.[9] To some extent, these labor policies have been brought about by pressures from the host-country governments. But one should not lose sight of the fact that these pressures also reflect the interests of those firms in hiring cheaper non-American labor.

Not all A labor will suffer equally by direct foreign investment.

At first it will be mainly those workers in trades or sectors that have to compete with B labor and the output of A/B firms. Other types of A labor—those engaged in personal services, governmental activities, and so forth—may even be beneficiaries of direct foreign investment, since the A/B firms might provide them with goods at lower prices than can the A/A firms. But given sufficient time, the A labor force will gradually transform itself away from jobs that place workers in competition with B workers and toward those jobs that do not directly compete with B workers. Of course this transformation will eventually adversely affect that portion of the A labor force that may initially have benefited from direct foreign investment.

Competition from the B labor force can have a number of consequences for the A labor force—all adverse. If the A labor market functions well, there will be a reduction in A wage rates. However, if wage rates are not allowed to fall in A, then we should expect high levels of unemployment. If we accept the inevitability of direct foreign investment, A labor in the long run will probably be better off with declining wage rates (and therefore higher capital formation in A) rather than unemployment. But wages and employment are not all that will be affected. In addition, economic pressures will build up to force a decline in a host of labor standards in A—safety, working conditions, and so forth. If direct foreign investment does not improve the wages of workers in the host country, the logical and bleak outcome of such investment must be that wage rates and labor standards in the wealthier countries must sink to those in the poorer countries. (It would seem that wage rates in the host country should rise because of direct foreign investment—but of course these expectations could be completely frustrated by rapid population increases.) If unions and the government in the investing country are able to stop wages from falling and labor standards from deteriorating, the result will then be unemployment (or "public service" jobs) and losses in productivity. Economic theory permits no other conclusions so long as A labor is shorn of its competitive advantages.

Direct foreign investment by A firms, particularly in manufacturing, raises important questions of equity and policy. The A labor force may have followed the advice of generations of economists to advance its welfare by limiting population increases, which now is in the interests of everybody. Yet if this advice were not followed in other countries, the conditions of labor in overcrowded high-population-growth countries would, through direct foreign investment, undermine the conditions of labor in the low-population-growth countries. Perhaps more basic is the responsibility of A capital. In a country such as the United States, there are many laws and policies designed to protect private capital and to nurture and encourage its growth. What is the economic philosophy underlying these favorable attitudes toward private capital accumulation? In the history of economic doctrine there is one overriding argument for this encouragement of private capital—that its growth will enhance the productivity and incomes of that country's workers. But when this capital is employed abroad rather than at home, a reexamination of the economic philosophy whereby the nurturing of private capital accumulation is always in the broad national interest is invited. Bearing in mind that some types of direct foreign investment can be in the national interest, the responsibility of the A government toward those A firms located abroad that do not advance this interest becomes questionable.

Yet great care must be exercised in any restrictions on foreign investment. Any government can enact confiscatory policies toward private capital, and direct foreign investment can provide a useful deterrent to such policies. And labor unions can become so unreasonable in their demands that the unorganized portion of a nation's labor force may be well served by the restraints that foreign investment may bring about on organized labor. Nevertheless, other methods for restraining the power of governments and labor unions could be devised that would be preferable.

American labor suffers in another way from direct foreign investment. The foreign exchange problems and the subsequent 1971 devaluation have led to greater American food exports, one of the few activities in which the United States has been able to maintain a competitive advantage. But, although Americans have been fortunate that their agriculture has been so productive, those higher exports have also led to higher food prices. Thus, the American industrial worker (and many other Americans) is squeezed not only by lower wages, or unemployment, but by higher food prices as well.

Of all types of direct foreign investment in manufacturing, that in which firms from the free-market countries locate in totalitarian countries raises questions beyond those of economic calculation. Such types of foreign investment essentially put free labor into competition with labor unable either to withhold their services or to bargain over the wage rate, and are most likely to lead to a weakening of democratic values.

7. The Transformation of the Economy of the Investing Country

Let us assume that most of A's direct foreign investment is in manufacturing in response to lower wage rates rather than to selling to protected markets. Let us also assume that A's wage rates are downward inflexible. What should happen to the A economy? The United States can be referred to, since it has been the most important country in this type of direct foreign investment. Under these conditions, American firms located in the United States would obviously have difficulties in competing in manufactures. These firms, it might be argued, might be able to compensate for their higher wage rates with superior technology or management. But since technology and management accompany American firms locating abroad, these compensations cannot be regarded as very dependable. Today, in fact, the main types of manufactured goods that the United States can export are limited to "sensitive" industries—such as aircraft, weapons, atomic energy production facilities—in which American government policy inhibits location in other countries. To some extent, however, the ability of the United States to export a wider range of manufactured goods from American locations was restored in the late 1970s because of sharp declines in the value of the dollar.

One should also expect declines in labor productivity and growth of the gross national product in the investing countries. That this has been the postwar experience of the United States and Great

Britain compared to other industrialized countries is quite clear.[10] That the declines in economic growth have not been greater can be attributed largely to a wide variety of tax credits and subsidies to firms that are tied to their investment levels. Although these kinds of aids are not ostensibly to discourage foreign investment, one can suggest that it is mainly the overseas investments and the ensuing declines in domestic capital formation that made these measures appear necessary.

The portion of the labor force in manufacturing industries should also diminish. The oft-noted fact that the United States is becoming a "service" economy is precisely what we should expect when its direct foreign investment is so heavily in manufacturing. The competition to the American labor force from foreign investment in manufacturing also explains why many Americans are eager to enter personal service work and public service, since these are precisely those activities most immune to competition from lower-wage foreign workers.

8. Political Problems

When production assets owned by the investing country are located in foreign countries, the uses of these assets are ultimately subject to the laws and will of the host countries. There are many actions that these host countries can take that are detrimental to the interests of the investing firms and ultimately to the investing countries. Should political differences arise between the investing and the host country, the latter can often exert leverage on the former by threatening expropriation, or at the least discriminatory treatment, against these firms. Put quite bluntly, these firms are nothing less than political hostages. This must necessarily add a new dimension to international political relations.

The owners of firms located abroad may sometimes become lobbyists for the host country in its political dealings with the investing country. They become lobbyists, of course, because the welfare of their operations in the host country often so heavily depends upon the goodwill of the host-country government. These lobbying operations, together with the "hostage" element, have on occasion resulted in investing countries supporting unpopular political regimes in host countries, and sometimes acting counter to their own long-term political interests.

The investing country also can have political problems because its firms overseas are such convenient scapegoats. When economic conditions deteriorate in a host country, the government of that country is more apt to blame the large foreign-owned corporation than itself for its problems.

9. A Summary

We argued that some types of direct foreign investment may be in the investing country's interest: investments in raw material production; investments in manufacturing when the output is sold in the protected market of the host country; investments that lead to a nontransportable output sold to the host country. Direct foreign investment can also be desirable if there is full employment in the investing country, and if the investments would not otherwise have been made. Locating abroad to remain competitive, although often given as an argument for direct foreign investment, was shown to be of less benefit than a devaluation of the investing country's currency.

By far the most adverse kind of direct foreign investment is in manufacturing in response to lower-wage labor—particularly when there is unemployment in the investing country, and particularly when, because of high population growth rates, the host country wage rates will not rise. Thus, although there are advantageous types of direct foreign investment and conditions under which such investment is in the investing country's interest, as a general proposition one cannot justify completely uncontrolled direct foreign investment —or its encouragement—as being in the economic interests of the investing country. I must remind the reader that this conclusion is based on purely nationalistic and economic criteria—and of course many will take issue with the selection of these criteria.

D. CAN THERE BE COMPARATIVE ADVANTAGE IN DIRECT FOREIGN INVESTMENT?

I will now turn to a question that I have not seen explored elsewhere: is there some sort of comparative advantage principle in the movement of direct foreign investment that is analogous to that believed to operate in trade? If there is, it should lead to some sort of specialization that will benefit both countries in our two-country model. I will limit myself mainly to manufacturing, and rely heavily upon Ricardo.

Before beginning the analysis, let us first reexamine the law of comparative advantage. As this term is generally used, it means that free trade—say between two countries in two products—will result in two-way trade, with each country specializing in the production of one product. (The two-way trade, however, may require some sort of trade imbalance adjustment mechanism.) The normative aspect of comparative advantage is that this specialization will enhance the average labor productivity, and hence the incomes, of *both* countries. If direct foreign investment is to lead to similarly desirable results, then this type of foreign investment should also be two-way—that is, each country must invest in the other. This necessity follows from the undeniable principle that if investment only flowed from one country to the other, labor productivity would increase only in that country receiving the investments. Thus, taking the law of comparative advantage to lead to product specialization in each country and an enhancement of labor productivity in both, we can pursue our original question by inquiring into the conditions necessary for a two-way flow of direct foreign investment.

There is, however, another sense in which there can be comparative advantage and specialization. As the term is generally used, comparative advantage refers to products. But it can also apply to the specialization of economic functions. Thus, individuals of different nationality may combine their efforts in producing goods, with each national group specializing in a different aspect of the productive effort. I will consider this possibility after first viewing specialization in its more usual sense, in which each territorially defined nation specializes in the production of some product.

Let us start with Ricardo and his England/Portugal cloth/wine example. Portugal is taken to be more efficient than England in the production of both products, as measured by the amount of labor needed to produce a unit of output, but comparatively more efficient in wine. Given these conditions, two-way trade takes place only after gold flows from England to Portugal (affecting internal money prices), and England specializes in cloth and Portugal in wine.

Ricardo really is not explicit about *why* Portuguese labor is more productive than English labor. Three reasons can be suggested. First, Portugal may have more productive capital per unit of labor. Second, Portuguese entrepreneurs may have knowledge superior to that of their English counterparts. Third, Portuguese labor may be more skilled, or better motivated, than English labor.

Because of the superiority of Portuguese productivity, Ricardo suggests that English businessmen might be expected to prefer to locate and produce in Portugal. If we assume that trade is taking place, which of these three explanations of the superiority of Portuguese productivity is consistent with direct foreign investment by England in Portugal? The first reason—that there is more capital per worker in Portugal—suggests that profit rates are lower, and wages are higher, in Portugal. Clearly, if this is the source of superior productivity, we should expect Portuguese investment in England rather than English businessmen locating in Portugal. The second explanation—that Portuguese entrepreneurs have superior knowledge—should also not lead to direct foreign investment by England in Portugal. English entrepreneurs will still be at a disadvantage if located in Portugal, unless they can acquire the same knowledge only by locating in Portugal. If this knowledge acquisition were a possibility, we might expect the English businessmen to return to England after they acquire this knowledge. If the knowledge differentials are maintained, one should in fact expect direct foreign investment only from Portugal to England. The third explanation of superior productivity in Portgual—that Portuguese workers are better skilled—can be attributed to education, training, work values, etc. Only with this explanation of superior Portuguese productivity might one expect English investment in Portugal. We can generalize: English direct foreign investment in Portugal will occur only if Portugal has some native nontransferable resource that is superior to that of England.

No matter which explanation of Portuguese superiority is accepted, there should not be two-way direct foreign investment. If Portuguese superiority is due either to higher capital/labor ratios or to entrepreneurial knowledge, investment should be one-way, from Portugal to England. If Portuguese superiority is attributable to worker skills, there should be one-way investment from England to Portugal. But one-way direct foreign investment is not comparative advantage: the average labor productivity rises only for the country receiving the direct foreign investment. If there is to be comparative advantage in direct foreign investment, one should require two-way investment, with investment moving from England to Portugal in wine production, and Portuguese investment to England in cloth. What conditions are necessary for this to occur?

The determination of these conditions requires a fairly complex argument. I hope to show that there are three necessary conditions for investment by English businessmen in Portugal and investment by Portuguese businessmen in England to occur simultaneously. (1) Some mechanism must exist such that monetary labor costs per unit of each product differ between the two countries; (2) there must be intersectoral immobility of capital in both countries; (3) the source of a country's relative labor productivity advantage must lie in the skills of labor itself, as opposed to entrepreneurial skills or higher capital/labor ratios.

Let us first determine why monetary labor costs per unit of output can differ between the two countries. Assume first, as did Ricardo, that Portuguese labor is absolutely more productive than English labor in both wine and cloth, but comparatively more productive in wine. Now we introduce trade. At first Portugal exports both products to England. Then, for two-way trade to occur, one of the following adjustment mechanisms must take place: gold flows from England to Portugal, or the value of the pound drops relative to that of the cruzero. As a result, monetary wage rates rise for Portuguese labor and fall for English labor. For two-way trade to occur, it will be necessary for these monetary wage rates to change to the degree that monetary labor costs per unit of wine are lower in Portugal while monetary labor costs per unit of cloth are lower in England. It should be noted that both trade and an adjustment mechanism must occur for these differences in monetary labor costs per unit of output to come about.

It would seem now that English wine producers have incentives to locate in Portugal, and Portuguese cloth producers have similar incentives to locate in England. But this may not occur, because trade will raise profits in cloth in England above that in wine, the reverse occurring in Portugal. Thus, English wine producers, rather than locating in Portugal, may instead enter the cloth business in England, while Portuguese cloth producers may enter the wine business in Portugal rather than locate cloth production in England. But such intersectoral movements of capital in each country will occur only if there are no substantial impediments to intersectoral movements of capital. If such impediments exist, one should then expect British wine producers to locate in Portugal and Portuguese cloth producers to locate in England.

But these two conditions—differences in monetary labor costs per unit of output, and intersectoral capital immobilities—although necessary to a two-way movement of foreign investment, may not be sufficient. If the original productive superiority of Portuguese labor were due to superior Portuguese entrepreneurs, one should expect Portuguese cloth producers to locate in England, but not English wine producers to locate in Portugal, where they would still be at a competitive disadvantage. The second possible explanation of superior Portuguese labor productivity, that of more capital per unit of labor, implies that the cost of capital is lower to Portuguese than to English businessmen. If this were the productivity differential source, then again English wine producers would be uncompetitive even though located in Portugal, unless such a location enables them to obtain capital on the same terms as their Portuguese competitors. But if the labor productivity differential is attributable to superior skills of Portuguese labor—or more broadly to any productive factor indigenous to Portugal—Portuguese wine producers would have no competitive advantage over British wine producers in Portugal. With this the source of productivity differentials, and assuming that trade and intersectoral capital immobilities exist, we should now expect English wine producers to locate in Portugal and Portuguese cloth producers to locate in England.

With these three conditions, there is not only two-way direct foreign investment but also a genuine law of comparative advantage at work. Cloth production by both English and Portuguese businessmen will take place in England because, compared to Portuguese workers, British *workers* have a comparative advantage in the production of cloth. And both Portuguese and British wine producers will locate in Portugal because the comparative advantage of that country's workers is in the production of wine.

A few words on the Heckscher-Ohlin model may be of interest. This model assumes complete homogeneity of capital and labor in both countries, and the same technology, so that comparative advantage is completely attributable to the capital/labor ratio in products and relative factor scarcity. Under these conditions, there clearly cannot be two-way direct foreign investment: investment should flow only from the relatively capital-abundant country to the relatively capital-scarce country. One would have to drop the assumptions of perfect intersectoral factor mobility in each country and homogeneous labor in both countries for there to be any possibility of two-way direct foreign investment.

Consider next the possibility of an "economic functional" view of comparative advantage. Let us assume that Englishmen, compared to

Portuguese, are generally superior as entrepreneurs, managers, and in technology. Now we should expect either (or possibly both) English direct foreign investment (including managers) to move to Portugal or (and) Portuguese labor to move to England—the latter less likely. There need not be any specialization by each country in products, but rather the specialization would be in economic function. Incomes of English entrepreneurs (etc.) should rise, while that of English workers should fall—and it is at least possible that the net effect would be beneficial to England as a whole. Much would depend on whether English workers could transform themselves into managers and engineers, which obviously would depend heavily upon the educational system and on opportunities for social and economic mobility. The reverse results would of course be obtained for Portugal. One need hardly point out that, although both countries could gain economically, economic class divisions would be sharpened by the association of economic class with nationality. Economic functional specialization surely typified many types of colonialism.

E. POLICIES AND ISSUES

Both the investing country and the host country can adopt a wide range of policies to either encourage or discourage direct foreign investment and to influence the pattern of that investment. The policy instruments available have been widely written about, so that we need consider this subject but briefly here.[11]

The host country can do many things to encourage the inflow of direct foreign investment. Among the policies that can be applied are the following: tariffs to protect internal markets from foreign competition; subsidies and tax benefits; promises of fair, nondiscriminatory treatment; special rights granted the firms to import; promises to enable the foreign-owned firm to convert its profits into the foreign exchange of the investing country for repatriation; a devaluation of the host country's currency. The nonexistence of such policies, of course, would tend to discourage direct foreign investment.

The host country may encourage direct foreign investment but at the same time be selective about which types of investment will be allowed. India, for example, while actively soliciting direct foreign investment, at the same time only issues licenses to foreign firms to operate in India after an Indian screening committee carefully reviews the applications for these licenses.

Many host countries also have policies designed to help them benefit most greatly from direct foreign investment. Thus, in order that foreign-owned firms should not drain the host country's foreign exchange, some host countries specify that these firms must export some percentage of their outputs or place restrictions on their imports.[12] Often the host country can increase its split of the income generated by the output of the foreign-owned firms by insisting that these firms increase their purchases of host-country inputs—this is an example of the so-called "domestic-content" laws. The host country also often insists that foreign-owned firms sell common stock to host-country citizens, and hire and train them.

The policies available to the investing country have not been as developed or widely discussed as those available to the host country. There are a number of reasons for this. First, much of the investing has been made by firms from the free market countries, in which control of firms tends to be minimal. Many of the host countries, on the other hand, have been those who exercise considerable control over their economies. Second, the host country is in a better position to exercise control, since the firms will operate on its soil. It would be a rash firm indeed that would invest in a country with a hostile government. Thus, the host country is in a good position to reduce or prohibit direct foreign investment, if it wishes to do so.

The investing country can do much to encourage direct foreign investment—taxes, insurance, treaties, and so forth—but there does not seem to be as much that can be done to prohibit it. Direct foreign investment involves an outflow of money, technology, management—all items that do not have to physically move across boundaries. These outflows could be prohibited, if at all, only by a country willing to exercise almost totalitarian control. Thus, investing countries face much greater problems in the discouragement rather than the encouragement of direct foreign investment. Perhaps the major weapon the investing country has in the discouragement of direct foreign investment is to withhold any type of political support of firms that locate abroad.

F. DIRECT FOREIGN INVESTMENT AND AMERICAN FOREIGN POLICY

Since the Second World War, American foreign policy has made use of direct foreign investment to advance its foreign political goals. There are many instances in which an American secretary of state, in an effort to reward a country acting consistently with American policies, has promised to encourage investment in that country. Theoretically, such investment, by improving living standards in other nations, would also make them more resistant to communism. To a considerable extent, these policies were successful—at least in raising living standards in the host countries. That they were not more so can sometimes be attributed to high population growth rates and corrupt and unstable governments. That the USSR and communists in the host countries have opposed American foreign investment lends some testimony to the thesis that direct foreign investment must have been at least partly effective in advancing American foreign political policy.

Official American policy in encouraging direct foreign investment also coincided nicely with the interests of many large American firms. These firms were, of course, motivated to locate abroad for other reasons: lower labor costs; to avoid tax payments; an enhanced bargaining position vis-à-vis American labor. Since these large firms unquestionably have a great deal of influence on American policy, one must question whether direct foreign investment was encouraged to help American foreign policy or to help large American firms.

I cannot argue against the use of direct foreign investment to advance American foreign policy goals. However, if the advancement of foreign policy were the purpose of the encouragement of such investment by American firms—as opposed to the advancement of the interests of these firms—then it can be argued that direct foreign investment should have been better controlled by the United States government. Rather than simply encouraging all direct foreign investment in all countries in all lines of economic activity, the United States government would have had some say in selecting the countries for investment and in selecting the types of economic activity.

The encouragement of direct foreign investment may indeed have helped American foreign political goals and even in many cases served humanitarian ends. Yet, in advancing foreign political policy, American encouragement of foreign investment has almost completely neglected its effect on the American economy. The lack of concern of the United States State Department with American economic interests is notorious, and has been criticized in many Congressional hearings. This accounts for the decision, in the Trade Expansion Act of 1962, to reduce the power of the State Department in economic negotiations and to centralize foreign economic policy in the White House.

Even if we accept the principle that official encouragement of direct foreign investment by the United States in order to contain communism is legitimate, the uncontrolled uses of such investment for this purpose may have been counterproductive. Direct foreign investment in some lines of activity may have damaged the performance of the American economy. It surely had an effect upon American unemployment problems, low growth rates in productivity and gross national product, and the necessity to devalue the dollar. A dynamic, prospering American economy is surely also important to the containment of communism, and to the extent that American direct foreign investment has created difficulties for its economy, it has been counterproductive. Ultimately, whether it is capitalism or communism that will win out will depend mainly on the performance of the American economy in comparison to the Soviet economy.

Notes

Chapter One

1. This figure is very much an estimate. The book value of American-owned firms abroad was close to $120 billion in 1975. If one adjusts for the fact that the inflation of the last few years is not reflected in the book values, the $150 billion figure in 1976 dollars is very conservative.

2. In 1970, sales of manufactured goods by American-owned firms abroad was $76.8 billion, while exports of manufactured goods from the United States were only $29.3 billion. See "The United States in the Changing World Economy" (Washington, D.C.: U.S. Government Printing Office), 1971, Chart 57.

3. See John Evans, *The Kennedy Round* (Cambridge: Harvard University Press) 1971.

4. For some history on the U.S. roles in these organizations, see I. Kravis, *Domestic Interests and International Obligations* (Philadelphia: University of Pennsylvania Press), 1963.

5. The political background to foreign economic policy could be read in such books as Benjamin J. Cohen (ed.), *American Foreign Economic Policy* (New York: Harper & Row), 1968, and William Diebold, *The United States and the Industrial World* (New York: Praeger), 1972.

6. As examples of the interest of American business firms in the aid programs, see the following reports, all published by the Government Printing Office: Gordon Grey Report (1950), Nelson Rockefeller Report (1950), William Paley Commission (1952), Randall Commission Report (1953), Watson Committee Report (1968).

7. For useful compendiums of views, the following can be consulted. Hearings before the Subcommittee on Foreign Economic Policy of the Joint Economic Committee, Congress of the United States, A Foreign Economic Policy for the 1970s (Washington: U.S. Government Printing Office), 1970; Committee on Finance, U.S. Senate, Multinational Corporations (Washington: U.S. Government Printing Office), 1973. George W. Ball (ed.), *Global Companies* (Englewood Cliffs, N.J.: Prentice Hall), 1975. The most spectacular attack on the multinational corporation in the United States has been R. J. Barnet and R. E. Muller, *Global Reach* (New York: Simon and Schuster), 1974. This book has been widely disseminated.

8. Such complaints are becoming more common. See, for example, R. A. Gordon, "Rigor and Relevance in a Changing Institutional Setting," *American Economic Review*, 66 (March 1976), 1–14.

Chapter Three

1. The following text could be consulted on offer curves: R. E. Caves and R. W. Jones, *World Trade and Payments* (Boston: Little, Brown), 1973.

2. Caves and Jones, p. 16.

3. My colleague, Franz Gehrels, assures me offer curves could be used even with trade imbalances. But to do this requires an advance specification of the amount of the imbalance. This seems to put the cart before the horse.

4. R. W. Jones employs the notion of an excess available for export, and cites Murray Kemp for also using this notion. R. W. Jones, "International Capital Movements and the Theory of Tariffs and Trade," *Quarterly Journal of Economics*, February 1967.

5. This assumes demand by B for A's goods is fairly price-elastic.

6. David Ricardo, *The Principles of Political Economy and Taxation* (Homewood, IL: R. D. Irwin), 1953, Chapter 7 (originally published in 1817).

7. Adam Smith, *The Wealth of Nations*, Modern Library Edition (New York: Random House), p. 395 (originally published in 1776).

8. E. Heckscher, "The Effects of Foreign Trade on the Distribution of Income," *Ekonomisk Tidskrift* (1919), reprinted in American Economic Association, *Readings in the Theory of International Trade* (Philadelphia: Blakiston), 1954, and B. Ohlin, *Interregional and International Trade* (Cambridge: Harvard University Press), 1933. For more detailed discussion, see Caves and Jones, *World Trade and Payments*.

9. John Williams, "The Theory of International Trade Reconsidered," *Economic Journal*, June 1929. Reprinted in American Economic Association, *Readings*.

10. I. Grossack and D. D. Martin, *Managerial Economics* (Boston: Little, Brown), 1973, Chapter 11.

11. One important study was by W. Leontief. For a review of this and others, see J. Bhagwati, "The Pure Theory of International Trade: A Survey," in American Economic Association and Royal Economic Society, *Surveys of Economic Theory*, Vol. II (New York: St. Martin's Press), 1965.

12. R. E. Baldwin and J. D. Richardson, *International Trade and Finance: Readings* (Boston: Little, Brown), 1974, p. 1.

13. D. B. Keesing, "Labor Skills and Comparative Advantage," *American Economic Review,* May 1966, reprinted in Baldwin and Richardson.

14. W. Gruber, D. Mehta, and R. Vernon, "The R&D Factor in International Trade and International Investment of U.S. Industries," *Journal of Political Economy,* February 1967.

15. Staffan Linder, *An Essay in Trade and Transformation* (New York: John Wiley), 1961.

16. Caves and Jones, *World Trade and Payments,* and P. Ellsworth and J. Lielh, *The International Economy* (New York: Macmillan), 1975.

Chapter Four

1. Because the expansion of output increases the wage rate, the output increase should be comparatively small in response to a higher price. But, because the wage rate fails to fall when output is reduced, output should fall greatly in response to a price reduction.

2. The results obtained here need not occur if there were some pretrade unemployment in the export sector. Also, even if there were no trade, any price changes could have the same effect upon real national income.

Chapter Five

1. Joan Robinson, "Beggar-My-Neighbor Remedies for Unemployment," *Essays on the Theory of Employment* (Oxford: Basil Blackwell), 1947, reprinted in American Economic Association, *Readings in the Theory of International Trade* (Philadelphia: Blakiston), 1950.

2. Originally, the Phillips curve was used to show the relation between unemployment and wage rates.

3. Max Wasserman and Ray Ware, *The Balance of Payments* (New York: Schenkman Boardman), 1965.

4. This and all other works by Keynes have recently been republished under the auspices of the Royal Economic Society by Macmillan (London).

5. See the chapter on the formation of the International Monetary Fund, in R. N. Cooper, *The Economics of Interdependence* (New York: McGraw-Hill), 1968.

6. R. A. Harrod, *The Life of John Maynard Keynes* (London: Macmillan), 1951.

7. A classic in the relation between stabilization policies and trade and payments balances is J. E. Meade, *The Balance of Payments* (London: Oxford University Press), 1951. For more on these problems, see R. M. Stern, *The Balance of Payments* (Chicago: Aldine), 1973.

8. See Harry G. Johnson, "The Case for Flexible Exchange Rates, 1969," in George Halm (ed.), *Approaches to Greater Flexibility in Exchange Rates: The Burgenstock Papers* (Princeton: Princeton University Press), 1970. Also Friedman's views in "Round Table on Exchange Rate Policy," *American Economic Review,* 59 (May, 1969), 357–369. Both are reprinted in Baldwin and Richardson, *International Trade and Finance,* along with other views.

9. This view is taken by two of my colleagues, Barbara Henneberry and James Witte. See "Stabilization Policy: Implications of Balance of Payments Constraints," Weltwirtscheftliches Archiv, 1976.

10. Hans Thorelli, *The Federal Antitrust Laws* (Baltimore: The Johns Hopkins Press), 1954.

11. For more on this, see D. Swann, *The Economics of the Common Market* (Middlesex, England: Penguin Books), 1970.

12. Harry G. Johnson, "The Implications of Free or Freer Trade for the Harmonization of Other Policies," in H. English (ed.), *World Trade and Trade Policy* (Toronto: University of Toronto Press), 1968. In this article, Johnson also discusses the relation between trade and internal stabilization.

13. James Meade made a valiant attempt to reconcile trade with governmental policies toward externalities. J. E. Meade, *Trade and Welfare* (London: Oxford University Press), 1955.

Chapter Six

1. Max Wasserman and Ray Ware, *The Balance of Payments* (New York: Schenkman Boardman), 1965

2. John Dunning made use of an "international transactions" matrix. See J. Dunning, "Multinational Enterprises and Trade Flows of Less-Developed Countries," *World Development,* Vol. 2 (February 1974), 131–138.

Chapter Seven

1. For an excellent exposition of this theorem, see M. Clement, R. Pfister, and K. Rothwell, *Theoretical Issues in International Economics* (Boston: Houghton-Mifflin), 1967. I have relied heavily upon the section of this book dealing with this theorem.

2. P. Samuelson, "International Factor-Price Equalization Once Again," *Economic Journal,* Vol. 59 (June 1946), 181–97. Reprinted in R. Caves and H. Johnson (eds.), *AEA Readings in International Economics* (Homewood, IL: R. D. Irwin), 1968.

3. Clement, Pfister, Rothwell, *Theoretical Issues*, p.18.

4. Samuelson, "International Factor-Price Equalization."

5. Clement, Pfister, Rothwell, p.18.

6. This is discussed in Clement, Pfister, Rothwell.

7. I. Grossack and D. Martin, *Managerial Economics* (Boston: Little, Brown), 1973, pp.406–409.

8. Travis, however, has proposed a way to bring intermediate goods into analysis. W. P. Travis, *The Theory of Trade and Protection* (Cambridge: Harvard University Press), 1964.

9. Samuelson, on page 68 of Caves and Johnson, *AEA Readings*.

10. R. A. Mundell, "International Trade and Factor Mobility," *Journal of Political Economy*, Vol. 47 (June 1957), 321–335, reprinted in Caves and Johnson, *AEA Readings*.

11. R. E. Caves, "International Corporations: The Industrial Economics of Foreign Investment," *Economica*, February 1971. Stephen Hymer, "The International Operations of National Firms: A Study of Direct Investment," unpublished doctoral dissertation, MIT, 1960. Charles Kindleberger, *American Business Abroad* (New Haven: Yale University Press), 1969, especially Chapter 1.

12. For an exposition of the product cycle thesis, See R. Vernon and L. Wells, Jr., *Economic Environment of International Business* (Englewood Cliffs, N.J.: Prentice-Hall), 1972, particularly pp.182–187.

13. Richard Robinson, *International Business Management* (New York: Holt, Rinehart, Winston), 1973, Chapter 8.

14. See, for example, "Statement of Paul Jennings, President, International Unions of Electrical, Radio, and Machine Workers," in A Foreign Economic Policy for the 1970s. Hearings before the Subcommittee on Foreign Economic Policy, 91st Congress (Washington, D.C.: U.S. Government Printing Office) 1970, pp.813–821.

15. "Hearings," p.39.

16. With multinational firms increasingly able to escape the sovereignty of individual nations, it is perhaps natural that international political bodies should seek the power to regulate and control these firms. The United Nations is already considering this. See United Nations, *Multinational Corporations in World Development* (New York), 1973.

17. I owe this point to my colleague, Richard Farmer, a frequent writer in the field of international business. He informs me that firms purposefully plan for different parts of a product to be produced in different countries in order to make expropriations unattractive to individual host countries.

18. Ross Robertson has given this as a major reason explaining the

growth of large U.S. firms. R. M. Robertson, *History of the American Economy* (New York: Harcourt, Brace, Jovanovich), 1973.

19. On this topic, see E. Kintner and M. Joelson, *An International Antitrust Primer* (New York: Macmillan), 1974.

20. Robert Z. Aliber, "A Theory of Direct Foreign Investment," in C. Kindleberger (ed.), *The International Corporation* (Cambridge: MIT Press), 1970.

21. For more on the increasing flow of direct foreign investment to the United States, see Arnold Sametz, "The Foreign Multinational Company in the U.S.," in J. Backman and E. Bloch (eds.), *Multinational Corporations, Trade and the Dollar* (New York: New York University Press), 1974.

22. See Robert Gilpin, *U.S. Power and the Multinational Corporation* (New York: Basic Books), 1975.

23. Many economic history books describe the economic interests in immigration policy. See, for example, Robertson, *History of the American Economy.*

24. Seev Hirsh has viewed foreign investment in this way, concentrating on differences of production costs in different countries. See Seev Hirsh, *Location of Industry and International Competitiveness* (Oxford: Clarendon Press), 1967.

Chapter Eight

1. See Ragnar Nurkse, "International Investment in the Light of 19th Century Experience," *Economic Journal*, 1951.

2. The transfer problem appears to have first been analyzed by Keynes in the context of the German reparations following World War I. See J. M. Keynes, "The German Transfer Problem," *Economic Journal*, Vol. 39 (March, 1929), 1–7, reprinted in American Economic Association, *Readings in the Theory of International Trade* (Philadelphia: Blakiston), 1950. There are other articles on the transfer mechanism in this same collection of readings.

3. It should be noted that the early classical economists, such as Smith and Ricardo, did not even distinguish between interest rates and profit rates.

4. For a criticism by Keynes, see J. M. Keynes, "Foreign Investment and National Advantage" *The Nation and the Athenaeum*, 35 (August 1924), 584–587. For details on British investment, see A. K. Cairncross, *Home and Foreign Investment, 1870–1913* (New York: Cambridge University Press), 1953.

Chapter Nine

1. J. M. Keynes, *The Economic Consequences of Mr. Churchill* (London: Hogarth Press), 1925. Churchill at that time was Chancellor of the Exchequer and had a large role in England's decision to return to the gold standard.

2. D. R. Hodgman, *National Monetary Policies and International Monetary Cooperation* (Boston: Little, Brown), 1974.

Chapter Ten

1. This is consistent with W. Dickerson Hogue, "The Foreign Investment Decision-Making Process," in R. W. Farmer, R. W. Stevens, and H. Schollhammer, *Readings in International Business* (Encino, California: Dickinson), 1972.

2. This is because part of the tariff, which is a tax, should be partly shifted in its incidence upon other countries. There is considerable literature on an "optimal" tariff from this viewpoint. See R. Caves and R. Jones, *World Trade and Payments* (Boston: Little, Brown), 1973, Chapter 12.

3. G. C. Hufbauer and F. Adler, *Overseas Manufacturing Investment and the Balance of Payments,* U.S. Treasury Department, Washington, D.C., 1968. For an exposition of this work, I have relied upon J. H. Dunning, *Studies in International Investment* (London: George Allen and Unwin), 1970.

4. According to this analysis, the investing country, A, could build plants in B, and at the same time borrow from B. Direct foreign investment by A in B can also result in indirect foreign investment by B to A. This model implicitly assumes fixed exchange rates.

Chapter Eleven

1. Of course, many developing countries often insist that firms located in them from the advanced industrial nations hire local citizens in important managerial and technical posts, as a way to obtain the transfer of technology.

2. For more on this, see E. W. Kintner and M. R. Joelson, *An International Antitrust Primer* (New York: Macmillan), 1974.

3. This writer served a term as program economist with the U.S. AID mission in India. The Indian government often "threatened" its own firms that it would permit the entry of firms from other countries.

4. Raymond Vernon, *Sovereignty at Bay* (New York: Basic Books), 1971.

5. There was a "case study" article on this in the August 1976 issue of *The New Yorker*.

6. From these second and third conditions, we can see why "traditional" international economic theory could support direct foreign investment as in the investing country's interest. This theory generally assumes: a fixed sized labor force; a perfectly working labor market; location abroad is made to sell to the protected market. But of course these assumptions are not always valid.

7. This argument is forcefully made by Gilpin. Robert Gilpin, *U.S. Power and the Multinational Corporation* (New York: Basic Books), 1975.

8. Reddaway explicitly assumed that if British firms did not locate in other countries, firms from other advanced nations would. W. B. Reddaway, *Effects of U.K. Direct Investment Overseas* (Cambridge, England: Cambridge University Press), 1968.

9. As a teacher in a large business school, my observations here might be useful. In the mid-sixties, students with majors in "international business" had no trouble finding jobs. But by the mid-seventies, the job market for American students in international business had largely dried up. Now the majority of our students majoring in international business are non-American.

10. As support for these facts, see *The United States in the Changing World Economy*, Vol. 2 (Washington, D.C.: U.S. Government Printing Office), 1971. In particular, see charts 1 through 5 in this volume. However, we must bear in mind that much of the high capital formation in host countries was capital formation by American firms—and could be considered American capital formation, although located outside the United States.

11. For a good exposition on these policy instruments, see S. Robock and K. Simmonds, *International Business and Multinational Enterprises* (Homewood, IL: R. D. Irwin), 1973.

12. This writer has published a proposal whereby the host country could be assured that DFI must improve its foreign exchange position. See I. M. Grossack, "Foreign-Owned Enterprise and the Balance of Payments: A Proposal," *Foreign Trade Review*, January 1973.

Index

251